Henry Clay Trumbull, H. Clay (Henry Clay) Trumbull

Children in the Temple

a hand-book for the Sunday school concert and a guide for the childrens preacher

Henry Clay Trumbull, H. Clay (Henry Clay) Trumbull

Children in the Temple
a hand-book for the Sunday school concert and a guide for the childrens preacher

ISBN/EAN: 9783337816018

Printed in Europe, USA, Canada, Australia, Japan

Cover: Foto ©Lupo / pixelio.de

More available books at **www.hansebooks.com**

Children in the Temple.

A HAND-BOOK

FOR THE

SUNDAY SCHOOL CONCERT;

AND A

GUIDE FOR THE CHILDREN'S PREACHER.

CONTAINING

A HISTORY OF CHILDREN'S WORSHIP; HINTS ON BIBLE READING, SINGING, PRAYER, AND PREACHING; FORMS FOR OPENING AND CLOSING SERVICE; CONCERT EXERCISES; SERMON PLANS; ETC.

By Rev. H. CLAY TRUMBULL,

Missionary Secretary of the American Sunday School Union for New England.

SPRINGFIELD, MASS.:
W. J. HOLLAND & CO.
1869.

Entered according to Act of Congress, in the year 1869, by
W. J. HOLLAND & Co.,
In the Clerk's Office of the District Court of Massachusetts.

SAMUEL BOWLES & COMPANY,
Printers, Binders and Electrotypers,
Springfield, Mass.

PREFACE.

THIS volume treats exclusively of children's worship, and of gatherings of children for religious exercises of a *general* rather than a *class* character. In this, it is believed to differ from any volume hitherto before the public. It includes the idea of the Sunday-School Concert, the monthly Missionary Meeting, the Anniversary, the Children's Church, and children's meetings for inquiry and prayer. It also presents, as germain to these, the matter of opening and closing exercises for the ordinary Sunday-school session—in fact, the whole subject of general religious exercises with or for children.

The book as now presented is a growth rather than a formation. The author having noted, in his wide observation of New England Sunday-schools, the value of attractive Bible recitations in the Sunday-school concert, and the evils growing out of the misuse of that service, purposed for a long time the publication of a collection of approved concert exercises, having especial reliance on a most valuable series prepared by Mrs. S. J. McCall, of Saybrook, Conn., for the children of her husband's parish. But, amid the pressure of other duties, he would have still delayed the work, had it not been for the impulse given to him by the proposal of the Rev. R. Crittenden, of Towanda, Penn., to perform a similar labor. Mr. C. was formerly successful among children as a pastor, and more recently has been richly blessed as a Sunday-school missionary. With a heart full of love for Jesus and the little ones, and a head full of plans for the benefit of the young, he was admirably fitted to go forward in such an undertaking. An agreement was made with him, by the writer of this, for a mutual prosecution of their work. He furnished choice lessons and other valuable material, and for a considerable time the book was in preparation under joint authorship. But, as the plan of the book grew beyond its original conception, a new arrangement was made, by which one author took the material furnished by both, and added to it his collections from other sources, and thus it came to its present shape. The patience of the publisher during all the delay and frequent changes has but newly evidenced his hearty personal sympathy with the object of the work.

Writings from either side of the water, on any point presented in the book, have been freely consulted, and, with full credit, quoted. The author's thanks are presented to the ministers and laymen whose important contributions of sermons, addresses, and schedules of exercises, are given and acknowledged in different parts of the volume. For what they have thus done for the cause represented in the work, many readers will be grateful.

It is useless to attempt a fuller description of the book in a prefatory note. It must tell its own story, on examination. The hope is not that it has exhausted, but that it has newly opened up—for further and better exposition, by others—the important theme which it presents. The author's prayer is, that the Saviour who loves the dear children may own and bless this effort to swell those hosannas of the children in the temple, which he deemed "perfected praise."

H. C. T.

HARTFORD, CT., Dec. 15, 1868.

CONTENTS.

PART I.—CHILDREN'S WORSHIP. ITS HISTORY, CHARACTER AND CLAIMS.

	PAGE.
The Children's Part in Worship,	11
Special Services for Children,	13
The Sunday School Concert,	14
The Children's Bible Service,	18
The Call for It,	19
Its Availability and Attractiveness,	28
Its Influence and Results,	29
How to Conduct it,	32

PART II.—THE CHILDREN'S SERVICE. ITS APPROPRIATE EXERCISES.

OPENING AND CLOSING EXERCISES.

Bible Reading,	42
Expository and Illustrative,	42
Interrogatory,	43
Simultaneous,	44
Responsive,	45
Elliptical,	47
Singing,	48
Prayer,	49
Prayer with Children,	51
Versions of the Lord's Prayer,	52
Specimen Forms of Opening and Closing Service,	54
Schedule I. By Henry P. Haven,	55
Schedule II. By Henry P. Haven,	58
Schedule III. By George Beal, Jr.,	63
Schedule IV. By The Rev. R. Newton, D. D.,	65

CONTENTS.

GENERAL EXERCISES.

	PAGE.
Forms of the Golden Text,	68
Letters,	68
Words,	69
Names,	69
Phrases,	70
Verses,	71
Illustrative and Proof Exercises,	72
Topical,	72
Historical,	72
Biographical,	72
Doctrinal,	73
Responsive,	73
General Questions,	75
Review Exercises,	75
Missionary Exercises,	78
Extended Topical Exercises,	79
Use of the Blackboard,	80
Caution as to Speech-Making,	81

PART III.—SPECIMEN BIBLE LESSONS FOR THE CHILDREN'S SERVICE.

Lesson I.	The Existence and Attributes of God as Exhibited in the Psalms,	86
Lesson II.	Prophecies Concerning Jesus Christ, with their Recorded Fulfillment,	101
Lesson III.	Thirty Prominent Events in Connection with the Life of Jesus Christ,	115
Lesson IV.	The Holy Ghost. His Titles, Emblems, Offices and Work,	130
Lesson V.	The Holy Scriptures,	140
Lesson VI.	Man. His Condition by Nature and by Grace,	151
Lesson VII.	The Parable of the Prodigal Son, Explained by Scripture,	159
Lesson VIII.	Prayer,	170
Lesson IX.	Giving to the Lord. A Lesson for Missionary Sunday,	177
Lesson X.	Scriptural History of Abraham,	187
Lesson XI.	Bible Mountains and their Lessons,	194
Lesson XII.	Music and Musical Instruments of the Bible,	204

SERMONS IN BIBLE LANGUAGE.

	PAGE.
Lesson XIII. The Good Shepherd,	213
Lesson XIV. God's Love.	220
Lesson XV. Jesus our Exemplar,	221

ILLUSTRATIONS OF CLASS MOTTOES.

Lesson XVI. Bible Lovers,	224
Lesson XVII. Workers for Jesus,	226
Suggestions to the Leader,	227

PART IV.—SERMONS AND ADDRESSES TO CHILDREN.

THE CHILDREN'S PREACHING SERVICE.

Bible Recitations Not Sufficient,	231
Rarity of Children's Preachers,	231
Claims of Children on the Ministry,	232
Inducements to Preach to Them,	234
Preaching to Them not an Easy Matter,	238
Where There's a Will There's a Way,	239
Preparation for the Work,	241
No Stereotyped Plan,	243
Old Time Practice,	244
Crumbs from the Adults' Table,	245

ELEMENTS OF SUCCESS.

Have Something to Teach,	249
Have a Plan of Teaching,	251
Use Simple Language,	255
Few Essentials to Hopeful Speech,	258
Questioning on the Truth Taught,	258
The Use of Illustration,	263
Preach Bible Truth,	268
Treat Sacred Themes Reverently,	271
Variety Desirable,	272
Keep Children's Minds Active,	274
Manner of Address,	274
Seating of the Children,	276

CONTENTS.

SPECIMEN DISCOURSES.

	PAGE.
The Ruling Power of Jesus. By The Rev. S. H. Tyng, D. D.,	278
Samson's Riddle, or the Slayer Slain. By The Rev. A. J. Gordon,	284
Against Temptation. By The Rev. R. T. Robinson,	288
Total Depravity. By The Rev. Alfred Taylor,	294
A Children's Service. By The Rev. J. H. Vincent,	300
Tasting God's Goodness. By The Rev. H. D. Ganse,	303
The Young Follower of Christ. By The Rev. F. D. Huntington, D. D.,	311
Outline of a Sermon on Reading. By The Rev. James M. Freeman,	317
Believing in Jesus. By Ralph Wells,	321
The Willow. By E. D. Jones,	325
Sketch of an Address on Besetting Sins. By William Reynolds,	330

OTHER MEETINGS FOR CHILDREN.

Expect Immediate Results from Preaching,	334
Children's Inquiry and Prayer Meeting,	337

APPENDIX.

HISTORICAL NOTES ON CHILDREN'S WORSHIP.

Worship by the Young in the Schools of the Prophets,	343
Care of Children by Ministers in the Early Church,	344
Children's Worship Commended in the Second Century,	344
Children's Claims Never Wholly Ignored by the Church,	344
Bible Recitations among the Waldenses in the Thirteenth Century,	344
Ignatius Loyola's Jesuit Schools in the Sixteenth Century,	345
Carlo Borromeo's Idea of Priestly Responsibility for Children, 1560-84,	345
Romish Zeal for Youth in Bohemia, 1584,	346
Revival among Moravian Children, 1727,	346
Children's Meeting in Penn., 1829,	346
Services for Children in Boston, 1834-5,	347
Worship for Children, Nismes, France, 1846,	347
English Plan for Children's Services, 1847,	347
Call for a Children's Chapel,	348
Children's Church in Glasgow, Scotland, 1861-3,	348
Separate Services in London, 1868,	349
Western Advocacy of Children's Church,	350
Books for the Leader of Children's Meetings,	350

PART I.

CHILDREN'S WORSHIP.

ITS HISTORY, CHARACTER AND CLAIMS.

CHILDREN IN THE TEMPLE.

THE CHILDREN'S PART IN WORSHIP.

SINCE the day* when "the chief priests and scribes" saw "the children crying in the temple," at Jerusalem, "and saying, Hosanna to the Son of David," and were "sore displeased," and made complaint of the sacrilege, but were met by the Saviour's assurance that this worship had divine approval, the struggle has been going on between the friends and opposers of children in the temple, and it is not quelled to-day.

Devout men, and reverent church dignitaries, not a few, have been loath to consider children as entitled to a full share in sanctuary services, and as fitted for an active part in God's public worship; but other followers of Jesus, ministers and people alike, have been

---

* Matt. xxi. 12-16.

ever glad to accept his teachings as to the place of the little ones;* and their response to those censuring any prominence of children in the temple service, has been in his rebuking words: "Have ye never read, Out of the mouth of babes and sucklings hast thou perfected praise?"

Jesus Christ "is the same, yesterday, and to-day, and forever." Should he now, in bodily presence, visit any sanctuary upreared to his praise, even if he found to condemn any money-changing or dove-selling, in pulpit, or pew, or choir, he would make no complaint of the decorous, hearty and outspoken worship of his holy name by those of tenderest years for such an offering.

And he would find more of such worship now, than ever before. His cause has made progress. His truth has gained power over the hearts of his people. Worship itself has more prominence in the exercises of God's house. While preaching is more valued, it is understood to be in no sense limited to pulpit efforts. Prayer and praise are assuming relatively greater importance, in the exercises of God's house and day. Many who formerly said, "O come let us hear two sermons to-day. Let us sit in silence before the preacher,"—and there rested their interest in sanctuary services,—now say, also, in reverence: "O come, let us worship and bow down; let us kneel before the Lord our Maker." "Let us come before his presence with thanksgiving, and make a joyful noise unto him with psalms."† And where worship is made

---
* See Appendix. † Psalms xcv. 2, 6.

prominent, the perfected praise of the youngest followers of Jesus is likely to be best appreciated.

Moreover, the hearts of the fathers are being turned to the children, by the power of God's Spirit; and the little ones of the fold of Jesus are now more generally accepted by his disciples as their example and their charge. "Except ye be converted, and become as little children, ye shall not enter into the kingdom of heaven;"* "Whosoever shall not receive the kingdom of God as a little child, shall in no wise enter therein;" † "Feed my lambs;" ‡ "Whoso shall receive one such little child in my name, receiveth me;" § "for of such is the kingdom of heaven;" ∥—these and kindred teachings of the Son of God have new force in the minds of his people; and while in every branch of the Christian church, the Sunday-school is provided for the formal instruction of children, and the young are cordially invited to a place with the adults as hearers at ordinary church services, the feeling is gaining ground that something more, in the way of general religious exercises for children, is needed to meet the requirements of their nature, and to conform to the teachings of Jesus in their behalf.

SPECIAL SERVICES FOR CHILDREN.

In England, the question of proper religious services for children has long attracted attention, and been a fruitful theme of discussion. For a third of a century

---

* Matt. xviii. 3.   † Luke xviii. 17.   ‡ John xxi. 15.
§ Matt. xviii. 5.   ∥ Matt. xix. 14.

some of the ablest writers for the Sunday-school cause, in that country, have earnestly advocated a system of separate or special services, for worship or preaching, or both, suited to the capacity or needs of the young, as essential to the full religious culture of those now in the Sunday-school. Such services have been finding more favor as their influence has become better known. Within a few years past, the evangelistic labors of the Rev. E. P. Hammond, among children in Great Britain, have called new attention to the value of children's meetings for inquiry, or prayer, or to hear preaching, or to join in acts of worship; and even where the immediate result of the meetings conducted by the evangelist have not met the expectations of lovers of the children, much good has come of later gatherings of similar character, under the quieter lead of the parish pastor or some of his home helpers. And now, reports of such meetings, conducted successfully and with rich accruing blessings, under the oversight of "The Children's Special Service Mission," or of individual workers, in particular localities, find a frequent place in the Sunday-school periodicals of the old world; and this mode of providing for the children is joyed over by many as furnishing the "missing link" between the Sunday-school and the sanctuary.

THE SUNDAY-SCHOOL CONCERT.

In this country, what is known as the "Sunday-School Concert" has been found a flexible means of providing a service for children, and of securing to them their place in the temple. In various stages of transition, this is now a widely popular religious service of the young, and as such is entitled to more attention than it has obtained in the Sunday-school literature of the day. Fugitive scraps in the periodicals, or occasional chapters in volumes treating of the whole Sunday-school system, comprise most that has been written on this agency. Its origin and history are still comparatively little known among Sunday-school men, and its capabilities for good are but now being appreciated by those who would do most for the spiritual welfare of the young. Hence, an attempt to develop the idea which its growing popularity indicates as in the mind of the Christian church, can hardly fail to be welcomed by the lovers of the little ones, and of him who took them in his arms and blessed them.

The Sunday-school concert was originally a monthly meeting for prayer in behalf of Sunday-schools, held in "concert" throughout the United States, on the *second* Monday evening of each month, in imitation of the monthly concert of prayer for missions, which had long been observed, in this and other lands, on the *first* Monday evening of the month. It gained a national prominence through its recommendation by the Board of Managers of the American Sunday-school Union, in September, 1824, and its growth in favor was thenceforward correspondent with the extension of the Sunday-school system.

Both the missionary and Sunday-school concerts were, after a time, changed from Monday to Sunday evenings; and gradually another change than that of the time of holding it took place in the latter, until it came to be counted rather as a meeting of children, than one for prayer in their behalf. This change has been lamented by some; but there are reasons for believing that it resulted from an increase, not from a diminution, of interest in the children's welfare.

At first, the Sunday-school was viewed only as a missionary agency to children not in Christian families, and the monthly meeting to pray for its success was of the friends of a novel instrumentality for the benefit of a limited class. But with the growth of the Sunday-school interest, children grew in prominence before the church, and new opinions gained ground, of their capacity to love and serve Jesus. The value of instructing them in Bible truth, (instead of merely indoctrinating them in catechetical forms, as was the old time practice,) was evidenced by the early conversion of very many in these new nurseries of piety, and gradually Christian parents came to perceive the advantage of the public teaching of God's word to their children, and the Sunday-school was taken to the heart of the church, as a precious agency for the spiritual culture of the younger members of its charge.

In its new prominence, the Sunday-school is, as a rule, prayed for in all religious meetings, and by Christians generally, rather than at a single service in the month, by only an interested few. The necessity of a special monthly prayer-meeting in its behalf is hardly more apparent than of a similar gathering in the interest of other church work—the pulpit preaching, the service of song, or social and family worship. Teachers are expected to meet often in prayer for their particular charge, and pastors and people are to supplicate, at all fitting times, God's blessing on church efforts among the most hopeful portion of the flock. But, with the passing away of the erroneous idea that the Sunday-school is purely an outside or missionary agency, the character of all the services in connection with it is naturally modified, elevated and improved. Hence, the prominence attained by the modern Sunday-school concert as the children's monthly meeting for worship.

That the name "Sunday-School Concert" is inappropriate to this service as now conducted, can hardly be questioned. It is liable to misapprehension, being supposed by some to refer merely to a singing exercise of the Sunday-school, while at the best it fails to indicate the character or design of the service. Indeed, in many places the term is no longer known. In New York and some other cities, the "Concert" is supplanted in great measure by the "Missionary Sunday" or "Missionary Meeting," when the children make their missionary offerings, hear from previous contributions, and listen to appropriate addresses. Now and then the "Children's Church," on the plan of Rev. Dr. Newton's exercise of preaching to the children, with questions freely put to them, and a part assigned them in the singing and prayers, has the half-Sabbath in every month formerly given to the concert.

Even where the old name is adhered to, there is by no means a uniformity of practice in the conduct of the exercises. In many places the Sunday-school concert is merely a monthly meeting of the children and their friends, where the little folks do the singing, and listen to short talks from pastor, superintendent, or others. But, extensively throughout New England and the Central States, and more or less in other parts of the country, the concert is now a monthly gathering of members of the Sunday-school and their friends, for *general* rather than for *class* exercises, at a time not conflicting with the ordinary sessions of the school—taking the place of the second regular service of the sanctuary, or held in the early evening.

Its exercises of worship, led by either pastor or superintendent, are suited to the capacity of children; and Bible recitations, by young and old alike, constitute one of its peculiar attractions. Indeed, it is chiefly from its value as a recitative Bible-service that it has so widely gained Christian approval.

THE CHILDREN'S BIBLE SERVICE.

The design of this recitative Bible-service is to connect the Sunday-school more immediately with the sanctuary, while full church services for children are yet so rare. By its occasional general exercises—monthly if not more frequent—it stores the minds of the young with the treasures of God's Word, and brings them to a love of his house and an active part in his worship. Stimulating them to "search the Scriptures," it tends, by its recitations, to aid them to "lay up the words of God in their heart and in their soul, and to keep them in the midst of their heart." Instead of praying, reading and singing only by proxy, as is too commonly the case with our adult congregations, the children are in this service to have each a part in its varied exercises, and thus unconsciously to be preparing to assume, in maturer years, the responsibilities of the social prayer-meeting, which so many professing Christians shirk. And by it they are to be brought under the more direct influence of the pastor, into closer association with the general congregation, and to a permanent place at the weekly preaching service for their benefit, to which it is likely to lead.

THE CALL FOR IT.

The propriety of such a service would hardly be questioned but for the latent heresy in the church as to the capabilities of childhood and the value of efforts to save the young—the heresy which manifested itself when the disciples much displeased Jesus by standing between him and the dear children brought by anxious mothers for his blessing, and which has never wholly died out from among Christ's people. But, in view of this heresy, it may be well, while urging the children's claim to the sanctuary services for at least one half-Sabbath in the month, to make mention of a few important truths.

I. *Children are not at present properly provided for in the " regular" Sabbath services which they are expected to attend.*

"The public services of the Lord's day do not meet the emergency," says a well-known English writer on this subject.* "Preaching, with a few happy exceptions, overshoots the juvenile portion of the congregation. The long, dry sermons which they often hear from Sunday to Sunday rather tend to associate feelings of distaste in their minds with the services of the temple, than to render the day to them 'a delight—the holy of the Lord and honorable.'" "How much of public preaching is utterly unintelligible and useless to them!" says the veteran American Sunday-school pastor,† in an appeal in behalf of the children. "Often, necessarily, of subjects beyond their reach. Often, unnecessarily, in language which they cannot comprehend."

Indeed, so prominent is the lack for children in the ordinary sanctuary services, that not a few distinguished Christian educators have questioned the propriety of taking children to church, while no provision is there made for their instruction. "I am by no means sure," said President Sears of Brown University, "of the good effect on children of sitting in listlessness, and acquiring habits of inattention in the house of God, when nothing is offered to them from the pulpit, and they are not expected to understand,

---

* Rev. J. F. Serjeant, in " Sunday-School Teaching," p. 4.
† Rev. Dr. Tyng, in " Forty Years' Experience in Sunday-Schools," p. 209.

or to have a part in, the exercises of worship." In like doubt, the Rev. Newman Hall, as Chairman of the English Congregational Union, enquired in his address at the autumnal meeting, in Sheffield, in 1866, "Should little children be encouraged to attend our public services? If those services are suited for adults will the children be interested? and if not, is it likely they will love the house and day of God."* With more of positiveness, a prize essay of the London Sunday-school Union † has declared distinctly against "the practice of taking little or ignorant children to the public services of the sanctuary," adding in pertinent suggestion, what may be thoughtfully considered even by those who are as yet unwilling to give it approval: "What habits are really formed by this practice? The habits of sleeping, of inattention and listlessness, of day-dreaming and vain thoughts, and of dislike and aversion to the Sabbath and the sanctuary. These habits are more or less formed in every child so trained, and cling to them in after life with an almost unconquerable force. Whence arise the complaints so often reiterated by pious persons, of wandering thoughts, distracted attention, incapability of fixing their minds on the preacher, but from the fact that for many years in early life they were forming the habit of hearing without attending—of sitting statue-like, without an effort to understand or to remember?"

---

*The Union Magazine for Sunday-School Teachers. London. June, 1867; p. 294.

† "The Sunday-School," by Louisa Davids, p. 215.

Would it not be well if so sad a lack were well supplied?

II. *The church has a duty of preaching Christ to the children, in addition to the instructions of the parent and the Sunday-school teacher.*

The young are the larger as well as the more impressible portion of the entire community. They, surely, should not be overlooked in the effort to "preach the Gospel to every creature." Family religious instruction is most deplorably deficient in even the most thoroughly evangelized communities; while in neighborhoods unblessed by the ministrations of the Gospel, the children receive almost no "nurture and admonition of the Lord." Since the first family there have been sad defects in the best households, and the church has been needed to supplement—although never to abrogate—the family institution. He would be a presumptuous father who would willingly dispense with the agency of the church and its ordinances in the religious training of his offspring.

The Sunday-school supplies, in a measure, an essential lack in the family for the spiritual culture of the young. "The one may give the advantage of solitary religious teaching. The other alone engrafts upon this, and adds to this, the social benefits and opportunities of pleasant religious relations and religious influences in association. Accordingly, the perfect scheme and the perfect operation are only to be found in the combination of the two."*

---

* Rev. Dr. Tyng's "Forty Years' Experience in Sunday Schools," p. 57.

But the Sunday-school should not be entirely disconnected from other services of the Lord's house. It should look to their identification with the people of God in all the temple ministrations. The command, "Feed my lambs," should be accepted as binding on the ministry and the entire church, as well as on the parent and the special teacher. The word of truth should be "rightly divided" from the pulpit to the children. Hence, such intermediate services as tend to this consummation, and link the Sunday-school to other exercises of the sanctuary, are likely to promote the true welfare of young and old, the salvation of souls, and the honor of the Great Head of the church.

III. *The giving to children a share in church services is no new idea of modern innovators. It is an old-time custom, to be venerated for its antiquity by lovers of the ancient landmarks.*

T. H. Horne says, in his Introduction to the Study of the Holy Scriptures, that at the Feast of the Passover the Jews were accustomed, during the celebration of that most sacred festival of the year, to clear the tables, "that the *children* might *inquire*, and *be instructed* in the nature of the feast. The text on which they generally discoursed was Deut. xxvi. 5–11."

When Moses was commanded to summon all Israel "to appear before the Lord," to hear the reading of the law, he was told of God to "gather the people together, men and women and *children*,"* and when Joel's inspired cry was to "blow the trumpet in Zion,"

---
* Deut. xxxi. 12.

to "call a solemn assembly," and to gather the people, he did not forget the injunction, "Gather the children,"* for these were never ignored in the plans of the theocracy. It was no meaningless utterance in which David gave thanks to God: "Out of the mouth of babes and sucklings hast thou ordained strength"†— or, as Jesus rendered it, when he approved the children's worship in the temple, "perfected praise."‡

IV. *In all study of church history it will be found that when Zion has prospered her children have been diligently "taught of the Lord," while in her days of sloth her prophets have lamented that "the young children lack bread and no man breaketh it unto them."* §

After the Jewish captivity, it was a popular saying among the scattered people of God, that "Jerusalem was destroyed because the instruction of the young was neglected;" and again, it was declared that "Even for the rebuilding of the temple the schools must not be interrupted." Those branches of the Christian church which have held the faith in its purity in seasons of general religious declension, have almost invariably been those which, like the Waldenses and Moravians, have given prominence to the public religious instruction of the young, while the Jews and Romanists, who have surprised the world by their hold on the faith of succeeding generations, have relied for success more on their work among children than upon all other endeavors to perpetuate their peculiar views.

It was in full recognition of the time-honored-cus-

---
* Joel ii. 16.   † Ps. viii. 2.   ‡ Matt. xxi. 16.   § Lam. iv. 4.

tom of instructing the children in the sanctuary, that the church at Roxbury, Mass., of which Rev. John Eliot, the Indian apostle, was pastor, declared by its record, "In 1674, 6th, 10th month," that "This day we *restored a primitive practice* for ye training up of our youth," and then described the assembling "every Sabbath after morning exercise," of the children, to be examined by the elders not only "in the Catechism," but in "whatever else may convene." And it was in a similar spirit that a few months later "the church in Norwich, in Connecticut Colony," regretting the "great degree of dangerous neglects of that which ought to be for the prevention of apostasie," solemnly renewed a covenant, the first clause of which was: "That our children shall be brought up in the Admonition of The Lord, as in our Families, so *in Publick;* that all the Males who are eight or nine years of age, shall be presented before the Lord in his Congregation every Lord's Day to be catechised, until they be about thirteen years in age." And such proofs might be multiplied indefinitely of the antiquity of public services for the religious culture of the young.

V. *Special sanctuary services for the children, in one form or another, are being clearly recognized as a necessity in the Christian church, and are finding favor with those most experienced in them.*

Nearly twenty years ago, a prominent English pastor, who had been highly successful as a preacher to children, while admitting the lack of provision for the young in ordinary Sabbath arrangements, declared: "Until the plan of separate services can be effectively adopted, that of *special services* will be the only means to remedy the defect."* The Rev. E. Spooner, in his admirable work, "Parson and People," † describes his successful attempt of a children's service. Together with portions of the prayer-book service, "two hymns are sung at due intervals, and then a sermonette, illustrated with anecdotes and even with pictures, follows; all is attention, the children enjoying thoroughly the service . . . and leaving the school with an impression of having joined in what they could understand and of having heard what they could remember." Mr. Spooner adds the testimony of others who have tried the experiment and become convinced of the permanent value of such services—in one instance after a twelve years' trial.

In our own country, many pastors have long held occasional preaching services for the children in the sanctuary, and many ecclesiastical bodies have warmly commended the extension of this practice. Bishop Janes is said ‡ to have remarked, in a Methodist Episcopal conference, that "the time is coming when there will be two sermons preached to children and youth where there is one to adults," and the Rev. Dr. Tyng declares: § "If every pastor would give one sermon on every Sunday, especially addressed to the young, and

---

* Addresses to Children. Rev. S. G. Greene; p. 7.
† American edition, pp. 138–141.
‡ The Sunday-School Index, p. 208.
§ Forty Years' Experience in Sunday-Schools, p. 210.

designed and prepared to teach them, he would find himself enlarging his direct usefulness in this particular work, and equally advancing the value and benefit of every other class of his public and private labors in religious instruction also.".

In many of our larger cities where there are two sessions of the Sunday-school, the second is given up to general exercises, with addresses from the pastor, or superintendent, or other competent instructors, and with a part assigned to the children in worship. There are not a few intelligent observers of the signs of the times, who believe that soon a full Sabbath service for the children will be as common in the Christian church as the Sunday-school is now, and that, in conducting it, more or less of such exercises as are here presented will be found of special value.

In view, then, of the present necessities of the children, of their claims on the church, of the teachings of the Bible with reference to them, of the approved practices of God's people in earlier days, and of the results of more recent experiment, it is surely not unreasonable to expect that at least one half-Sabbath, in each month shall be given, even now, to such a sanctuary service for the young as is here commended and illustrated, even though the church is yet unprepared to accept the views of those large-hearted Christ following leaders in its ministry, who see and urge the importance of providing services at which the children may worship in God's house, and receive the word of truth from the lips of his ambassador on the return of each Lord's day of blessing.

ITS AVAILABILITY AND ATTRACTIVENESS.

A peculiar advantage of this monthly recitative Bible service is found in the fact that it is almost everywhere available, attractive, and popular.

In many places, the Sunday-school is suspended during a portion of the year—in cities, for the summer months; in the country, for the winter. Even then, the lamentable gulf of intermitted religious effort may be spanned by the children's monthly meeting. Without commending Sunday-school vacations, it is safe to say that where the children are not taught God's word each week, they can, at all events, be gathered for worship as often as once a month.

Not all churches have pastors; nor do all pastors feel that they can preach acceptably to children. But all have the Bible, and from that the children can ever learn beautiful and precious passages, to recite to their own profit and to the good of those who rightly hear them.

Even mission schools, as branches of church schools or as independent organizations, can have a monthly Bible service, where impressive and effective lessons may be added to the usual Sabbath teachings, and where any lack in the poorer taught classes may be measurably supplied by well conducted general exercises.

Rarely is any religious meeting better attended than

one in which the children have a share. They are themselves glad to be recognized by the church, and to be given a part in worship. They can be always relied on for their presence and aid. Parents are pleased to have their children thus prominent, and to witness their enjoyment of the service, and many who attend church at no other time, will come with the little ones to their monthly meeting. It is a matter of fact, that in hundreds of country churches, a crowded house on Sunday-school concert afternoon or evening, attests the popularity of such a meeting where only thin congregations are found at the ordinary Sabbath services; and many pastors particularly prize it for the opportunity it gives them of preaching Christ to the unevangelized.

ITS INFLUENCE AND RESULTS.

Whatever induces Bible study is so far advantageous. However passive hearers may "receive the word with all readiness of mind," those always are "more noble," who, like the Bereans, "search the Scriptures daily whether these things are so."* To the young, especially, God's "word is a shield and buckler." Every additional lesson of Scripture renders the armor more complete and secure.

In this service the exercises are chiefly biblical. Bible study is essential to a share in them; and in such study the mind is expanded, for "the entrance of

---
* Acts xvii. 11.

God's word giveth light; it giveth understanding to the simple." *

Moreover, those who give expression anew to what they have learned, by reciting it literally or re-stating its substance, increase thereby their hold upon that truth, and gain in mental grasp and reach.

There is a natural unwillingness to take an active part before others in God's worship, but this very repugnance to "well-doing" is what should be overcome. The earlier in life the effort is made, the better. Children manifest less of this feeling than adults. They can easily be led along to take any part assigned them, and when rightly trained they are competent to edify believers, and to instruct, rebuke, and exhort others in the words of inspired wisdom. Many a father now rejoices in hope, who was led to the Sunday-school concert by the entreaties of his little girl, and, remaining there from its attractiveness, at length yielded his heart to the Saviour of whom he was there first taught.

And there is no place where the older ones will be more ready to take a part in worship than the children's meeting. For the children's sake, from the influence of the very atmosphere of the service, and because the part assigned to them is so easy of performance, adults, whose voices are heard in no other religious meeting, are often sharers in the recitations of the Sunday-school concert. In many a New England community, almost the entire congregation will

---
* Ps. cxix. 130.

be found on "concert afternoon" in the country church, as interested participants in the services, parents rising with their children to repeat proof texts, and even adult or aged non-professors sharing recitations with the youngest. Of course the influence of such co-operative Bible study will be widely manifest for good. A pastor in Eastern Connecticut declared, after a few months' trial of such a service, that he was surprised at the quickening it gave his people in the search for truth. Where before, as he visited in his parish, he heard only of the crops, or weather, or neighborhood gossip, he now found all wide awake about the last concert lesson, or the topic announced for the next. He would be asked what he thought of this passage, or where was proof of that doctrine, or there would be serious words uttered as to the great theme of a recent service. Indeed the atmosphere in which he moved was so different that he could actually write his sermons with half the time and toilsome effort before demanded, and his own love of the Bible was correspondingly increased,—and his experience is by no means solitary.

In the children's service has often commenced a work of grace resulting in many new-born souls. Eight hundred and twenty persons, mostly young, were received into church communion during less than a year, from one hundred Sunday-schools in Pennsylvania, from which the author of this book has received report. A watch of the "conversation" of those young believers furnished witness that those who had previously received the most faithful Christian instruction became the most active and efficient workers in God's vineyard. And the church which received the largest accession in a given time was one which devoted the afternoon of every Lord's day to a congregational Bible school, including all classes and ages, from the infant to the grand parent.

HOW TO CONDUCT IT.

The idea of a children's Bible service being admitted as good, it is yet necessary that that idea be properly carried out, else the labor is lost—and well is it if there be no worse result. That the Sunday-school concert has been often perverted and abused by reliance on silly exercises or sillier speakers, until it was little above the "moral drama" in its tone and tendency, can no more be denied than that the pulpit has had some very poor and some sadly heretical preachers in it, while words of divine truth have been wrested by them "that are unlearned and unstable" "unto their own destruction." But it would be surely unwise to condemn a service for searching the Scriptures, or to object to the ministry or the Bible, because of abuses of that which God has approved. It may be well, however, to suggest a few points as worthy of note in arranging for and conducting the children's service.

I. *The Bible should be the text-book of the service.* Children love variety, and are entitled to it. But there is ample material in the Bible to gratify their proper desire for diversity. That is adequate to furnish lessons, "new and old," which edify while they interest, and are "profitable" to make "wise unto salvation through faith which is in Christ Jesus."

The Bible is little enough studied at the best. Its beauties are unfamiliar to too many who have long had it at hand. The children need its holy lessons, and in the few public services for their benefit, they are entitled to the privileges of its study and recitation. Let them learn miscellaneous selections for the day-school or the home circle, but in their sanctuary service let them rejoice in what God has prepared for them. The only excuse which charity can furnish for pastors and superintendents who so often substitute other lessons for the Bible in this service, is, that they are themselves ignorant of the adaptiveness of Scripture to such exercises. It is not too much to say that the widest experience has shown that Scripture recitations may be made more permanently attractive, while far more impressive and profitable to those of all ages, than the best of miscellaneous selections.

Occasionally, a Scripture truth may be easiest committed by the infant class in verse, or a stanzas or so of a hymn may be added in illustration of the quoted text, but the necessity of using other language than the Bible in the service is rare, for it will be found in the end, as a prominent Bible student* has said, that "God knows best how to write a book for his own children," or as a foremost Sunday-school worker† has

---

* Rev. Prof. Stowe.   † E. D. Jones of St. Louis.

declared, as the result of his experience among the little ones: "God never made anything more attractive to the children than the Bible."

II. *The singing should be carefully looked to.* It will naturally have prominence in such a service, and this is well, for it is the choicest mode of praise on earth or in heaven; and "it is good to sing praises unto our God; for it is pleasant; and praise is comely."* Sunday-school music is a recognized power in our land. It has already driven from our streets in great measure the vulgar melodies which were before so rife. It has lightened many a heavy burden in homes of poverty and sorrow, and has drawn multitudes to the house of God, and instrumentally not a few to the fold of Jesus.

Sharp criticisms have been made with obvious propriety on particular hymns or tunes, or classes of either, but none who are fair-minded and well-informed can fail to commend this music as a whole, as comparing most favorably in devotional character and in Christian tone and taste with that generally found in collections for adults, or heard from fashionable choirs. But care should be taken in the selection of hymns and tunes for the monthly meeting. An appropriateness to the time and the theme of the service should be manifest in all that is sung. And nothing should be given out unless it is likely to prove a help to the children in their service of worship, and in their gain of profitable impressions from the lessons of the day.

---

* Ps. cxlvii. 1.

III. *Great caution should be observed as to the speakers—if any are admitted.* There are many machine-talkers at hand for such an occasion, ready and anxious to exercise their gifts. Some have mirth-provoking stories with which to set the school in a laugh. Others have threadbare anecdotes and illustrations, already more familiar to the children than the most precious portions of the Bible they have assembled to study. Some are serious, but prosy, pointless, or long-winded. Let none of these be called on. Allow no false delicacy to prevent the passing them by if they are present. The children's eternal interests must not be trifled with nor needlessly endangered.

It is better to have no speaking than that which is profitless, and indeed it should rarely be a reliance or made particularly prominent. Bible recitations are more satisfactory to all than most of the talk at such times. But whatever is said should be brief, pointed, and earnest, with a bearing on the theme of the day. He who is not likely to speak thus, should not be heard.

IV. *The lessons should be distributed " without partiality."* As a rule, one scholar or class should not occupy more time in recitation than is assigned to others. All should be treated as nearly alike as possible, that neither modesty be endangered on the one hand, nor envy or ill-feeling be provoked on the other. Of course, this caution does not apply to the dividing of a large school into sections, for recitations at different concerts.

V. *The exercises should not partake of the character of an exhibition.* Tableaux or dramatic representations of any kind, should not be tolerated. No child should be lifted on to the platform or led to the front, to be the gazing stock of the congregation. The service is rather one of Scripture recitation to the pastor or superintendent, who is its leader, or of direct praise to Jesus, than of addresses to a miscellaneous audience for their approval or criticism. It is marred by whatever calls particular attention to the manner of presenting the truth, or to the person presenting it; and the injury is likely to be considerable to the scholar who faces the smiles of an admiring audience, or perhaps receives the murmur of gentle applause, and is commended in the local paper as having "rendered her part admirably, throwing into it much heart and feeling," or as having "given with much oratorical effect" his impressive "declamation."

VI. *The children should, as far as practicable, have a share in all parts of the service.* In the singing they will naturally be prominent. They should join or alternate with the leader in Bible reading. Even in prayer their voices may properly be heard. Some superintendents pray in simple language, and have the children repeat after them each clause as it is uttered. In other cases, the Lord's prayer may be used in concert at the close of extemporaneous prayer.

VII. *The entire service should be a unit, tending in all its parts to the enforcing of a single great thought.*
Two hundred children may recite two hundred dis-

connected texts in such a way as only to confuse the hearers, and to send them from the service with no well defined idea of the object of the meeting, or the nature of the truth presented. On the contrary, if the Bible reading, the singing, the prayers, the remarks of each speaker, and all the recitations, have reference to the one theme of the day, all present, from the youngest to the most mature, are likely to be seriously impressed by the truth of that theme, and to carry it away in the mind, where, with God's blessing, it may be productive of that faith which "cometh by hearing."*

The mind cannot grasp a legion of great truths at a single effort, and the rapid disconnected repetition of these can hardly fail to perplex, rather than to benefit, even the intelligent and earnest seeker. The flashing in quick succession of all the prismatic colors on a printed page, is less likely to clearly exhibit its text, than the steady beaming on it of the combined rays, through a well-cut lens. So, both children and adults are better taught by the systematic presentation of a truth in repeated yet harmonious instructions, than by any jumble of fragmentary teachings even of Divine utterance.

VIII. *Life and promptness should be shown in all the exercises.* The pulse of a child beats quicker than that of an adult. There is with the child a natural repugnance to long metres. The time-honored doxology may be profitably learned and sung by old and young,

---

* Rom. x. 17.

but the fact remains that short metre, in praise and prayer and all devotional exercises, is best adapted to edify the children.

Nothing should drag. Mere business matters should not be introduced, lest they divert the children from the one purpose of the meeting. Readings, hymns, recitations should be prearranged, that there may be a prompt passing from one thing to another. It is said of a prominent Sunday-school worker of Illinois* that he never enters his desk as superintendent without having every part of his duty carefully planned. "He knows just what he is going to do, and the order of doing it. His chapter is selected and read and prayed over, his hymn has also been read over some times, as he remarked, at least twenty times, before he feels that he has entered into the spirit of it and is prepared to read it before his school." †

One coming thus prepared by study and prayer, is likely to infuse his spirit of love for Christ, for the truth, and for the dear children, into all the exercises, and the fire of that divine love will radiate from the leader so as to impart light and life to all who are in the house, and the entire service will tend to the children's welfare and their Saviour's honor.

---
* Wm. Reynolds of Peoria.
† Report of Ninth Conv. of Ill. S. S. Teach. Assoc.

PART II.

THE CHILDREN'S SERVICE.

ITS APPROPRIATE EXERCISES.

EXERCISES FOR THE CHILDREN'S SERVICE.

THE exercises of the children's service cannot be well conducted on any stereotyped plan. To be fresh they must be often varied; and this desirable variety is not easily secured by ministers and superintendents without aid from others, since it involves the use of more time in preparation than they can readily give for such a purpose. Hence, it is proposed to furnish specimen exercises, which have proved on trial attractive and profitable, that they may be at the command of all workers for the children. As preliminary to these, comments on different portions of the service may not be out of place.

OPENING AND CLOSING EXERCISES.

Attention should be given to the opening and closing exercises no less than to those which are more prominent and central. No part should be so dull and unattractive that the children will long to have it done with, to give place to that which alone is pleasing. They can be taught to love Bible reading and prayer as well as the singing, if they are wisely led.

In many Sunday-schools and children's meetings the formal exercises at the opening and close of service are an attraction to both young and old. This may always be the case, if sufficient attention, in a right spirit, is given to their preparation, and they are properly used.

BIBLE READING.

EXPOSITORY AND ILLUSTRATIVE READING.

If the leader reads a portion of Scripture by himself, let him select a brief one, suited to the children's comprehension—one of narrative, command, or practical exhortation,—and to this let him add (if any comment is made) merely a few words of explanation or illustration, to fasten attention to its teachings. To do this wisely, requires previous careful study, and the exercise of sound judgment. "Both written and oral teaching are to a large extent dependent on illustration for any attractions which they may possess,"* yet "illustrations of divine truths are .... dangerous unless well guarded so as never to withdraw attention from the Bible." †

It will be well to study Groser's treatise on Illustrative Teaching as preliminary to this public illustration of Scripture, and the annual volumes of The Biblical

---

* Illustrative Teaching, W. H. Groser, p. 6.
† The Sabbath-School Index, R. G. Pardee, p. 87.

THE CHILDREN'S BIBLE SERVICE. 43

Treasury, published by the London Sunday-School Union, and The Land and the Book, by Rev. Dr. W. M. Thomson, also Rev. Dr. Richard Newton's series of sermons to children, will be found of use in supplying illustrations of Scripture or desirable incidents and lessons.

The following are named as examples of passages suitable to be read at the children's service:

> Abraham's Trial of Faith. Gen. xxii. 1-14.
> The Blessings for Obedience. Deut. xxviii 1-14.
> David's Triumph over Goliath. I. Sam. xvii. 38-50.
> Naaman and the Little Maid. II. Kings v. 1-14.
> The Excellence of Wisdom. Prov. iv. 1-15.
> Exhortation to Early Piety. Eccl. xii. 1-14.
> Visit of the Wise Men to Jesus. Matt. ii. 1-12.
> The Crucifixion. Mark xv. 15-38.
> Christ's Resurrection. Luke xxiv. 1-15.
> Obedience and Courage Enjoined. Eph. vi. 1-13.
> Love to God and to Man a Duty. I. John iv. 7-21.
> The Heavenly Jerusalem. Rev. xxi. 10-25.

The parables and the miracles of Jesus are also particularly well adapted for such reading.

INTERROGATORY READING.

After reading the selection, the leader may ask such questions, to be answered by the assembly, as will tend to fasten the truth taught in the passage. In doing this, he should consider the principles laid down in J. G. Fitch's Art of Questioning, and by Rev. J. B. Draper, in his essays on Our Lessons and How to Teach Them.*

---

* See S. S. World, July, 1868.

Take, for example, the following questions, given by Draper, on Luke v. 1–11, one for each verse:

1. For what reason did the people press upon Jesus?
2. How were the owners of the two ships employed?
3. Whose ship did Jesus choose to enter?
4. After his sermon, what command did he give to the fishermen?
5. What answer was given by Peter?
6. How did the fishermen succeed in their fishing?
7. What did they do with the large quantity of fish which they caught?
8. What effect did the miracle have upon Peter?
9. And what effect upon his companions?
10. How did Jesus comfort Peter?
11. What did the disciples do when they came to land?

SIMULTANEOUS READING.

These selections, or indeed any portion of the Bible, may be read simultaneously by leader and assembly; but to ensure in such reading, harmony and distinctness of utterance, instead of the confused jumble of voices which is heard in a room where all read at the same time, but not in concert, it is essential that such breath-pauses be made at intervals in the reading, as will enable all to note the measure given by the leader, and to keep together in their utterances. The dashes in the following selection, from I. Cor. xiv. 7–9, will indicate these desirable rests, and a few experiments with a school, in reading with and then without them, will convince all of their value:

"And even things — without life — giving sound, — whether pipe or harp—except they give—a distinction—in the sounds,—

how shall it be known—what is piped or harped?—For if the trumpet—give an uncertain sound,—who shall prepare himself—to the battle?—So likewise ye,—except ye utter—by the tongue—words easy to be understood,—how shall it be known—what is spoken?"

RESPONSIVE READING.

Responsive or alternate readings are not equally suited to all portions of the Bible, especially by the common arrangement of verses. Such a division frequently mars the sense, in the transition from leader to assembly, although in other instances it is eminently proper.

The verses of some chapters are naturally divided into two parts, and can be responsively read with good effect. Take, for example, the tenth chapter of Proverbs. The first half of each verse may be read by the leader. The remainder, (as printed in italics,) forms the response by the assembly.

1 The proverbs of Solomon. A wise son maketh a glad father:
But a foolish son is the heaviness of his mother.
2 Treasures of wickedness profit nothing:
But righteousness delivereth from death.
3 The Lord will not suffer the soul of the righteous to famish:
But he casteth away the substance of the wicked.
4 He becometh poor that dealeth with a slack hand:
But the hand of the diligent maketh rich.

It is a good suggestion of Mr. Waldo Abbott's[*] that in the alternate readings of Scripture, the chil-

---

[*] Our Sunday-School, Waldo Abbott, p. 54.

dren "be led by the assistant [superintendent] who should stand at the further end of the room."

THE PSALMS FOR RESPONSIVE READING.

The Psalms are peculiarly suited to responsive use in public worship. Indeed it was for just this that they were obviously designed. "They are all poetical, not merely imaginative and expressive of feeling, but stamped externally with that peculiar character of parallelism, which distinguishes the higher style of Hebrew composition from ordinary prose. . . . They are all ecclesiastical lyrics, psalms or hymns, intended to be permanently used in public worship."* "In all, or nearly all of them," says one, in commending an admirable version of the Psalms arranged according to the original parallelisms,† "the two parts, *lead* and *response*, are clearly traceable throughout. Thought answers to thought, emotion to emotion, and the responsive utterance by leader and people develops the beauty and power of their inspired words in a much higher degree than can be realized by the ordinary mode of reading by alternate verses."

In illustration of this, take the sixty-seventh Psalm. The *lead* is printed in Roman letters, and the *response* in italics:

1 God be merciful unto us and bless us;
   And cause his face to shine upon us.

---

*Alexander on the Psalms.
† The Book of Psalms arranged according to the Original Parallelisms for Responsive Reading. Mason Brothers, New York.

THE CHILDREN'S BIBLE SERVICE.

2 That thy way may be known upon earth,
Thy saving health among all nations.
3 Let the people praise thee, O God;
Let all the people praise thee.
4 O let the nations be glad and sing for joy:
*For thou shalt judge the people righteously,
And govern the nations upon earth.*
5 Let the people praise thee, O God:
Let all the people praise thee.
6 Then shall the earth yield her increase;
And God, even our own God, shall bless us.
7 God shall bless us;
And all the ends of the earth shall fear him.

In many of the Psalms, the two parts, (*lead* and *response,*) are so readily distinguished, that the assembly can read the response from the common version when the leader has read the lead. For example, the leads being given in a portion of the one hundred and nineteenth Psalm, the responses can be readily supplied:

9 Wherewithal shall a young man cleanse his way?
10 With my whole heart have I sought thee:
11 Thy word have I hid in mine heart,
12 Blessed art thou, O Lord:
13 With my lips have I declared all the judgment of thy mouth.
15 I will meditate in thy precepts,
16 I will delight myself in thy statutes.

ELLIPTICAL READING.

By the elliptical method of reading, any portion of Scripture can be properly read in alternation, and rarely can narrative be read alternately in any other way without injury to the sense in the transition.

The assembly must be charged not to begin until the leader stops; but then to read until the next period. It is understood that when the leader reads a whole verse, the next verse is to be read by the assembly. In example, take the parable of the prodigal son, Luke xv. 11–24. The ellipses are to be supplied by the assembly, the leader reading as follows:

11 And he said,——
12 And the younger of them said to his father,——
13 And not many days after, the younger son gathered all together, and took his journey into a far country,——
14 And when he had spent all there arose a mighty famine in that land;——
15 And he went and joined himself to a citizen of that country;——
16 And he would fain have filled his belly with the husks that the swine did eat:——
17 And when he came to himself he said,——
20 And he arose and came to his father. But when he was yet a great way off, his father saw him and had compassion, and ran, and fell on his neck, and kissed him. And the son said unto him,——
22 But the father said to his servants,——

SINGING.

Concerning the singing, the suggestions made by Philip Phillips, in his Singing Pilgrim, may well be considered by those who lead in this exercise at the children's service. In explanation of the points named in his book, Mr. Phillips remarked at one of the great conventions of Sunday-school workers:* "If the lesson of the day [or the topic of the service] is about faith, sing a hymn of faith; if about Jesus, sing of Jesus. .... To interest scholars in the hymn, see that all always engage in singing it. Give them before they commence a clear idea of what they are about to sing. Let the superintendent, in a word or two, refer to the sentiment of the hymn. Then we may expect to have singing with the spirit and with the understanding also. ..... The great power of adaptation may be wonderfully applied in our singing. Sing not according to a plan laid out and stereotyped a week ahead. Suit your selections to the feeling that exists at the time."

Amid the variety of hymn and music-books for the children, many Sunday-schools are now having the hymns they prefer, printed in large type on muslin sheets, or on the Norwich Song Roll,† to be suspended in sight of all in the room. This plan is of especial value in the children's service, where all the exercises are general, and where it is so desirable to secure harmony, and unity of purpose, for there is a gain in having the children's eyes all fastened on the same point, or all looking towards the leader.

PRAYER.

"As to the *prayer*, a volume of directions might be given, and after all the good sense and discretion of

---
* Ninth Illinois Convention.
† Manufactured by H. V. Edmonds, Norwich, Conn.

the superintendent must be the main directory," is the statement of the Teacher Taught,* concerning the opening exercises of the Sunday-school—and the remarks are equally applicable to the children's service. But the suggestions made on this subject which follow that statement in the volume referred to, can hardly fail to profit one who is to lead children in their devotions.

"Let not the prayer degenerate into a sermon," says a valued Sunday-school writer,† "for when we are asking blessings from God, we ought not, with the same breath, to be directing the scholars. Let figurative language be avoided, as children form the strangest conceptions from many ordinary phrases. The language can hardly be too simple, or the prayer too short."

The same writer makes this further suggestion, as to prayer for the children, to follow a brief prayer for the teachers and other adults: "Let the superintendent offer a prayer *with* the children, as follows: 'O Lord God, thou art very great and good'—then children repeat. 'We thank thee for giving us food to eat and clothes to wear'—children repeat. 'Take us under thy kind care this Sabbath day'—children repeat, and so on to the end. There can be no objection to this prayer being a suitable form if preferred; it either may or may not conclude with the Lord's prayer."

---

* By F. A. Packard, Am. S. S. Union.
† Louisa Davids in The Sunday-school.

One of the most successful workers* among the children in our country, always leads the children thus in prayer in his Sunday-school, or in other services which he conducts for them. The following report † was made of his prayer with an infant class, which he taught by way of illustration at a Sunday-school convention in Washington, D. C.

After singing with the children one verse of the hymn,

"Jesus loves me, this I know,"

he said: "Now let us pray to this Saviour who loves us so much. You repeat after me.—[The children bowed their heads and prayed.]

"Dear Saviour,—we do thank thee—for coming so far—to save us.—We remember—how thou wast a little boy—in Bethlehem's manger;—how thou didst go about—doing good;—without any home;—men ill-treating thee;—until at last, after thirty-three years—thou didst die for me—on Calvary.—O Saviour!—help me—to call thee—*my* Saviour,—and to love thee—like thy little child.—May I show my love to thee,—by trying to keep—all thy commandments;—by being very kind to everybody;—by keeping the Sabbath-day,—by not saying bad words,—by helping my father and mother.—From a good distance off—a stranger has come—to tell us about thee.—Dear Saviour! help the stranger-man;—give him a word to speak,—give me a heart to listen;—and bless all that I love,—make them all thy children,—and in a little while—may we meet thee in heaven—for Jesus' sake. Amen."

"Perhaps you think you cannot pray thus," says another intelligent friend of the Sunday-school,‡ in

---

* Ralph Wells.   † Sunday-school Times, Jan. 4. 1868.
‡ R. G. Pardee in The Sunday-school Times.

comment on this style of prayer, "but you can learn— you can learn. Think what specific things you wish to thank God for, what to ask of Him, and your prayers will change for the better. The children love such prayer, delight in it, think they are worth praying for, and learn to pray, and the children ought to be taught thus to pray."

"During the time of prayer," suggests a valued English writer, "let the scholars clasp their hands in front, and let them close their eyes; if these members of the body are thus secured . . . . much disorder will be prevented."* At all events, "they should have some uniform position. If old enough, let them incline their heads forward. If not, let them stand."† This is in schools where kneeling is not the habit.

"A few moments' silent and thoughtful secret prayer by the teachers and children as they come to their places, is a blessed opening," says Dr. Tyng, ‡ " and a most encouraging sight. It seems to say in its expressive form of utterance, 'we are all here ready before the Lord, to hear all things that are commanded of Him.' It inspires hopeful anticipations. The Lord the Spirit seems to be in the place, and the work of the day begins with the dew upon the grass."

VERSIONS OF THE LORD'S PRAYER.

There is a growing readiness, even among those who are least inclined to liturgical services, to use fre-

---

* The Teachers' Companion, R. N. Collins, p. 91.
† Our Sunday-school, W. Abbott, p. 55.
‡ Forty Years Experience in Sunday-school, p. 108.

quently in public worship the sublime form of prayer commended by our blessed Lord. And surely this is well. "Its petitions are so simple and direct, that children of very tender age understand and appreciate them, yet so comprehensive and far-reaching, in the generalizations which evidently underlie them, that the profoundest theologians have failed to exhaust their meaning."*

When employed in the children's service, care should be taken as to the form followed. To prevent confusion, either the form given in Matt. vi. 9–13, according to our common English version, or that prescribed in the prayer-book of the Episcopal Church, should be adhered to. Some are strenuous as to the use of one of these, while many prefer the other. In favor of the one, it is said that it is the more accurate scriptural version. For the other is claimed the merit of wide use in the Episcopal, Methodist, Hugenot, and other churches with established liturgies. Certainly, either formula is admissible, unless with high ritualists who would forbid any departure in prayer from the phraseology of the prayer-book or of a particular translation of the Scriptures.

The two forms are appended, and it will be seen that the third word, used as "who" or "which," will indicate the form adopted by the leader, and thus enable the assembly to follow, "nothing doubting":

(From Matt. vi. 9–13.)
Our Father which art in heaven,
   Hallowed be thy name.

---

* The Golden Censer, John S. Hart, p. 5.

Thy kingdom come.
Thy will be done in earth, as it is in heaven.
Give us this day our daily bread.
And forgive us our debts, as we forgive our debtors.
And lead us not into temptation,
But deliver us from evil:
For thine is the kingdom,
And the power, and the glory, forever. Amen.

(From the Prayer-Book.)
Our Father who art in heaven,
Hallowed be thy name.
Thy kingdom come.
Thy will be done on earth, as it is in heaven.
Give us this day our daily bread.
And forgive us our trespasses, as we forgive those who trespass against us;
And lead us not into temptation;
But deliver us from evil:
For thine is the kingdom,
And the power, and the glory, forever and ever. Amen.

SPECIMEN FORMS

OF OPENING AND CLOSING EXERCISES.

A few specimen schedules of opening and closing exercises for a children's service are given herewith, for the benefit of those who are inexperienced in their preparation, and as suggestive of other forms in great variety.

The first two are arranged from the plans of the Sunday-school of the Second Congregational Church, New London, Ct., which are prepared annually by the superintendent, Henry P. Haven, and printed on sheets for distribution in the school:

SCHEDULE I.

At the tap of the bell, all bow their heads in silent prayer. At a second tap, the assembly rises. The leader says:

Gather the people together, men and women, and children, and the stranger that is within thy gates, that they may hear, and that they may learn, and fear the Lord your God, and observe to do all the words of this law. Deut. xxxi. 12.

In concert, all repeat:

Hear, O Israel! The Lord our God is one Lord.
And thou shalt love the Lord thy God, with all thine heart, and with all thy soul, and with all thy might.
Thou shalt fear the Lord thy God and serve him. Deut. vi. 4, 5, 13.

The superintendent says:

Ye shall diligently keep the commandments of the Lord your God, and his testimonies, and his statutes, which he hath commanded thee.
And thou shalt do that which is right and good in the sight of the Lord, that it may be well with thee. Deut. vi. 17, 18.

The assembly responds:

And the Lord commanded us to do all these statutes, to fear the Lord our God, for our good always, that he might preserve us alive, as it is at this day.
And it shall be our righteousness, if we observe to do all these commandments before the Lord our God, as he hath commanded us. Deut. vi. 24, 25.

The assembly chants:

O sing unto the Lord a | new— | song;
Sing unto the | Lord— | all the | earth;
Sing unto the Lord ; | bless his | name ;
Show forth his sal | vation, from | day to | day,
Declare his glory a | mong the | heathen :
His wonders a | mong | all | people.
For the Lord is great and greatly | to be | praised ;
He is to be | feared a | bove all | gods.
O worship the Lord in the | beauty of | holiness ;
Fear be | fore him, | all the | earth.

The assembly being seated, the leader reads a selection from the New Testament, having reference to the topic of the day.

All rising, an appropriate Psalm is read responsively by leader and assembly.

In concert, all repeat:

Blessed be the God and Father of our Lord Jesus Christ, who hath blessed us with all spiritual blessings in heavenly places in Christ. Eph. i. 3.

The assembly being seated, a hymn is sung.

All being in a position for prayer [kneeling, bowing forward the head, standing, or sitting with the eyes covered by the hand, as may be the practice,] prayer is offered by the leader, closing with the Lord's prayer, in which all unite.

The school rises. The leader says:

So they read the book of the law of God distinctly and gave the sense, and caused them to understand the reading. Neh. viii. 8.

Passages appropriate to the theme of the day are read responsively by the assembly, in divisions.

The assembly being seated, a hymn is sung:

Rising, all recite, in concert, this statement of Christian doctrines, in the language of Scripture:

ALL MEN ARE SINNERS.

For there is not a just man upon earth that doeth good, and sihneth not. Eccl. vii. 20.

Wherefore as by one man sin entered into the world, and death by sin; and so death passed upon all men, for that all have sinned. Rom. v. 12.

ALL MUST BE CONVERTED.

Jesus answered and said unto him, Verily, verily, I say unto thee, except a man be born again he cannot see the kingdom of God. John iii. 3.

Not by works of righteousness which we have done, but according to his mercy he saved us, by the washing of regeneration, and renewing of the Holy Ghost. Titus iii. 5.

JESUS THE ONLY SAVIOUR.

This is a faithful saying and worthy of all acceptation, that Christ Jesus came into the world to save sinners. I. Tim. i. 15.

Neither is there salvation in any other, for there is none other name under heaven given among men, whereby we must be saved. Acts iv. 12.

FINAL DESTINY OF THE RIGHTEOUS AND THE WICKED.

The hour is coming, in the which all that are in the graves shall hear his voice, And shall come forth, they that have done good to the resurrection of life, and they that have done evil to the resurrection of damnation. John v. 28, 29.

These shall go away into everlasting punishment, but the righteous into life eternal. Matt. xxv. 46.

For the foregoing statement, the apostles' creed may be substituted, if preferred.

The general exercises for the day follow this opening service.

At their close, the assembly rises, as at the opening, at the tap of the bell.

The leader says:

This book of the law shall not depart out of thy mouth; but thou shalt meditate therein day and night, that thou mayest observe to do according to all that is written therein: for then thou shalt make thy way prosperous, and then thou shalt have good success. Josh. i. 8.

The assembly responds:

All Scripture is given by inspiration of God, and is profitable for doctrine, for reproof, for correction, for instruction in righteousness: that the man of God may be perfect, thoroughly furnished unto all good works. II. Tim. iii. 16, 17.

A hymn is sung, followed by the doxology to close the service.

SCHEDULE II.

Rising at the tap of the bell, all recite in concert:

This is the day which the Lord hath made;
We will rejoice and be glad in it. Ps. cxviii. 24.
Hear my prayer O Lord!
Give ear to my supplications: Ps. cxliii. 1.
Unto thee, O Lord, do I lift up my soul!
O my God, I trust in thee. Ps. xxv. 1, 2.
Show me thy ways, O Lord;
Teach me thy paths. Ps. xxv. 4.
For thou art the God of my salvation;
On thee do I wait all the day. Ps. xxv. 5.

THE CHILDREN'S BIBLE SERVICE.

Trust in the Lord with all thine heart;
And lean not unto thine own understanding.
In all thy ways acknowledge him,
And he shall direct thy paths. Prov. iii. 5, 6.

This is a faithful saying, and worthy of all acceptation, that Christ Jesus came into the world to save sinners. I. Tim. i. 15.

Still standing, the assembly chants:

I will lift up mine eyes unto the hills,
From whence | cometh .. my | help.
My help cometh from the Lord,
Which made | heaven .. and | earth.
He will not suffer thy foot to be moved:
He that keepeth thee | will not | slumber.
Behold, he that keepeth Israel
Shall not | slumber .. nor | sleep.
The Lord shall preserve thee from all evil:
He shall pre- | serve thy | soul.
The Lord shall preserve thy going out, and thy coming in,
From this time forth, and even forevermore. | A- | men.

The assembly being seated, selections from the Scriptures, appropriate to the topic of the day, are read by the leader.

A hymn is sung.

All rising, selections from the twenty-seventh Psalm, as follows, are read responsively by leader and assembly:

The Lord is my light and my salvation;
Whom shall I fear?
The Lord is the strength of my life;
Of whom shall I be afraid?
One thing have I desired of the Lord,
That will I seek after;

That I may dwell in the house of the Lord all the days of my life.
To behold the beauty of the Lord,
And to inquire in his temple.
For in the time of trouble he shall hide me in his pavilion;
In the secret of his tabernacle shall he hide me;
He shall set me up upon a rock.
Therefore will I offer in his tabernacle sacrifices of joy;
I will sing, yea, I will sing praises unto the Lord.
Hear, O Lord, when I cry with my voice;
Have mercy also upon me, and answer me.
When thou saidst, Seek ye my face;
My heart said unto thee, Thy face, Lord, will I seek,
Thou hast been my help; leave me not,
Neither forsake me, O God of my salvation!
Teach me thy way, O Lord!
And lead me in a plain path, because of mine enemies.
I had fainted unless I had believed to see the goodness of the Lord
In the land of the living.
Wait on the Lord!
Be of good courage, and he shall strengthen thine heart;
Wait I say on the Lord!

In concert, all say:

The Lord our God be with us; let him not leave us nor forsake us; that he may incline our hearts unto him, to walk in all his ways and to keep his commandments. I. Kings viii. 57, 58.

The assembly being seated, a hymn is sung.

Prayer is offered, closing with the Lord's prayer, in which all unite.

All rising, the following selections are read, in alternation by leader and assembly, from the teachings of Christ in the sermon on the mount:

Remember the words of the Lord Jesus. Acts xx. 35.

Blessed are the poor in spirit: for theirs is the kingdom of heaven. Matt. v. 3.

Blessed are they which do hunger and thirst after righteousness: for they shall be filled.—Matt. v. 6.

Blessed are the merciful: for they shall obtain mercy. Matt. v. 7.

Blessed are the pure in heart: for they shall see God." Matt. v. 8.

Blessed are the peace-makers: for they shall be called the children of God. Matt. v. 9.

Blessed are they which are persecuted for righteousness' sake: for theirs is the kingdom of heaven. Matt. v. 10.

Let your light so shine before men, that they may see your good works and glorify your Father which is in heaven. Matt. v. 16.

Love your enemies, bless them that curse you, do good to them that hate you, and pray for them which despitefully use you, and persecute you. Matt. v. 44.

When thou doest alms, let not thy left hand know what thy right hand doeth. Matt. vi. 3.

When thou prayest, enter into thy closet, and when thou hast shut thy door, pray to thy Father which is in secret; and thy Father which seeth in secret shall reward thee openly. Matt. vi. 6.

If ye forgive men their trespasses, your heavenly Father will also forgive you. Matt. vi. 14.

But if ye forgive not men their trespasses, neither will your Father forgive your trespasses. Matt. vi. 15.

Ask, and it shall be given you; seek, and ye shall find; knock, and it shall be opened unto you. Matt. vii. 7.

For every one that asketh receiveth; and he that seeketh findeth; and to him that knocketh it shall be opened. Matt. vii. 8.

Enter ye in at the strait gate: for wide is the gate, and broad is the way, that leadeth to destruction, and many there be which go in thereat. Matt. vii. 13.

Because strait is the gate, and narrow is the way, which leadeth unto life, and few there be that find it. Matt. vii. 14.

The assembly being seated, a hymn is sung.

The general exercises for the day follow. At their

close, the assembly rises, at the tap of the bell, and the ten commandments are recited in concert.

The leader says:

These are the commandments, which the Lord commanded Moses for the children of Israel in Mount Sinai. Lev. xxvii. 34.

In concert, all recite:

1. Thou shalt have no other gods before me.
2. Thou shalt not make unto thee any graven image, or any likeness of any thing that is in heaven above, or that is in the earth beneath, or that is in the water under the earth: thou shalt not bow down thyself to them, nor serve them: for I the Lord thy God am a jealous God, visiting the iniquity of the fathers upon the children unto the third and fourth generation of them that hate me; and showing mercy unto thousands of them that love me, and keep my commandments.
3. Thou shalt not take the name of the Lord thy God in vain; for the Lord will not hold him guiltless that taketh his name in vain.
4. Remember the Sabbath-day, to keep it holy. Six days shalt thou labor, and do all thy work: but the seventh day is the Sabbath of the Lord thy God: in it thou shalt not do any work, thou, nor thy son, nor thy daughter, thy man-servant, nor thy maid-servant, nor thy cattle, nor thy stranger that is within thy gates: for in six days the Lord made heaven and earth, the sea, and all that in them is, and rested the seventh day: wherefore the Lord blessed the Sabbath-day, and hallowed it.
5. Honor thy father and thy mother: that thy days may be long upon the land which the Lord thy God giveth thee.
6. Thou shalt not kill.
7. Thou shalt not commit adultery.
8. Thou shalt not steal.
9. Thou shalt not bear false witness against thy neighbor.
10. Thou shalt not covet thy neighbor's house, thou shalt not covet thy neighbor's wife, nor his man-servant, nor his

maid-servant, nor his ox, nor his ass, nor any thing that is thy neighbor's. Ex. xx. 3-17.

The leader says:

The sum of the commandments, as given by our Lord Jesus Christ, in the gospel according to St. Mark, twelfth chapter, twenty-ninth, thirtieth, and thirty-first verses, reads:—

Assembly recites:

The first of all the commandments is, Hear, O Israel; the Lord our God is one Lord: And thou shalt love the Lord thy God with all thy heart, and with all thy soul, and with all thy mind, and with all thy strength: this is the first commandment. And the second is like, namely this, Thou shalt love thy neighbor as thyself.

The assembly being seated, a hymn is sung.

Prayer is offered, followed by the benediction, if a minister leads.

SCHEDULE III.

A third example of opening and closing exercises is adapted from the plans presented by George Beal, Jr., in his Manual of the Second Congregational Sabbath-school of Cohasset, Mass:

The bell strikes *twice* for the assembly to come to order.

It strikes *once* for the assembly to chant, as follows:

The Lord is in his holy temple, let all the earth keep | silence be- | fore him. Oh, worship the Lord in the beauty of | holiness; fear be- | fore him | all the earth.

The Lord is nigh unto them that are of a broken heart; and saveth | such as | be of a | contrite | spirit.

Oh, come let us worship and bow down; let us kneel before the | Lord our | maker. |

For he is our God, and we are the people of his | pasture, | and the | sheep of his | hand.

The bell strikes *once* for the assembly to assume a proper position for prayer. While all is quiet, prayer is offered, closing with the Lord's prayer, in which all join.

All rising, a hymn is sung.

After the reading by the leader, (the assembly being seated,) of a portion of Scripture suited to the theme of the day, the assembly rises, and in concert all recite:

Great is the Lord, and greatly to be praised;
And his greatness is unsearchable.
The Lord is righteous in all his ways,
And holy in all his works.
The Lord is nigh unto all them that call upon him,
To all that call upon him in truth. Ps. cxlv. 3, 17, 18.
Seek ye the Lord while he may be found;
Call ye upon him while he is near.
Let the wicked forsake his way,
And the unrighteous man his thoughts:
And let him return unto the Lord,
And he will have mercy upon him;
And to our God, for he will abundantly pardon. Is. lv. 6, 7.

The assembly, by divisions, (as males and females, or from opposite sides of the room,) recites responsively a portion of the nineteenth Psalm.

The law of the Lord is perfect, converting the soul:
The testimony of the Lord is sure, making wise the simple.
The statutes of the Lord are right, rejoicing the heart:
The commandment of the Lord is pure, enlightening the eyes.
The fear of the Lord is clean, enduring forever:
The judgments of the Lord are true and righteous altogether.

More to be desired are they than gold; yea, than much fine gold:
Sweeter also than honey, and the honeycomb.
Moreover by them is thy servant warned:
And in keeping of them there is great reward.
Who can understand his errors?
Cleanse thou me from secret faults.
Keep back thy servant also from presumptuous sins; let them not have dominion over me:
Then shall I be upright, and I shall be innocent from the great transgression.

All in concert recite:

Let the words of my mouth, and the meditation of my heart, be acceptable in thy sight, O Lord, my strength and my redeemer.

A hymn is sung.
General exercises follow.
At the conclusion of these, the bell strikes *twice*, to command attention. Notices are then given out, or announcements made.
The bell strikes *once*, for the assembly to arise.
A hymn is sung.
Prayer closes the services.

SCHEDULE IV.

In a little work* prepared by the Rev. Dr. Richard Newton, of Philadelphia, for the Sunday-schools of his church, are given plans for opening and closing services, for each Sabbath in the month. One of these is

---

*Offices of Devotion for the use of Sunday Schools.

given herewith, as appropriate to any service for the children.

Singing.

Reading of Scripture.

Responsive Selection.

WISDOM'S COUNSEL.

Superintendent. My son, forget not my law: but let thine heart keep my commandments. Prov. iii. 1.

Scholars. For length of days, and long life, and peace shall they add to thee. Prov. iii. 2.

Superintendent. Let not mercy and truth forsake thee: bind them about thy neck, write them upon the table of thine heart. Prov. iii. 3.

Scholars. So shalt thou find favor and good understanding in the sight of God and man. Prov. iii. 4.

Superintendent. Trust in the Lord with all thine heart, and lean not to thine own understanding. Prov. iii. 5.

Scholars. In all thy ways acknowledge him, and he shall direct thy paths. Prov. iii. 6.

Superintendent. Happy is the man that findeth wisdom, and the man that getteth understanding. Prov. iii. 13.

Scholars. For the merchandise of it is better than the merchandise of silver, and the gain thereof than fine gold. Prov. iii. 14.

Superintendent. She is more precious than rubies; and all the things thou canst desire are not to be compared unto her. Prov. iii. 15.

Scholars. Length of days is in her right hand, and in her left hand riches and honor. Prov. iii. 17.

Scholars. She is a tree of life to them that lay hold upon her, and happy is every one that retaineth her. Prov. iii. 18.

The superintendent says: Let us pray.

Then follows a prayer suited to the occasion, and to

the theme of the service, closing with the Lord's prayer, in which all join.

The superintendent adds the prayer :

The grace of our Lord Jesus Christ, and the love of God, and the fellowship of the Holy Ghost, be with us all evermore. Amen.

After the general exercises, a simple prayer closes the service.

Other forms of opening and closing exercises can be found in Dr. Newton's Offices of Devotion, and Mr. Beal's Cohasset Manual, already referred to, and in Philip Phillip's Singing Pilgrim, the Sunday School Reader, for Opening Service and Class Study, by Rev. J. H. Vincent, and The New Sunday School Manual, by Carlton & Porter.

GENERAL EXERCISES.

In the general exercises of the children's service, there is room for great variety. Rules to govern in their arrangement have already been indicated. Whatever is now added by way of example may be so modified or altered in use, by any minister or superintendent, as to better adapt it to the assembly for which it is employed, and each form here given will be likely to suggest a number of similar ones on the same general plan, and thus the list can be extended indefinitely.

Before presenting any of the more elaborate exercises, it may be well to give some of the simpler forms, employed by beginners or in communities where, as yet, there is a shrinking from whatever of this character involves much study or effort to make it ready for use. These may also prove serviceable as supplementary to the extended exercises, or at the close of an ordinary Sunday-school session.

FORMS OF THE GOLDEN TEXT.

A call is made for passages of Scripture containing a particular word, previously designated, or beginning with a given letter or phrase, known as the Golden Text.

Each person present may recite such a text, or in a large school one division may recite at one meeting, and another at the next.

The following are examples of the Golden Text:

LETTERS.

Texts beginning with some letter of the alphabet:

Examples.—A—Ask and it shall be given you. Matt. vii. 7.
B—Be of the same mind one toward another. Rom. xii. 16.

Texts beginning with the letter that begins the scholar's Christian name:

Examples.—William—Wisdom is the principal thing, &c., Prov. iv. 7.
Sarah—Search the Scriptures, &c. John v. 39.

Texts beginning with the letter that begins the name of the month on which the service is observed:

Examples.—January—Judge not that ye be not judged, &c. Matt. vii. 1.
August—A soft answer turneth away wrath, &c. Prov. xv. 1.

WORDS.

Texts commencing with such words as Blessed, Cursed, Come, Go, Praise, Pray, Seek, Trust, etc. :

Examples.—Blessed—Blessed are the pure in heart, for they shall see God. Matt. v. 8.
Cursed—Cursed be he that setteth light by his father or his mother. Deut. xxvii. 16.

Texts containing such words as Faith, Love, Grace, Wisdom, Heart, Life, Death, Heaven, Hell, etc. :

Examples.—Faith—Watch ye, stand fast in the faith, quit you like men, be strong. I. Cor. xvi. 13.
Love—For this is the love of God, that we keep his commandments. I. John v. 3.

NAMES.

Texts which contain the name of any person present who has a Scripture name :

Examples.—Mary—But one thing is needful, and Mary hath chosen that good part, &c. Luke x. 42.
Samuel—And the child Samuel ministered unto the Lord before Eli. I. Sam. iii. 1.

Texts which contain the name of either of the twelve tribes of Israel, of the four evangelists, of the twelve apostles, of the mountains, cities, or rivers of Palestine :

Examples.—Benjamin—And of Benjamin he said, The beloved of the Lord shall dwell in safety by him ; and the Lord shall cover him all the day long. Deut. xxxiii. 12.
Mark—He came to the house of Mary, the mother of John, whose surname was Mark, where many were gathered together, praying. Acts xii. 12.

Thomas—Jesus saith unto him, Thomas, because thou hast seen me thou hast believed; blessed are they which have not seen and yet have believed. John xx. 29.

Mount of Olives—And he came out and went, as he was wont, to the Mount of Olives. Luke xxii. 39.

Jerusalem—O Jerusalem, Jerusalem, thou that killest the prophets and stonest them which are sent unto thee, &c. Matt. xxiii. 37.

Jordan—Then went out to him Jerusalem, and all Judea, and all the region round about Jordan. Matt. iii. 5.

Texts containing different names or titles given to God the Father:

Example.—God of hosts—O Lord God of hosts, hear my prayer: give ear, O God of Jacob. Ps. lxxxiv. 8.

Texts containing different names or titles given to Jesus Christ:

Example.—Wonderful—And his name shall be called Wonderful, Counsellor, &c. Is. ix. 6.

Texts containing different names or titles given to the Holy Spirit:

Example.—Comforter—But the Comforter, which is the Holy Spirit, &c. John xiv. 26.

Texts containing different descriptive names of the Holy Scriptures:

Example.—Lamp—Thy word is a lamp unto my feet, and a light unto my path. Ps. cxix. 105.

PHRASES.

Texts commencing with, And it came to pass, Verily, verily, etc. :

Example.—And it came to pass, when the time was come that

he should be received up, he steadfastly set his face to go to Jerusalem. Luke ix. 51.

Verily, Verily, I say unto you, he that receiveth whomsoever I send receiveth me. John xiii. 20.

Texts containing I will, Thou shalt, The fear of the Lord, etc:

Example.—Peter said unto him, Lord, why cannot I follow thee now? *I will* lay down my life for thy sake. John xiii. 37.

Then saith Jesus unto him, Get thee hence, Satan: for it is written, *Thou shalt* worship the Lord thy God, and him only shalt thou serve. Matt. iv. 10.

Come ye children, hearken unto me: I will teach you *the fear of the Lord*. Ps. xxxiv. 11.

VERSES.

The first or last verses of the different books of the Bible:

Example.—The first of Genesis—In the beginning God created the heaven and the earth.

The last of Hosea—Who is wise, and he shall understand these things? prudent, and he shall know them? &c.

The last verses of the various psalms:

Example.—Psalm xcix. 9.—Exalt the Lord our God, and worship at his holy hill; for the Lord our God is holy.

The last verses of the different chapters of the gospels:

Example.—Mark xiii. 37.—And what I say unto you, I say unto all, Watch.

The last verses of the different chapters of the epistles:

Example.—I. Cor. xiii. 13.—And now abideth faith, hope, charity, these three; but the greatest of these is charity.

ILLUSTRATIVE AND PROOF EXERCISES.

Besides the various forms of the Golden Text, there are in common use at the children's service many simple modes of illustrating subjects, bringing out history or biography, or proving doctrines in Scripture language:

TOPICAL.

Each person present is requested to recite some passage from the Bible on the subject of Faith, Prayer, Humility, Temperance, The Sabbath, Sin, Charity, Death, Heaven, The Judgment, etc.

HISTORICAL.

To one class or division is assigned the Bible history of Jerusalem before its occupancy by the Jews, to another its history before the building of the first temple, to another its history until the time of the captivity, to another its history from the return of the Jews to the coming of Christ, to another its history in the days of Jesus as the Son of Man, etc.

And thus of Hebron, or Bethlehem, or Shechem, of the tribes of Israel or Judah, of the Edomites, or of the early church.

BIOGRAPHICAL.

A call is made for the main facts in the history of a patriarch, as Abraham; a commander, as Gideon; a matron, as Rebecca; a prophet, as Daniel; a King, as David; an apostle, as Peter, etc.

By arrangement, one person, or one class, can recite four or five verses in this history, and the next person or class can follow with as many more, in chronological order, and thus through the record.

DOCTRINAL.

The request is made for Scripture recitations in proof of certain truths or doctrines which are stated, as, That man is by nature sinful ; That the finally impenitent are hopelessly lost ; That there is fulness of salvation through faith in Christ, etc. All present may have an opportunity of reciting the proof passages, to bring out an accumulation of Bible testimony in defense of the truth. Sometimes it is requested that as far as possible there be no repetition of texts—that each person shall recite one not previously quoted by another. This necessitates the memorizing of a number of passages, and of watchfulness while others are reciting. At the same time it adds interest to the exercise, and evidences the wonderful richness of the treasures of God's Word.

The different clauses of the apostle's creed may be thus re-enforced by Scripture, or truths may be brought out as applicable to the special circumstances of the times, or the needs of the assembly.

RESPONSIVE.

A question asked in one text, may be answered in another. The leader can ask all the questions, and the members of the assembly can answer them, or the teachers can put the questions, and their scholars can respond. Or this last order can be reversed, the scholars questioning and the teachers replying. A similar arrangement may be made between two divisions of the school—two Bible classes, or the older and younger classes,—or between those who are members of the school and those who are not.

Those who are to propound the questions, can look them out from the Bible and give them, in advance of the meeting, on slips of paper, to those who are to answer them. The latter must then search out the responses, and have them ready in season for the service at which they are to be recited.

EXAMPLE.

Question—Who shall ascend into the hill of the Lord? or who shall dwell in his holy place? Ps. xxiv. 3.

Answer—He that walketh uprightly, and worketh righteousness, and speaketh the truth in his heart. Ps. xv. 2.

Question—What shall we do that we might work the works of God? John vi. 28.

Answer—This is the work of God, that ye believe on him whom He hath sent. John vi. 29.

Question—If a man die, shall he live again? Job xiv. 14.

Answer—Marvel not at this: for the hour is coming in the which all that are in the graves shall hear his voice, and shall come forth; they that have done good unto the resurrection of life; and they that have done evil, unto the resurrection of damnation. John v. 28, 29.

Question—Shall we give, or shall we not give? Mark xii. 15.

Answer—Every man according as he purposeth in his heart, so let him give; not grudgingly, or of necessity; for God loveth a cheerful giver. II. Cor. ix. 7.

GENERAL QUESTIONS.

A general question may be given out by the leader, to be replied to, in Bible language or otherwise, by each member of the assembly. Thus:

What think ye of Christ?
What must I do to be saved?
What is it to live a Christian life?
What one text of the Bible would you preserve, if all the rest must be destroyed?

Sometimes a question of practical importance to all is asked, to be replied to in writing at the next meeting, and these answers are read by their writers or by the leader, and briefly commented on. Thus each one is requested to give a reason for believing that Jesus is *his* Saviour, or to state *his* hindrances to a Christian life or faith.

REVIEW EXERCISES.

The children's service is often made useful as a monthly or quarterly review exercise. The lessons studied in the Sunday-school from week to week are taken up at the close of the month, and proof texts are called for in support of the truths taught.

In some places it is the practice for members of the congregation to recite consecutively, at a quarterly children's meeting, the texts of the pastor's sermons for the last three months, thus bringing to mind not only the Scripture passages, but the lessons of their enforcement in the Sabbath preaching.

In some instances the pastors cluster the lessons of the month in skillful grouping, to enforce some grand truth which runs through them all, and this they illustrate in a brief talk suited to the comprehension of the children.

Rev. W. E. Knox, pastor of the Presbyterian church at Rome, N. Y., has been peculiarly successful in a line of effort kindred to this. His school studies the series of Graduated Sunday-school Text-books prepared by his brother, Rev. Charles E. Knox. Different classes having commenced the series at different times, all five of the volumes are in use at one time in his school. It is his habit to run over the lesson for the day in the several books, to find in each some illustration of one truth which he then presents for consideration. As these lessons had no designed connection with each other, except chronologically, it would not seem easy to discover in those for every Sabbath such identity of teaching as would make this plan available; but a reference to his note-book for these services not only shows his own ingenuity and sound wisdom, but also illustrates the unity and harmony of the word of God, and goes to prove that "*all* Scripture is given by inspiration of God, and is profitable for doctrine, for reproof, for correction, for instruction in righteousness."

A few sample schedules are appended, as employed by Mr. Knox, in his service with the children, showing as they do the ease with which various Bible lessons may, at a monthly service of review, be made to impress some central and important truth.

For one Sabbath, the lessons to be commented on were as follows:

The call of Jesus to Peter and Andrew. Matt. iv. 17-22.
The struggle with Beelzebub, in casting out devils. Luke x. 14-26.
The harvest of souls pointed out by Jesus. John iv. 35-42.
The parable of the ten virgins at the marriage. Matt. xxv. 1-9.
The imprisonment of Peter and John for preaching. Acts iv. 1-7.

The truth enforced was,

THE CHRISTIAN LIFE ILLUSTRATED.

Wherein is a Christian's life like fishing?
Wherein is a Christian's life like fighting?
Wherein is a Christian's life like farming?
Wherein is a Christian's life like marrying?
Wherein is a Christian's life like law-breaking?

Another Sabbath showed these lessons:

The coming of Jesus to the Mount to preach. Matt. v.
The traveler from Jerusalem to Jericho. Luke x.
The angel at the pool of Bethesda. John v.
The departing lord distributing the talents. Matt. xxv.
The disciples shown to have been with Jesus. Acts 4.

The subject announced was,

THE TRAVELERS:

The Divine traveler—What he saw.
The lonely traveler—What he suffered.
The angelic traveler—Where he descended.
The princely traveler—What he distributed.
The apostolic travelers—Whom they had been with.

Again, these were the lessons:

Jesus heals the leper. Matt. viii. 3.
Publicans and sinners come to hear Jesus. Luke xv. 1.
The Jews wonder at the knowledge of Jesus   John vii. 15.
The King sends away the condemned. Matt. xxv. 41.
The disciples preach with boldness. Acts iv. 31.

The truth presented was,

THE MIGHTY POWER OF JESUS:

His touch cleanses the filthiest.
His voice draws the vilest.
His knowledge astonishes the wisest.
His wrath dismays the stoutest.
His grace emboldens the weakest.

MISSIONARY EXERCISES.

The children's missionary meeting is often alternated with their service of general Bible exercises. If there is a juvenile missionary association in the school or congregation, the president of that takes the lead at the missionary meeting, as the pastor or superintendent does at the ordinary children's service. The missionary meeting is held one month, and the service with general exercises the next. Or, where the children's service is observed weekly, the missionary meeting has the first Sabbath in each month. The hymns and passages of Scripture are then selected with reference to the missionary character of the service. Texts are called for to illustrate the duty and manner of giving to advance the cause of Christ, or of making personal endeavor for souls. Or Bible incidents are asked for, showing how the early disciples performed missionary service, and the results of such enterprise.

If the school or congregation assists in the support of a Sunday-school or other missionary, his letters will be read at the missionary meeting, and statements may be made by scholars or teachers designated for the purpose, as to the history or progress of particular missions. And the free-will offerings of the children, through their class circles or auxiliary societies, may be presented to the treasurer, and by him reported for the month, or more, included in the returns.

EXTENDED TOPICAL EXERCISES.

In addition to the simpler forms for the exercises of the children's service thus outlined, there are in use in many schools extended and carefully prepared Bible exercises on particular themes, arranged anew for each month's service. These are best explained in the examples which follow. They cost much time and study in their preparation, and they can be used only by a special assignment to each class or division of the school of its particular portion in advance of the day of recitation, that the proper passages may be looked out and committed to memory in season for the service. But the beauty and value of these exercises far more than repay all the labor involved in their arrangement or use, and none who employ them will be likely to deem the simpler forms more desirable or attractive, except for beginners in such services, or as supplementary, in occasional instances, to the extended schedules.

USE OF THE BLACKBOARD.

In connection with all the exercises herein designated—both simple and elaborate—the blackboard can be made serviceable. The Golden Text for the day may be written on the board. So may the topic assigned for illustration or proof. An initial text of Scripture on the day's theme, may have a place there. Or, the subject of the exercises may be presented by a synopsis on the board, for explanation and comment by the leader, when the recitations are concluded. But let it be borne in mind that "the only justifiable use of the blackboard in a Sabbath-school is in order to make Bible truths more clear and attractive in the eyes of teachers and scholars."* It is to be hoped that neither in the children's service nor in the Sunday-school will any human exposition of Scripture truth be made a substitute for the Divinely inspired Word. Bible texts memorized by the children would be likely to prove better spiritual food for them, than would the most accurate and ingenious other presentation of the truth taught in those texts, if there must be a choice between the two. But the blackboard can be so employed as to aid in fastening the inspired phraseology in the children's minds, as well as in indicating its exposition, and thus it is used by many a superintendent or pastor. By it, the Christian teacher is enabled

---

*The Sabbath School Index, p. 114.

to fulfill the spirit of the command as to the words of the law, which came to Israel; "and thou shalt bind them for a sign upon thine hand, and they shall be as frontlets between thine eyes. *And thou shalt write them upon the posts of thy house, and on thy gates.*" *

CAUTION AS TO SPEECH-MAKING.

Brief and appropriate addresses on the theme of the Bible recitations for the day, may properly follow any of the exercises here commended. But caution must be observed on this point, for speech-making to children has been sadly overdone. The habit still prevalent in many places, of looking up "speakers" for the Sunday-school concert, or the monthly missionary meetings, as though they were to be a chief reliance and attraction, is by no means to be approved. One aim of this book is to press the superior advantages of fitting exercises of worship, and of Bible-recitations for the children, over miscellaneous declamations on their part or on the part of any of the vast host of platform story-tellers whose services have been in such command before them.

Addresses and sermons to children have their place, and a very important one it is; but that whole subject is treated by itself in a subsequent portion of this volume. The Sunday school concert as a recitative Bible-service, has proved so valuable where best known, that it deserves prominence as a distinct meeting of the children even where they are preached to at stated

---
* Deut. vi. 8, 9.

seasons. Perhaps the Bible service might, to advantage alternate, month by month, with the preaching service, or the two forms of service might be judiciously combined.

It is not the purpose of this work to portray a model or ideal service for universal use among children in the temple; but rather to show what in this line has been approved in practice, and to suggest thoughts which may be of value to those interested in arranging, conducting and improving such services, until the day when the best energies of the church and ministry shall be directed thither.

PART III.

SPECIMEN BIBLE LESSONS

FOR

THE CHILDREN'S SERVICE.

SPECIMEN BIBLE LESSONS

FOR

THE CHILDREN'S SERVICE.

THE lessons which follow were collected by the author of this volume in a wide field of observation and experience. Almost without exception, they have been already used successfully by pastors or superintendents in children's meetings. But little time will now be required to prepare them for use in any school or congregation. If each teacher has a book, the required references may be written therefrom on cards or slips of paper, and distributed to the scholars a week or more previous to the day of recitation, to give sufficient time for the committal of the texts. The cards should be numbered to correspond with the figures in the book, that the references may be readily called for in order.

If, in recitation, there should be any failure of a scholar to respond, the teacher should recite or read the required passage, that there be no break in the chain of proofs. It will be well also for the leader to repeat any passage not given so as to be clearly heard, although with a little effort each scholar can be taught to recite audibly and with distinctness.

The opening and closing exercises introductory to some of the lessons which follow, may be used appropriately at the ordinary sessions of the Sunday-school.

LESSON I.

THE EXISTENCE AND ATTRIBUTES OF GOD, OUR CREATOR, KING, FATHER, AND BENEFACTOR, AS EXHIBITED IN THE PSALMS OF DAVID.

(Originally prepared for the Sunday School of the Asylum Hill Congregational Church, Hartford, Ct.)

INTRODUCTORY EXERCISES.

At the call to order the assembly rises.

The leader says:

Hearken unto me, O ye children: . . . Hear instruction and be wise, and refuse it not. Prov. viii. 32, 33.

The assembly responds:

Seek ye out of the book of the Lord, and read. Isa. xxxiv. 16.

Leader. Every house is builded by some man; but he that built all things is God. Heb. iii. 4.

Of him, and through him, and to him are all things. Rom. xi. 36.

In him we live, and move, and have our being. Acts xvii. 28.

Know therefore this day, and consider it in thine heart, that the Lord he is God in heaven above, and upon the earth beneath: there is none else. Deut. iv. 39.

Assembly. Thou art worthy, O Lord, to receive glory and honor and power: for thou hast created all things, and for thy pleasure they are and were created. Rev. iv. 11.

Leader. The Lord our God is righteous in all his works which he doeth. Dan ix. 14.

A God of truth and without iniquity, just and right is he. Deut. xxxii. 4.

He is the living God, and steadfast for ever, and his kingdom that which shall not be destroyed, and his dominion shall be even unto the end. Dan. vi. 26.

And he doeth according to his will in the army of heaven, and among the inhabitants of the earth: and none can stay his hand, or say unto him, What doest thou? Dan. iv. 35.

Assembly. Thine, O Lord, is the greatness and the power, and the glory and the victory, and the majesty: for all that is in the heaven and in the earth is thine; thine is the kingdom, O Lord, and thou art exalted as head above all. I. Chron. xxix. 11.

Leader. The Lord by wisdom hath founded the earth; by understanding hath he established the heavens. Prov. iii. 19.

With him is wisdom and strength, he hath counsel and understanding. Job xii. 13.

The Lord searcheth all hearts, and understandeth all the imaginations of the thoughts. I. Chron. xxviii. 9.

Neither is there any creature that is not manifest in his sight: but all things are naked and opened unto the eyes of him with whom we have to do. Heb. iv. 13.

Assembly. O the depth of the riches both of the wisdom and knowledge of God! how unsearchable are his judgments, and his ways past finding out! Rom. xi. 33.

All, in concert, say:

To God only wise, be glory through Jesus Christ for ever. Amen. Rom. xvi. 27.

The assembly being seated, a hymn is sung.

> Praise to God, the great Creator;
> Praise to God from every tongue.—[*Happy Voices, Hymn* 9.

> Praise the Lord when blushing morning
> Wakes the blossoms fresh with dew.—[*Golden Shower, p.* 43.

Or any hymn of similar character.

All rising, Job. xxxviii. 1–18 and xl. 7–14 are read in alternation by leader and assembly:

Leader. Then the Lord answered Job out of the whirlwind and said,
Assembly. Who is this that darkeneth counsel
By words without knowledge?
Leader. Gird up now thy loins like a man;
For I will demand of thee, and answer thou me.
Assembly. Where wast thou when I laid the foundations of the earth?
Declare, if thou hast understanding.
Leader. Who hath laid the measures thereof, if thou knowest?
Or who hath stretched the line upon it?
Assembly. Whereupon are the foundations thereof fastened!
Or who laid the corner-stone thereof;
Leader. When the morning stars sang together,
And all the sons of God shouted for joy?
Assembly. Or who shut up the sea with doors,
When it brake forth, as if it had issued out of the womb?
Leader. When I made the cloud the garment thereof,
And thick darkness a swaddling-band for it,
Assembly. And brake up for it my decreed place,
And set bars and doors,
Leader. And said, Hitherto shalt thou come, but no further:
And here shall thy proud waves be stayed?
Assembly. Hast thou commanded the morning since thy days;
And caused the day-spring to know his place;
Leader. That it might take hold of the ends of the earth,
That the wicked might be shaken out of it?
Assembly. It is turned as clay to the seal;
And they stand as a garment.
Leader. And from the wicked their light is withholden,
And the high arm shall be broken.
Assembly. Hast thou entered into the springs of the sea?
Or hast thou walked in the search of the depth?

THE CHILDREN'S BIBLE SERVICE. 89

Leader. Have the gates of death been opened unto thee?
Or hast thou seen the doors of the shadow of death?
Assembly. Hast thou perceived the breadth of the earth?
Declare if thou knowest it all.
Leader. Gird up thy loins now like a man:
I will demand of thee, and declare thou unto me.
Assembly. Wilt thou also disannul my judgment?
Wilt thou condemn me, that thou mayest be righteous?
Leader. Hast thou an arm like God?
Or canst thou thunder with a voice like him?
Assembly. Deck thyself now with majesty and excellency;
And array thyself with glory and beauty.
Leader. Cast abroad the rage of thy wrath:
And behold every one that is proud, and abase him.
Assembly. Look on every one that is proud, and bring him low;
And tread down the wicked in their place.
Leader. Hide them in the dust together;
And bind their faces in secret.
Assembly. Then will I also confess unto thee
That thine own right hand can save thee.

Prayer is offered, closing with the Lord's prayer, in which all unite.

All rising, the assembly unite in singing a hymn.

> Come, sound his praise abroad,
> And hymns of glory sing.
> [*Am. S. S. Hymn Book, p.* 52.

All being seated, the leader reads the first fourteen verses of the first chapter of St. John's Gospel, adding a few words of explanation as to the identity of the Word with Jesus Christ.

The members of the infant department rise and recite as follows, from the Infant Catechism, (one scholar giving a question and the next an answer, and so on, as in responsive recitations of Scripture):

Q.—Who made the world? who dress'd the earth?
Who gave the flowers and fruits their birth?

A.—'Twas God, by whose almighty power
The shower falls and blooms the flower.

Q.—Who placed the glorious sun on high?
Who spread abroad the starry sky?

A.—'Twas God, who said, Let there be light;
'Twas God, who made the heavens so bright.

Q.—Who made this little frame of mine?
Who made my soul, almost divine?

A.—God's wondrous power my body framed,
And from his breath my spirit came.

Q.—And who is God? Where does he dwell?
How great he is no tongue can tell.

A.—He dwells in heaven too far to see,
And yet he stoops to look on me.

Q.—How near is God? Does he e'er come
To see me in my earthly home?

A.—Yes; near thy path and round thy bed,
He hears whatever there is said.

Q.—How good is God! I've heard it said
He counts the hairs upon my head.

A.—He hears the ravens when they call;
He watches when the sparrows fall.

Q.—Can God love me?—so great, so high,—
Me, in my helpless infancy?

A.—Yes, when on earth he came to dwell
He loved the little children well.

Q.—What were the words he kindly said
   When on their heads his hands he laid?

A.—Suffer the lambs to come to me;
   Like such must my disciples be.

[In teaching this lesson to the children, the questions and answers should be fully explained. The rhyming is useful in impressing the lesson when it is fairly understood.]

All rising, the leader says:

Remember now thy Creator in the days of thy youth. Eccl. xii. 1.

The assembly responds:

My father, thou art the guide of my youth. Jer. iii. 4.

Leader. Trust in the Lord with all thine heart; and lean not unto thine own understanding. Prov. iii. 5.

Assembly. Though he slay me, yet will I trust in him. Job xiii. 15.

Leader. In all thy ways acknowledge him, and he shall direct thy paths. Prov. iii. 6.

All being seated, a hymn is sung.

How gentle God's commands,
How kind his precepts are.
   [*Song Flowers, p.* 29.

GENERAL EXERCISES.

The leader says: The Psalms are full of evidences of God's existence, as shown in his works of creation and providence. It was not the purpose of the Psalmist to declare, in so many words, a truth which it seems impossible should be doubted; and when such declarations are made, it is only that they may serve as incentives to trust, or as a ground of supreme consolation.

1. Will the first division [or class*] repeat some of the verses in which David in this way affirms the existence of God?

Division [or class] No. 1 rises, and its members recite, simultaneously or in consecutive order, as follows:

The Lord liveth; and blessed be my Rock; and let the God of my salvation be exalted. Psalms xviii. 46.

That men may know that thou, whose name alone is JEHOVAH, art the Most High over all the earth. Psalms lxxxiii. 18.

For the Lord is great, and greatly to be praised: he is to be feared above all gods.

For all the gods of the nations are idols; but the Lord made the heavens.

Say among the heathen that the Lord reigneth: the world also shall be established that it shall not be moved: he shall judge the people righteously. Psalms xcvi. 4, 5, 10.

2. *Leader.* Do any deny the existence of God? and who are they?

Div. No. 2. The fool hath said in his heart, There is no God. They are corrupt, they have done abominable works, there is none that doeth good. Psalms xiv. 1.

3. *Leader.* Even without the Bible, are there not proofs enough of God's existence in his works, to leave men without excuse for disbelief?

Div. No. 3. The heavens declare the glory of God; and the firmament sheweth his handywork.

---

* Each class can take a section of this lesson, or two or more sections can be assigned to one class.

Day unto day uttereth speech, and night unto night sheweth knowledge.

There is no speech nor language, where their voice is not heard. Psalms xix. 1, 2, 3.

4. *Leader.* Is God the absolute sovereign of the universe?

Div. No. 4. The Lord hath prepared his throne in the heavens; and his kingdom ruleth over all. Psalms ciii. 19.

The Lord reigneth, he is clothed with majesty; the Lord is clothed with strength, wherewith he hath girded himself: the world also is established, that it cannot be moved. Psalms xciii. 1.

5. *Leader.* Repeat some passage in which the Psalmist asserts God's sovereign rule over the world of nature.

Div. No. 5. In his hand are the deep places of the earth: the strength of the hills is his also.

The sea is his, and he made it: and his hands formed the dry land. Psalms xcv. 4, 5.

Whatsoever the Lord pleased, that did he in heaven, and in earth, in the seas, and all deep places.

He causeth the vapors to ascend from the ends of the earth; he maketh lightnings for the rain; he bringeth the wind out of his treasuries. Psalms cxxxv. 6, 7.

6. *Leader.* And over angels and men.

Div. No. 6. For who in the heaven can be compared unto the Lord? who among the sons of the mighty can be likened unto the Lord? Psalms lxxxix. 6.

For the kingdom is the Lord's: and he is the governor among the nations. Psalms xxii. 28.

For God is the King of all the earth: sing ye praises with understanding. Psalms xlvii. 7.

7. *Leader.* Does God himself, through the mouth of the inspired Psalmist, assert his sovereignty?

Div. No. 7. Be still and know that I am God: I will be exalted among the heathen, I will be exalted in the earth. Psalms xlvi. 10.

8. *Leader.* God is a rightful sovereign; (1st.) because he created all things. How does David express this?

Div. No. 8. Know ye that the Lord he is God: it is he that hath made us, and not we ourselves; we are his people, and the sheep of his pasture. Psalms c. 3.

The heavens are thine, the earth also is thine: as for the world, and the fullness thereof, thou hast founded them.

The north and the south thou hast created them: Tabor and Herman shall rejoice in thy name. Psalms lxxxix. 11, 12.

9. *Leader.* He is a rightful sovereign; (2d.) because he preserves, and sustains the works which he has created. What does David say of this?

Div. No. 9. He watereth the hills from his chambers: the earth is satisfied with the fruit of thy works.

He causeth the grass to grow for the cattle, and herb for the service of man: that he may bring forth food out of the earth.

These wait all upon thee; that thou mayest give them their meat in due season.

That thou givest them, they gather: thou openest thine hand, they are filled with good.

Thou hidest thy face, they are troubled: thou takest away their breath, they die, and return to their dust.

Thou sendest forth thy spirit, they are created: and thou renewest the face of the earth. Psalms civ. 13, 14, 27, 28, 29, 30.

10. *Leader.* Is not this a reason why God should be worshiped and obeyed?

Div. No. 10. O come, let us worship and bow down : let us kneel before the Lord our maker.

For he is our God ; and we are the people of his pasture, and the sheep of his hand. To-day if ye will hear his voice,

Harden not your heart. Psalms xcv. 6, 7, 8.

11. *Leader.* Is God's reign eternal?

Div. No. 11. Before the mountains were brought forth, or ever thou hadst formed the earth and the world, even from everlasting to everlasting, thou art God. Psalms xc. 2.

Thy throne is established of old : thou art from everlasting. Psalms xciii. 2.

12. *Leader.* Is God subject to change? or is he " the same, yesterday, and to-day, and forever?"

Div. No. 12. Of old hast thou laid the foundation of the earth : and the heavens are the work of thy hands.

They shall perish, but thou shalt endure : yea, all of them shall wax old like a garment ; as a vesture shalt thou change them, and they shall be changed :

But thou art the same, and thy years shall have no end. Psalms cii. 25, 26, 27.

The counsel of the Lord standeth for ever, the thoughts of his heart to all generations. Psalms xxxiii. 11.

13. *Leader.* Is he a God of infinite power?

Div. No. 13. O Lord God of hosts, who is a strong Lord like unto thee ? or to thy faithfulness round about thee ? Psalms lxxxix. 8.

14. *Leader.* Is God as far above earthly beings in majesty as in power?

Div. No. 14. Bless the Lord, O my soul. O Lord my God, thou art very great ; thou art clothed with honor and majesty.

Who coverest thyself with light as with a garment : who stretchest out the heavens like a curtain :

Who layeth the beams of his chambers in the waters : who

maketh the clouds his chariot: who walketh upon the wings of the wind:

Who maketh his angels spirits; his ministers a flaming fire. Psalms civ. 1, 2, 3, 4.

15. *Leader.* Is he an infinitely wise, an omniscient God?

Div. No. 15. He that planted the ear, shall he not hear? he that formed the eye, shall he not see?

He that chastiseth the heathen, shall not he correct? he that teacheth man knowledge, shall not he know? Psalms xciv. 9, 10.

For there is not a word in my tongue, but, lo, O Lord, thou knowest it altogether.

Thou hast beset me behind and before, and laid thine hand upon me.

Such knowledge is too wonderful for me; it is high, I cannot attain unto it.

Yea, the darkness hideth not from thee; but the night shineth as the day: the darkness and the light are both alike to thee. Psalms cxxxix. 4, 5, 6, 12.

Great is our Lord, and of great power: his understanding is infinite. Psalms cxlvii. 5.

16. *Leader.* God is not only himself all-wise, but the source of all true wisdom for man.

How did David become wise?

Div. No. 16. Thou through thy commandments hast made me wiser than mine enemies: for they are ever with me.

I have more understanding than all my teachers: for thy testimonies are my meditation.

I understand more than the ancients, because I keep thy precepts. Psalms cxix. 98, 99, 100.

The fear of the Lord is the beginning of wisdom: a good understanding have all they that do his commandments: his praise endureth for ever. Psalms cxi. 10.

17. *Leader.* How has David expressed the truth of God's omnipresence—or that he is an everywhere-present God?

Div. No. 17. Whither shall I go from thy Spirit? or whither shall I flee from thy presence?

If I ascend up into heaven, thou art there: if I make my bed in hell, behold, thou art there.

If I take the wings of the morning, and dwell in the uppermost parts of the sea;

Even there shall thy hand lead me, and thy right hand shall hold me. Psalms cxxxix. 7, 8, 9, 10.

18. *Leader.* We have heard the Psalmist's testimony to the existence of God, his rightful sovereignty, and the perfection of his natural attributes,—his unchangeableness, omnipotence, and omnipresence. Let us next consider those passages in which his moral attributes are affirmed,—his holiness, justice, truth, goodness, and mercy.

In what verses does David declare the holiness of God?

Div. No. 18. But thou art holy, O thou that inhabitest the praises of Israel. Psalms xxii. 3.

The Lord is righteous in all his ways, and holy in all his works. Psalms cxlv. 17.

Rejoice in the Lord, ye righteous; and give thanks at the remembrance of his holiness. Psalms xcvii. 12.

19. *Leader.* What does he say of his justice?

Div. No. 19. Thou dost establish equity, thou executest judgment and righteousness in Jacob. Psalms xcix. 4.

Justice and judgment are the habitation of thy throne. Psalms lxxxix. 14.

20. *Leader.* What is said of his truth?

Div. No. 20. For the word of the Lord is right; and all his works are done in truth. Psalms xxxiii. 4.

Thy word is true from the beginning: and every one of thy righteous judgments endureth for ever. Psalms cxix. 160.

21. *Leader.* The Psalmist loved especially to celebrate the mercy of God. Repeat some verses in which he proclaims it.

Div. No. 21. But thou, O Lord, art a God full of compassion, and gracious, long-suffering, and plenteous in mercy and truth. Psalms lxxxvi. 15.

O give thanks unto the Lord; For he is good: for his mercy endureth forever.

O give thanks unto the God of gods: for his mercy endureth forever. Psalms cxxxvi. 1, 2.

22. *Leader.* Does God's mercy, infinite though it is, lessen his just anger against sin?

Div. No. 22. For thou art not a God that hath pleasure in wickedness: neither shall evil dwell with thee.

The foolish shall not stand in thy sight: thou hatest all workers of iniquity. Psalms v. 4, 5.

God judgeth the righteous, and God is angry with the wicked every day.

If he turn not, he will whet his sword; he hath bent his bow, and made it ready. Psalms vii. 11, 12.

Kiss the Son, lest he be angry, and ye perish from the way, when his wrath is kindled but a little. Blessed are all they that put their trust in him. Psalms ii. 12.

23. *Leader.* The longest Psalm, [which is it?] is full of the excellence of God's law. Repeat some of the verses which especially declare this.

Div. No. 23. And I will delight myself in thy commandments, which I have loved.

My hands also will I lift up unto thy commandments, which I have loved; and I will meditate in thy statutes.

The law of thy mouth is better unto me than thousands of gold and silver.

Thy word is a lamp unto my feet, and a light unto my path. Psalms cxix. 47, 48, 72, 105.

24. *Leader.* May this God of infinite greatness and of infinite holiness be the refuge and trust of his children?

Div. No. 24. The Lord is my rock, and my fortress, and my deliverer; my God, my strength, in whom I will trust; my buckler, and the horn of my salvation, and my high tower. Psalms xviii. 2.

God is our refuge and strength, a very present help in trouble.

Therefore will not we fear, though the earth be removed, and though the mountains be carried into the midst of the sea;

Though the waters thereof roar and be troubled, though the mountains shake with the swelling thereof. Psalms xlvi. 1, 2, 3.

25. *Leader.* Will God surely save those who rightly put trust in him?

Div. No. 25. The righteous cry, and the Lord heareth, and delivereth them out of all their troubles.

The Lord redeemeth the soul of his servants: and none of them that trust in him shall be desolate. Psalms xxxiv. 17, 22.

But the salvation of the righteous is of the Lord: he is their strength in the time of trouble.

And the Lord shall help them, and deliver them: he shall deliver them from the wicked, and save them, because they trust in him. Psalms xxxvii. 39, 40.

Blessed be the Lord, who daily loadeth us with benefits, even the God of our salvation. Psalms lxviii. 19.

26. *Leader.* Are we assured of God's watchful care of all who are his?

Div. No. 26. Behold, he that keepeth Israel shall neither slumber nor sleep.

The Lord is thy keeper: the Lord is thy shade upon thy right hand.

The sun shall not smite thee by day, nor the moon by night.

The Lord shall preserve thee from all evil: he shall preserve thy soul.

The Lord shall preserve thy going out and thy coming in from this time forth, and even for evermore. Psalms cxxi. 4, 5, 6, 7, 8.

Yea, though I walk through the valley of the shadow of death, I will fear no evil: for thou art with me; thy rod and thy staff they comfort me. Psalms xxiii. 4.

Leader. Let us all unite with the Psalmist in blessing and praise to God—our Creator, King, Father, and Benefactor.

All rising, recite in concert:

Bless the Lord, ye his angels, that excel in strength, that do his commandments, hearkening unto the voice of his word.

Bless ye the Lord, all ye his hosts; ye ministers of his, that do his pleasure.

Bless the Lord, all his works in all places of his dominion: Bless the Lord, O my soul. Psalms ciii. 20, 21, 22.

Blessed be the Lord God, the God of Israel, who only doeth wondrous things.

And blessed be his glorious name forever: and let the whole earth be filled with his glory; Amen, and Amen. Psalms lxxii. 18, 19.

An appropriate hymn is sung, as:

>Praise the Lord who reigns above
>And keeps his courts below. [*Happy Voices, p.* 172.

The service is then closed with the benediction, if the pastor is present.

LESSON II.

OLD TESTAMENT PROPHECIES CONCERNING JESUS CHRIST, WITH THEIR FULFILLMENT AS RECORDED IN THE NEW TESTAMENT.

For opening exercises, either of the schedules already given may be used, with variations, as follows:

OPENING SENTENCES.

Leader. This is a faithful saying, and worthy of all acceptation, that Christ Jesus came into the world to save sinners. I. Tim. i. 15.

Assembly. To the Lord our God belong mercies, and forgivenesses, though we have rebelled against him. Dan. ix. 9.

All. The blood of Jesus Christ his Son cleanseth us from all sin. I. John i. 7.

Or,

Leader. God anointed Jesus of Nazareth with the Holy Ghost and with power; who went about doing good and healing all that were oppressed of the devil; for God was with him. Acts x. 38.

Assembly. God also hath highly exalted him and given him a name which is above every name. Phil. ii. 9.

All. Neither is there salvation in any other; for there is none other name under heaven given among men, whereby we must be saved. Acts iv. 12.

SCRIPTURE READINGS.

To be read in alternation by leader and assembly:

Ho, every one that thirsteth, come ye to the waters, &c. Isaiah lv.

To be read by the leader, and briefly explained by him:

Luke ii. 8-20.

HYMNS.

All hail the power of Jesus name !—*Coronation.*
Come let us sing of Jesus.—*Song Flowers.*
I think when I read that sweet story of old.—*S. S. Hosanna.*

CHANT.

The people that walked in darkness have seen a great light, &c. Isa. ix. 2, 6, 7.

In this exercise, thirty prophecies are named, with their corresponding fulfillment or re-affirmation. A teacher can announce the prophecy and his class recite its fufillment. Or, one class can announce the prophecy, and the next class the fulfillment. Or these two plans may be combined, so that each class may have a share in the exercise, whether the school be large or small. Where more than one verse is included in a reference, the several scholars of a class may each recite one; or the entire class may recite them in concert.

The leader will announce the subject of the prophecy, in each case, as he calls on the class or division for recitation.

GENERAL EXERCISES.

Leader. What was the prophecy as to the birthplace of Jesus?

Teacher of Class No. 1. But thou, Bethlehem Ephratah, though thou be little among the thousands of Judah, yet out of thee shall he come forth unto me that is to be ruler in Israel;

whose goings forth have been from of old, from everlasting. Micah v. 2.

Leader. What is the record of the fulfillment of this prophecy?

Class No. 1. Jesus was born in Bethlehem of Judea in the days of Herod the King. Matt. ii. 1.

Leader. What was the prophecy as to the homage he should receive?

Teacher of Class No. 2. The kings of Tarshish and of the isles shall bring presents: the kings of Sheba and Seba shall offer gifts.

Yea, all kings shall fall down before him: all nations shall serve him. Psalms lxxii. 10, 11.

Leader. Will you show its fulfillment?

Class No. 2. Behold, there came wise men from the east to Jerusalem.

And when they were come into the house, they saw the young child with Mary his mother, and fell down, and worshiped him: and when they had opened their treasures, they presented unto him gifts; gold, and frankincense, and myrrh. Matt. ii. 1, 11.

Leader. As to his being a dweller in Egypt?

Teacher of Class No. 3. When Israel was a child, then I loved him, and called my son out of Egypt. Hos. xi. 1.

Leader. Its fulfillment?

Class No. 3. When he arose, he took the young child and his mother by night, and departed into Egypt:

And was there until the death of Herod: that it might be fulfilled which was spoken of the Lord by the prophet, saying, Out of Egypt have I called my son. Matt. ii. 14, 15.

Leader. As to the forerunner of his ministry?

Teacher of Class No. 4. The voice of him that crieth in the wilderness, Prepare ye the way of the Lord, make straight in the desert a highway for our God. Isa. xl. 3.

Leader. Its fulfillment?

Class No. 4. In those days came John the Baptist, preaching in the wilderness of Judea,

And saying, Repent ye: for the kingdom of heaven is at hand. Matt. iii. 1, 2.

Leader. As to his humility?

Teacher of Class No. 5. Behold my servant, whom I uphold; mine elect, in whom my soul delighteth; I have put my spirit upon him: he shall bring forth judgment to the Gentiles.

He shall not cry, nor lift up, nor cause his voice to be heard in the street. Isa. xlii. 1, 2.

Leader. Its fulfillment?

Class No. 5. But when Jesus knew it, he withdrew himself from thence: and great multitudes followed him, and he healed them all:

And charged them that they should not make him known. Matt. xii. 15, 16.

Leader. As to the guilelessness of his life?

Teacher of Class No. 6. He had done no violence, neither was any deceit in his mouth. Isa. liii. 9.

Leader. Its fulfillment?

Class No. 6. For we have not an high priest which cannot be touched with the feeling of our infirmities; but was in all points tempted like as we are, yet without sin. Heb. iv. 15.

Leader. As to his being rejected by his brethren?

Teacher of Class No. 7. I am become a stranger unto my brethren, and an alien unto my mother's children. Psalms lxix. 8.

Leader. Its fulfillment?

Class No. 7. He came unto his own, and his own received him not. John i. 11.

For neither did his brethren believe in him. John vii. 5.

Leader.   As to the style of his preaching?

Teacher of Class No. 8.   I will open my mouth in a parable: I will utter dark sayings of old.   Psalms lxxviii. 2.

Leader.   Its fulfillment?

Class No. 8.   All these things spake Jesus unto the multitude in parables; and without a parable spake he not unto them:

That it might be fulfilled which was spoken by the prophet, saying, I will open my mouth in parables; I will utter things which have been kept secret from the foundation of the world. Matt. xiii. 34, 35.

Leader.   As to his working of miracles?

Teacher of Class No. 9.   Then the eyes of the blind shall be opened, and the ears of the deaf shall be unstopped.

Then shall the lame man leap as an hart, and the tongue of the dumb sing: for in the wilderness shall waters break out, and streams in the desert.   Isa. xxxv. 5, 6.

Leader.   Its fulfillment?

Class No. 9.   Jesus answered and said unto them, Go and shew John again those things which ye do hear and see:

The blind receive their sight, and the lame walk, the lepers are cleansed, and the deaf hear, the dead are raised up, and the poor have the gospel preached to them.

And blessed is he, whosoever shall not be offended in me. Matt. xi. 4–6.

Then gathered the chief priests and the Pharisees a council, and said, What do we? for this man doeth many miracles. John xi. 47.

The superintendent recites:

Blessed be the Lord God of Israel, who hath with his hands fulfilled that which he spake with his mouth.   II. Chronicles vi. 4.

How God anointed Jesus of Nazareth with the Holy Ghost, and with power: who went about doing good, and healing all that were oppressed of the devil; for God was with him.   Acts x. 38.

The pastor if present, may recite :

For by him were all things created that are in heaven, and that are in earth, visible and invisible, whether they be thrones, or dominions, or principalities, or powers : all things were created by him and for him :

And he is before all things, and by him all things consist.

And he is the head of the body, the church: who is the beginning, the first-born from the dead ; that in all things he might have the pre-eminence.

For it pleased the Father, that in him should all fulness dwell. Col. i. 16–19.

All rising, recite in concert :

But God commendeth his love toward us, in that, while we were yet sinners, Christ died for us. Rom. v. 8.

A hymn is sung.

  Saviour, like a shepherd lead us,
  Much we need thy tender care.
      [*Golden Chain.*

Leader. What was the prophecy as to the public entry of Jesus into Jerusalem?

Teacher of Class No. 10. Rejoice greatly, O daughter of Zion ; shout, O daughter of Jerusalem : behold, thy King cometh unto thee : he is just, and having salvation ; lowly, and riding upon an ass, and upon a colt the foal of an ass. Zech. ix. 9.

Leader. What is the record of its fulfillment?

Class No. 10. And when they drew nigh unto Jerusalem, and were come to Bethphage, unto the mount of Olives, then sent Jesus two disciples,

Saying unto them, Go into the village over against you, and straightway ye shall find an ass tied, and a colt with her : loose them and bring them unto me.

And if any man say aught unto you, ye shall say, the Lord hath need of them ; and straightway he will send them.

All this was done, that it might be fulfilled which was spoken by the prophet, saying,

Tell ye the daughter of Sion, Behold, thy King cometh unto thee, meek, and sitting upon an ass, and a colt the foal of an ass. Matt. xxi. 1–5.

Leader. As to his betrayal by a friend?

Teacher of Class No. 11. For it was not an enemy that reproached me; then I could have borne it: neither was it he that hated me that did magnify himself against me; then I would have hid myself from him:

But it was thou, a man mine equal, my guide, and mine acquaintance.

We took sweet counsel together, and walked unto the house of God in company. Psalms lv. 12–14.

Yea, mine own familiar friend, in whom I trusted, which did eat of my bread, hath lifted up his heel against me. Psalms xli. 9.

Leader. Its fulfillment?

Class No. 11. I speak not of you all: I know whom I have chosen: but that the Scripture may be fulfilled, He that eateth bread with me hath lifted up his heel against me.

When Jesus had thus said, he was troubled in spirit, and testified, and said, Verily, verily, I say unto you, that one of you shall betray me. John xiii. 18, 21.

And Judas Iscariot, one of the twelve, went unto the chief priests, to betray him unto them. Mark xiv. 10.

Leader. As to the price of his purchase?

Teacher of Class No. 12. And I said unto them, If ye think good, give me my price; and if not, forbear. So they weighed for my price thirty pieces of silver. Zech. xi. 12.

Leader. Its fulfillment?

Class No. 12. Then one of the twelve, called Judas Iscariot, went unto the chief priests,

And said unto them, What will ye give me, and I will deliver him unto you? And they covenanted with him for thirty pieces of silver. Matt. xxvi. 14, 15.

Leader. As to the use made of his purchase-money?

Teacher of Class No. 13. And the Lord said unto me, Cast it unto the potter: a goodly price that I was prized at of them. And I took the thirty pieces of silver, and cast them to the potter in the house of the Lord. Zech. xi. 13.

Leader. Its fulfillment?

Class No. 13. And the chief priests took the silver pieces, and said, It is not lawful for to put them into the treasury, because it is the price of blood.

And they took counsel, and bought with them the potter's field, to bury strangers in. Matt. xxvii. 6, 7.

Leader. As to his patience and silence under suffering?

Teacher of Class No. 14. He was oppressed, and he was afflicted, yet he opened not his mouth: he is brought as a lamb to the slaughter, and as a sheep before her shearers is dumb, so he openeth not his mouth. Isa. liii. 7.

Leader. Its fulfillment?

Class No. 14. And when he was accused of the chief priests and elders, he answered nothing.

Then said Pilate unto him, Hearest thou not how many things they witness against thee?

And he answered him to never a word; insomuch that the governor marvelled greatly. Matt. xxvii. 12–14.

Leader. As to his being smitten on the head?

Teacher of Class No. 15. They shall smite the judge of Israel with a rod upon the cheek. Micah v. 1.

Leader. Its fulfillment?

Class No. 15. And they spit upon him, and took the reed, and smote him on the head. Matt. xxvii. 30.

Leader. As to his being condemned with criminals?

Teacher of Class No. 16. And he was numbered with the transgressors; and he bare the sin of many, and made intercession for the transgressors. Isa. liii. 12.

Leader. Its fulfillment?

Class No 16. And with him they crucify two thieves; the one on his right hand, and the other on his left.

And the Scripture was fulfilled, which saith, And he was numbered with the transgressors. Mark xv. 27, 28.

Leader. As to his being nailed to the cross?

Teacher of Class No. 17. The assembly of the wicked have inclosed me: they pierced my hands and my feet. Psalms xxii. 16.

Leader. Its fulfillment?

Class No. 17. And they crucified him. Matt. xxvii. 35.

Then saith he to Thomas, Reach hither thy finger, and behold my hands: and reach hither thy hand, and thrust it into my side: and be not faithless, but believing. John xx. 27.

Leader. As to gall and vinegar being offered him?

Teacher of Class No. 18. They gave me also gall for my meat; and in my thirst they gave me vinegar to drink. Psalms lxix. 21.

Leader. Its fulfillment?

Class No. 18. They gave him vinegar to drink, mingled with gall: and when he had tasted thereof, he would not drink. Matt. xxvii. 34.

Leader. As to his side being pierced?

Teacher of Class No. 19. They shall look upon me whom they have pierced, and they shall mourn for him, as one mourneth for his only son, and shall be in bitterness for him, as one that is in bitterness for his first-born. Zech. xii. 10.

Leader. Its fulfillment?

Class No. 19. But one of the soldiers with a spear pierced his side, and forthwith came there out blood and water. John xix. 34.

Leader. As to the preservation of his every bone?

Teacher of Class No. 20. He keepeth all his bones: not one of them is broken. Psalms xxxiv. 20.

Leader. Its fulfillment?

Class No. 20. But when they came to Jesus, and saw that he was dead already, they brake not his legs:
For these things were done, that the Scripture should be fulfilled, A bone of him shall not be broken. John xix. 33, 36.

Leader. As to his suffering death?

Teacher of Class No. 21. He hath poured out his soul unto death. Isa. liii. 12.

Leader. Its fulfillment?

Class No. 21. Jesus, when he had cried again with a loud voice, yielded up the ghost. Matt. xxvii. 50.

The superintendent recites:

Certainly this was a righteous man. Luke xxiii. 47.
Truly this was the Son of God. Matt. xxvi. 54.

The pastor may add:

But those things, which God before had shewed by the mouth of all his prophets, that Christ should suffer, he hath so fulfilled.

Repent ye therefore, and be converted, that your sins may be blotted out. Acts iii. 18, 19.

All, rising, recite in concert:

When thou saidst, Seek ye my face; my heart said unto thee, Thy face, Lord, will I seek. Psalms xxvii. 8.

A hymn is sung:

I will sing for Jesus.

[*Singing Pilgrim.*

Leader. What was the prophecy as to the division of the garments of Jesus as spoils?

Teacher of Class No. 22. They part my garments among them, and cast lots upon my vesture. Psalms xxii. 18.

Leader. What is the record of its fulfillment?

Class No. 22. Then the soldiers, when they had crucified Jesus, took his garments, and made four parts, to every soldier a part; and also his coat: now the coat was without seam, woven from the top throughout.
They said therefore among themselves, Let us not rend it, but cast lots for it, whose it shall be: that the Scripture might be fulfilled, which saith, They parted my raiment among them, and for my vesture they did cast lots. These things therefore the soldiers did. John xix. 23, 24.

Leader. As to his finding rest in the grave of the wealthy?

Teacher of Class No. 23. And he made his grave with the wicked, and with the rich in his death. Isa. liii. ix.

Leader. Its fulfillment?

Class No. 23. When the even was come, there came a rich man of Arimathea, named Joseph, who also himself was Jesus' disciple:
He went to Pilate, and begged the body of Jesus. Then Pilate commanded the body to be delivered.
And when Joseph had taken the body, he wrapped it in a clean linen cloth,
And laid it in his own new tomb, which he had hewn out in the rock: and he rolled a great stone to the door of the sepulchre, and departed. Matt. xxvii. 57–60.

Leader. As to his resurrection?

Teacher of Class No. 24. For thou wilt not leave my soul in hell; neither wilt thou suffer thine Holy One to see corruption. Psalms xvi. 10.

Thy dead men shall live, together with my dead body shall they arise. Awake and sing, ye that dwell in dust: for thy dew is as the dew of herbs, and the earth shall cast out the dead. Isa. xxvi. 19.

Leader. Its fulfillment?

Class No. 24. And the angel answered and said unto the woman, Fear not ye: for I know that ye seek Jesus, which was crucified.

He is not here: for he is risen, as he said. Come, see the place where the Lord lay. Matt. xxviii. 5, 6.

Leader. As to his ascension?

Teacher of Class No. 25. Thou hast ascended on high, thou hast led captivity captive: thou hast received gifts for men; yea, for the rebellious also, that the Lord God might dwell among them. Psalms lxviii. 18.

Leader. Its fulfillment?

Class No. 25. And it came to pass, while he blessed them, he was parted from them, and carried up into heaven. Luke xxiv. 51.

Leader. As to his sitting at the right hand of God?

Teacher of Class No. 26. The Lord said unto my Lord, sit thou at my right hand, until I make thine enemies thy footstool. Psalms cx. 1.

Leader. Its fulfillment?

Class No. 26. Who, being the brightness of his glory, and the express image of his person, and upholding all things by the word of his power, when he had by himself purged our sins, sat down on the right hand of the Majesty on high. Heb. i. 3.

Leader. As to the righteousness of his rule?

Teacher of Class No. 27. Thy throne, O Lord, is for ever and ever: the sceptre of thy kingdom is a right sceptre.

Thou lovest righteousness, and hatest wickedness; therefore

God, thy God, hath anointed thee with the oil of gladness above thy fellows. Psalms xlv. 6, 7.

Leader. Its fulfillment?

Class No. 27. I can of mine own self do nothing: as I hear, I judge: and my judgment is just; because I seek not mine own will, but the will of the Father which hath sent me. John v. 30.

Leader. As to his mission as the Saviour of sinners?

Teacher of Class No. 28. The people that walked in darkness have seen a great light: they that dwell in the land of the shadow of death, upon them hath the light shined. Isa. ix. 2.

And a man shall be as a hiding place from the wind, and a covert from the tempest; as rivers of water in a dry place, as the shadow of a great rock in a weary land. Isa xxxii. 2.

Leader. Its fulfillment?

Class No. 28. There is therefore now no condemnation to them which are in Christ Jesus, who walk not after the flesh, but after the Spirit. Rom. viii. 1.

In whom we have redemption through his blood, even the forgiveness of sins. Col. i. 14.

Leader. As to his becoming the chief corner-stone and sure foundation of the church?

Teacher of Class No. 29. Therefore thus saith the Lord God, Behold, I lay in Zion for a foundation a stone, a tried stone, a precious corner-stone, a sure foundation: he that believeth shall not make haste. Isa. xxviii. 16.

Leader. Its fulfillment?

Class No. 29. Wherefore also it is contained in the Scripture, Behold, I lay in Sion a chief corner-stone, elect, precious: and he that believeth on him shall not be confounded.

Unto you therefore which believe he is precious: but unto them which be disobedient, the stone which the builders disallowed, the same is made the head of the corner. I. Pet. ii. 6, 7.

For other foundation can no man lay than that is laid, which is Jesus Christ. I. Cor. iii 11.

Leader. What Old Testament prophecies of Christ are yet unfulfilled?

Teacher of Class No. 30. Of the increase of his government and peace there shall be no end, upon the throne of David, and upon his kingdom, to order it, and to establish it with judgment and with justice from henceforth even forever. The zeal of the Lord of hosts will perform this. Isa. ix. 7.

He shall have dominion also from sea to sea, and from the river unto the ends of the earth. Psalms lxxii. 8.

Leader. Are these reaffirmed in the New Testament?

Class No. 30. He shall be great, and shall be called the Son of the Highest: and the Lord God shall give unto him the throne of his father David:

And he shall reign over the house of Jacob forever; and of his kingdom there shall be no end. Luke i. 32, 33.

Leader. Behold the Lamb of God, which taketh away the sin of the world! John. i. 29.

Assembly. Worthy is the Lamb that was slain to receive power, and riches, and wisdom, and strength, and honor, and glory, and blessing. Rev. v. 12.

All. Blessing, and honor, and glory, and power, be unto him that sitteth upon the throne, and unto the Lamb, for ever and ever. Rev. v. 13.

LESSON III.

THIRTY PROMINENT EVENTS IN CONNECTION WITH THE LIFE OF JESUS CHRIST.

OPENING SENTENCES.

Leader. Dost thou believe on the Son of God? John ix. 35.
Assembly. Lord, I believe; help thou mine unbelief. Mark ix. 24.
Leader. Unto you therefore which believe he is precious. I. Peter ii. 7.

SCRIPTURE READINGS.

To be read responsively by leader and assembly:
Psalm ii.
To be read elliptically, as explained on page 47.
Acts x. 34-43.

CHANT.

Luke i. 68-72.

HYMN.

How precious is the story
Of our Redeemer's birth.
[*Happy Voices*, p. 26.

Thou dear Redeemer, dying Lamb,
I love to hear of thee.
[*Song Flowers*, p. 76.

Jesus is our dearest friend,
So tender, tried and true.
[*Golden Censer*, p. 34.

GENERAL EXERCISES.

Each quoted passage, entire, may be recited by a single class in concert; or each member of the class may recite a single text of the passage, until all are given; or each teacher may recite a portion, and his class the remainder; or in any other way the lesson may be so assigned as to give to all their share, according to the size of the school.

Leader. What is said in the word of God, of the rejoicing in heaven over the birth of the holy child Jesus?

Class No. 1. And there were in the same country shepherds abiding in the field, keeping watch over their flock by night.

And, lo, the angel of the Lord came upon them, and the glory of the Lord shone round about them: and they were sore afraid.

And the angel said unto them, Fear not: for, behold, I bring you good tidings of great joy, which shall be to all people.

For unto you is born this day in the city of David a Saviour, which is Christ the Lord.

And this shall be a sign unto you; Ye shall find the babe wrapped in swaddling clothes, lying in a manger.

And suddenly there was with the angel a multitude of the heavenly host praising God, and saying,

Glory to God in the highest, and on earth peace, good will toward men. Luke ii. 8-14.

Leader. What is said of the welcome given to the divine child by some of the wise men of earth?

Class No. 2. Now when Jesus was born in Bethlehem of Judea, in the days of Herod the king, behold, there came wise men from the east to Jerusalem,

Saying, Where is he that is born King of the Jews? for we have seen his star in the east, and are come to worship him.

And when they were come into the house, they saw the young child with Mary his mother, and fell down and worshiped him: and when they had opened their treasures, they presented unto him gifts; gold, and frankincense, and myrrh. Matt. ii. 1, 2, 11.

Leader. What is the record of his exhibition of heavenly wisdom, while yet but a child?

Class No. 3. Now his parents went to Jerusalem every year at the feast of the passover.

And when he was twelve years old, they went up to Jerusalem, after the custom of the feast.

And when they had fulfilled the days, as they returned, the child Jesus tarried behind in Jerusalem; and Joseph and his mother knew not of it.

But they, supposing him to have been in the company, went a day's journey; and they sought him among their kinsfolk and acquaintance.

And when they found him not, they turned back again to Jerusalem, seeking him.

And it came to pass, that after three days they found him in the temple, sitting in the midst of the doctors, both hearing them, and asking them questions.

And all that heard him were astonished at his understanding and answers. Luke ii. 41–47.

Leader. In what spirit did Jesus conduct himself towards his parents when they had found him in the temple?

Class No. 4. And he went down with them, and came to Nazareth, and was subject unto them: but his mother kept all these sayings in her heart.

And Jesus increased in wisdom and stature, and in favour with God and man. Luke ii. 51, 52.

The infant class rises, and recites as follows:

Teacher. Did Christ come into the world as a little child?

Scholars. Jesus became a little child,
Holy and humble, meek and mild.

Teacher. How did he grow up?

Scholars. In wisdom and in stature too,
The holy child, our Saviour grew.

[*Scriptural Lessons.*

No selfish grief he ever felt,
No anger in his bosom dwelt;
But thoughts of love, of praise, and prayer,
Like cloudless sunshine rested there.

[*Tract Primer.*

The entire assembly rising, a hymn is sung:

Long ago the Lord of glory
Lived on earth a little child.

[*Am. S. S. Hymn Book, p.* 306.

Leader. What is told of the preparation of Jesus for his special ministry?

Class No. 5. And it came to pass in those days, that Jesus came from Nazareth of Galilee, and was baptized of John in Jordan.

And straightway coming up out of the water, he saw the heavens opened, and the Spirit like a dove descending upon him:

And there came a voice from heaven, saying, Thou art my beloved Son, in whom I am well pleased. Mark i. 9-11.

Leader. Was Jesus ever tempted to sin?

Class No. 6. And Jesus being full of the Holy Ghost returned from Jordan, and was led by the Spirit into the wilderness,

Being forty days tempted of the devil. Luke iv. 1, 2.

In all points tempted like as we are, yet without sin. Heb. iv. 15.

For in that he himself hath suffered being tempted, he is able to succour them that are tempted. Heb. ii. 18.

Leader. What is recorded of the commencement of his public ministry?

Class No. 7. Now when Jesus had heard that John was cast into prison, he departed into Galilee;

From that time Jesus began to preach, and to say, Repent: for the kingdom of heaven is at hand. Matt. iv. 12, 17.

And he came to Nazareth, where he had been brought up: and, as his custom was, he went into the synagogue on the sabbath-day, and stood up for to read. Luke iv. 16.

Leader. In Matthew xi. 2, 3, we are told:

Now when John had heard in the prison the works of Christ, he sent two of his disciples,

And said unto him, Art thou he that should come, or do we look for another?

Will you tell me what answer Jesus sent back to John?

The entire assembly rises and responds:

Jesus answered and said unto them, Go and shew John again those things which ye do hear and see:

The blind receive their sight, and the lame walk, the lepers are cleansed, and the deaf hear, the dead are raised up, and the poor have the gospel preached to them. Matt. xi. 4, 5.

Leader. Will you give an instance of Christ's healing of the sick?

Class No. 8. And he arose out of the synagogue, and entered into Simon's house. And Simon's wife's mother was taken with a great fever; and they besought him for her.

And he stood over her, and rebuked the fever; and it left her: and immediately she arose and ministered unto them.

Now when the sun was setting, all they that had any sick with divers diseases brought them unto him; and he laid his hands on every one of them, and healed them. Luke iv. 38–40.

Leader. Can you tell of his restoring sight to the blind?

Class No. 9. And when Jésus departed thence, two blind men followed him, crying, and saying, Thou Son of David, have mercy on us.

And when he was come into the house, the blind men came to him: and Jesus saith unto them, Believe ye that I am able to do this? They said unto him, Yea, Lord.

Then touched he their eyes, saying, According to your faith be it unto you.

And their eyes were opened; and Jesus straitly charged them, saying, See that no man know it. Matt. ix. 27-30.

Leader. Is there any mention of his making the lame to walk?

Class No. 10. And they come unto him, bringing one sick of the palsy, which was borne of four.

And when they could not come nigh unto him for the press, they uncovered the roof where he was: and when they had broken it up, they let down the bed wherein the sick of the palsy lay.

When Jesus saw their faith, he said unto the sick of the palsy, Son, thy sins be forgiven thee.

I say unto thee, Arise, and take up thy bed, and go thy way into thine house.

And immediately he arose, took up the bed, and went forth before them all; insomuch that they were all amazed, and glorified God, saying, We never saw it on this fashion. Mark ii. 3-5, 11, 12.

Leader. Did Jesus ever cleanse a leper?

Class No. 11. And there came a leper to him, beseeching him, and kneeling down to him, and saying unto him, If thou wilt, thou canst make me clean.

And Jesus, moved with compassion, put forth his hand, and touched him, and saith unto him, I will: be thou clean.

And as soon as he had spoken, immediately the leprosy departed from him, and he was cleansed. Mark i. 40-42.

Leader. Do you recall the story of his restoring hearing and speech to the deaf and dumb?

Class No. 12. And they bring unto him one that was deaf, and had an impediment in his speech; and they beseech him to put his hand upon him.

And he took him aside from the multitude, and put his fingers into his ears, and he spit, and touched his tongue;

And looking up to heaven, he sighed, and saith unto him, Ephphatha, that is, Be opened.

And straightway his ears were opened, and the string of his tongue was loosed, and he spake plain. Mark vii. 32-35.

Leader. Is any instance recorded of his raising the dead to life?

Class No. 13. Then they took away the stone from the place where the dead was laid. And Jesus lifted up his eyes and said, Father, I thank thee that thou hast heard me.

And I knew that thou hearest me always: but because of the people which stand by I said it, that they may believe that thou hast sent me.

And when he thus had spoken, he cried with a loud voice, Lazarus, come forth.

And he that was dead came forth, bound hand and foot with grave-clothes: and his face was bound about with a napkin. Jesus saith unto them, Loose him, and let him go. John xi. 41-44.

Leader. What is the record of his preaching to the poor?

Class No. 14. And he taught in their synagogues, being glorified of all. Luke iv. 15.

And the common people heard him gladly. Mark xii. 37.

The pastor, if present, may add:

My brethren, have not the faith of our Lord Jesus Christ, the Lord of glory, with respect of persons.

If ye fulfil the royal law according to the Scripture, Thou shalt love thy neighbor as thyself, ye do well :

But if ye have respect to persons, ye commit sin, and are convinced of the law as transgressors. James ii. 1, 8, 9.

Leader. Are any incidents given which go to show our Saviour's habit of prayer?

Class No. 15. And in the morning, rising up a great while before day, he went out, and departed into a solitary place, and there prayed. Mark i. 35.

And when he had sent the multitudes away, he went up into a mountain apart to pray; and when the evening was come he was there alone. Matt. xiv. 23.

And it came to pass in those days, that he went out into a mountain to pray, and continued all night in prayer to God. Luke vi. 12.

Leader. What is the record of his transfiguration?

Class No. 16. And after six days Jesus taketh Peter, James, and John his brother, and bringeth them up into a high mountain apart,

And was transfigured before them: and his face did shine as the sun, and his raiment was white as the light.

And, behold, there appeared unto them Moses and Elias talking with him.

Then answered Peter and said unto Jesus, Lord, it is good for us to be here: if thou wilt, let us make here three tabernacles; one for thee, and one for Moses, and one for Elias.

While he yet spake, behold, a bright cloud overshadowed them: and behold a voice out of the cloud, which said, This is my beloved Son, in whom I am well pleased; hear ye him. Matt. xvii. 1–5.

Leader. Did Jesus on any occasion assume to forgive sin?

Class No. 17. When Jesus saw their faith he said unto the sick of the palsy, Son, thy sins be forgiven thee. Mark ii. 5.

Wherefore I say unto thee, Her sins, which are many, are forgiven; for she loved much: but to whom little is forgiven, the same loveth little.

And he said unto her, Thy sins are forgiven. Luke vii. 47, 48.

Leader. How did Jesus show his love for little children?

Class No. 18. And they brought young children to him, that he should touch them: and his disciples rebuked those that brought them.

But when Jesus saw it, he was much displeased, and said unto them, Suffer the little children to come unto me, and forbid them not: for of such is the kingdom of God.

Verily I say unto you, Whosoever shall not receive the kingdom of God as a little child, he shall not enter therein.

And he took them up in his arms, put his hands upon them, and blessed them. Mark x. 13-16.

The infant class recites:

Teacher. Did Jesus show love to children while on earth?

Scholars. The little ones he took and blest,
And clasp'd them to his tender breast.

Teacher. What did Jesus say about little children?

Scholars Suffer the young to come to me;
Of such the saints in heaven shall be.

Teacher. Does he still regard the young?

Scholars. Though on his glorious throne above,
Children he still regards with love.

Teacher. Will God hear the praises of children?

Scholars. Yes! God will hear the hymns they raise,
And Jesus loves an infant's praise.

[*Scriptural Lessons.*

All rising, a hymn is sung :

> Around the throne of God in heaven
> Ten thousand children stand.
>
> [*Golden Chain, p.* 118.

Leader. Do you remember the story of the triumphal entry of Jesus into Jerusalem?

Class No. 19. And they brought the colt to Jesus, and cast their garments on him; and he sat upon him.

And many spread their garments in the way; and others cut down branches off the trees, and strewed them in the way.

And they that went before, and they that followed, cried, saying, Hosanna; Blessed is he that cometh in the name of the Lord :

Blessed be the kingdom of our father David, that cometh in the name of the Lord: Hosanna in the highest. Mark. xi. 7-10.

Leader. In what incident did Jesus give an example of humility to his followers?

Class No 20. He riseth from supper, and laid aside his garments; and took a towel, and girded himself.

After that he poureth water into a basin, and began to wash the disciples' feet, and to wipe them with the towel wherewith he was girded.

So after he had washed their feet, and had taken his garments, and was set down again, he said unto them, Know ye what I have done to you?

Ye call me Master and Lord: and ye say well; for so I am.

If I then, your Lord and Master, have washed your feet; ye also ought to wash one another's feet. John xiii. 4, 5, 12-14.

Leader. Will you recite the record of his institution of the Memorial Supper?

Class No. 21. Now when the even was come, he sat down with the twelve.

And as they were eating, Jesus took bread and blessed it, and brake it, and gave it to the disciples, and said, Take, eat; this is my body.

And he took the cup, and gave thanks, and gave it to them; saying, Drink ye all of it;

For this is my blood of the new testament, which is shed for many for the remission of sins.

But I say unto you, I will not drink henceforth of this fruit of the vine, until that day when I drink it new with you in my Father's kingdom. Matt. xxvi. 20, 26-29.

Leader. What are we told of his agony in Gethsemane?

Class No. 22. And he was withdrawn from them about a stone's cast, and kneeled down, and prayed,

Saying, Father, if thou be willing, remove this cup from me: nevertheless, not my will, but thine, be done.

And there appeared an angel unto him from heaven, strengthening him.

And being in an agony he prayed more earnestly: and his sweat was as it were great drops of blood falling down to the ground. Luke xxii. 41-44.

Leader. How and by whom was Jesus betrayed?

Class No. 23. And immediately, while he yet spake, cometh Judas, one of the twelve, and with him a great multitude with swords and staves, from the chief priests and the scribes and the elders.

And he that had betrayed him had given them a token, saying, Whomsoever I shall kiss, that same is he; take him, and lead him away safely.

And as soon as he was come, he goeth straightway to him, and saith, Master, master; and kissed him.

And they laid their hands on him, and took him. Mark xiv. 43-46.

Leader. Did the other disciples of Jesus remain with him in the hour of his betrayal by Judas?

Class No. 24. Then all the disciples forsook him, and fled.

And they that had laid hold on Jesus led him away to Caiaphas the high priest, where the scribes and the elders were assembled.

But Peter followed him afar off unto the high priest's palace, and went in, and sat with the servants, to see the end.

Now Peter sat without in the palace : and a damsel came unto him, saying, Thou also wast with Jesus of Galilee.

But he denied before them all, saying, I know not what thou sayest. Matt. xxvi. 56–58, 69, 70.

Leader. In what way was Jesus treated after his arrest and trial?

Class No. 25. Then the soldiers of the governor took Jesus into the common hall, and gathered unto him the whole band of soldiers.

And they stripped him, and put on him a scarlet robe.

And when they had platted a crown of thorns, they put it upon his head, and a reed in his right hand : and they bowed the knee before him, and mocked him, saying, Hail, King of the Jews!

And they spit upon him, and took the reed, and smote him on the head.

And after that they had mocked him, they took the robe off from him, and put his own raiment on him, and led him away to crucify him. Matt. xxvii. 27–31.

Leader. Will you give the record of his crucifixion?

Class No. 26. And when they were come to the place, which is called Calvary, there they crucified him, and the malefactors, one on the right hand, and the other on the left.

And a superscription also was written over him in letters of Greek, and Latin, and Hebrew, THIS IS THE KING OF THE JEWS. Luke xxiii. 33, 38.

Leader. What is said of the burial of Jesus?

Class No. 27. When the even was come, there came a rich man of Arimathea, named Joseph, who also himself was Jesus' disciple :

He went to Pilate, and begged the body of Jesus. Then Pilate commanded the body to be delivered.

And when Joseph had taken the body, he wrapped it in a clean linen cloth, and laid it in his own new tomb, which he had hewn out in the rock: and he rolled a great stone to the door of the sepulchre, and departed. Matt. xxvii. 57-60.

Leader. Did Jesus remain in the tomb?

Class No. 28. And very early in the morning, the first day of the week, they came unto the sepulchre at the rising of the sun.

And they said among themselves, Who shall roll us away the stone from the door of the sepulchre?

And when they looked, they saw that the stone was rolled away: for it was very great.

And entering into the sepulchre, they saw a young man sitting on the right side, clothed in a long white garment; and they were affrighted.

And he saith unto them, Be not affrighted: ye seek Jesus of Nazareth, which was crucified: he is risen; he is not here: behold the place where they laid him. Mark xvi. 2-6.

Leader. Did the disciples see Jesus after his resurrection?

Class No. 29. Now when Jesus was risen early the first day of the week, he appeared first to Mary Magdalene, out of whom he had cast seven devils.

After that he appeared in another form unto two of them, as they walked, and went into the country.

Afterward he appeared unto the eleven as they sat at meat, and upbraided them with their unbelief and hardness of heart, because they believed not them which had seen him after he was risen. Mark xvi. 9, 12, 14.

To whom also he showed himself alive after his passion by many infallible proofs, being seen of them forty days, and speaking of the things pertaining to the kingdom of God. Acts i. 3.

Leader. What is the closing record of the life of Jesus on earth?

Class No. 30. And he led them out as far as to Bethany, and he lifted up his hands, and blessed them.

And it came to pass, while he blessed them, he was parted from them, and carried up into heaven.

And they worshiped him, and returned to Jerusalem with great joy:

And were continually in the temple, praising and blessing God. Amen. Luke xxiv. 50–53.

Leader. Are these all the incidents in the life of Jesus on earth?

All, rising, recite :

And there are also many other things which Jesus did, the which, if they should be written every one, I suppose that even the world itself could not contain the books that should be written. John xxi. 25.

The leader responds :

But these are written, that ye might believe that Jesus is the Christ, the Son of God; and that believing ye might have life through his name. John xx. 31.

The pastor may add :

God, who at sundry times and in divers manners spake in time past unto the fathers by the prophets,

Hath in these last days spoken unto us by his Son, whom he hath appointed heir of all things, by whom also he made the worlds;

Who being the brightness of his glory, and the express image of his person, and upholding all things by the word of his power, when he had by himself purged our sins, sat down on the right hand of the Majesty on high. Heb. i. 1–3.

Therefore we ought to give the more earnest heed to the things which we have heard, lest at any time we should let them slip. Heb. ii. 1.

All, rising, respond :

Let us run with patience the race that is set before us, looking unto Jesus the author and finisher of our faith. Heb. xii. 1, 2.

The assembly still standing, a closing hymn is sung :

> O for a thousand tongues to sing
> My great Redeemer's praise.

It may be well for the leader to ask such occasional questions, in the course of the foregoing lesson, as will bring out the explanation of points not likely to be understood by all. For instance: To Class No. 7, What was a synagogue? To Class No. 11, What was a leper? To Class No. 16, What is the meaning of transfiguration? To Class No. 26, What was the mode of crucifixion? To Class No. 28, How long did Jesus remain in the tomb? etc., etc.

If the lesson entire is deemed too long for a single exercise, or if there are too many texts for a small school, it may easily be shortened by the omission of some of the Scripture incidents.

LESSON IV.

THE HOLY GHOST—HIS TITLES, EMBLEMS, OFFICES, AND WORK.

[Arranged from an exercise prepared for the Congregational Church Sunday School, Saybrook, Conn., by Mrs. S. J. McCall.]

OPENING SENTENCES.

Leader. God hath from the beginning chosen you to salvation, through sanctification of the Spirit, and belief of the truth. II. Thess. ii. 13.

Assembly. The love of God is shed abroad in our hearts by the Holy Ghost. Romans xv. 16.

All. Create in me a clean heart, O God; and renew a right spirit within me.

Cast me not away from thy presence; and take not thy Holy Spirit from me. Psalms li. 10, 11.

SCRIPTURE READING.

In alternation by leader and assembly:
Isaiah xi. 1–9.

HYMN.

Gracious Spirit, love divine!
Let thy light within me shine.

[*Song Flowers*, p. 13.

GENERAL EXERCISES.

[For a Golden Text, used as designated on page 68, the words Convert and Renew, in their various forms, may be announced.]

Leader. What is the first mention in the Bible of the Spirit of God?

Class No. 1. And the earth was without form, and void; and darkness was upon the face of the deep. And the SPIRIT OF GOD moved upon the face of the waters. Gen. i. 2.

Leader. Is the Spirit of God called by any other title, or name, in the Scriptures?

Class No. 2. For there are three that bear record in heaven, the Father, the Word, and the HOLY GHOST: and these three are one. I. John v. 7.

Leader. Any other title?

Class No. 3. But the COMFORTER, which is the Holy Ghost, whom the Father will send in my name, he shall teach you all things, and bring all things to your remembrance, whatsoever I have said unto you. John xiv. 26.

Leader. Any other?

Class No. 4. And I will pray the Father, and he shall give you another Comforter, that he may abide with you for ever;

Even the SPIRIT OF TRUTH; whom the world cannot receive, because it seeth him not, neither knoweth him: but ye know him; for he dwelleth with you, and shall be in you. John xiv. 16, 17.

Leader. Has he yet another title?

Class No. 5. If ye then, being evil, know how to give good gifts unto your children: how much more shall your heavenly Father give the HOLY SPIRIT to them that ask him? Luke xi. 13.

The infant class, rising, recite as follows:

Teacher. Does God know all you do and say?
Scholars. Yes: and my thoughts too, night and day.
Teacher. Have you an evil heart within?
Scholars. Yes: or I should not always sin.
Teacher. How does your heart its evil show?
Scholars. By sinful words and actions too.

Teacher. And does not sin God's anger move?
Scholars. Yes: for I sin against his love.
Teacher. What wages then must sin obtain?
Scholars. Present and everlasting pain.
Teacher. And can you save yourself from woe?
Scholars. I cannot save myself, I know.
Teacher. Who can your sinful heart renew?
Scholars. God's Spirit only makes it new.
Teacher. Who only can direct your youth?
Scholars. The Holy Spirit, God of truth. [*Scriptural Lessons.*

The assembly rising, a hymn is sung:

>Glory to the Father give—
>Praise him, and adore. [*Happy Voices, p.* 178.

Leader. The Holy Spirit is likened in the Scriptures to a variety of emblems. Do you recall where he is likened to the *wind?*

Class No. 6. The wind bloweth where it listeth, and thou hearest the sound thereof, but canst not tell whence it cometh, and whither it goeth: so is every one that is born of the Spirit. John iii. 8.

And when the day of Pentecost was fully come, they were all with one accord in one place.

And suddenly there came a sound from heaven as of a rushing mighty wind, and it filled all the house where they were sitting.

And they were all filled with the Holy Ghost, and began to speak with other tongues, as the Spirit gave them utterance. Acts ii. 1, 2, 4.

>The Spirit like some heavenly wind,
> Blows on the sons of flesh,
>New models all the carnal mind,
> And forms the man afresh.

Leader. Can you recite any passage wherein the Spirit is likened to *water?*

Class No. 7. But whosoever drinketh of the water that I shall give him shall never thirst; but the water that I shall give him shall be in him a well of water springing up into everlasting life. John iv. 14.

(But this spake he of the Spirit, which they that believe on him should receive: for the Holy Ghost was not yet given; because that Jesus was not yet glorified.) John vii. 39.

>His love within us, shed abroad,
>   Life's ever-springing well;
>Till God in us, and we in God,
>   In love eternal dwell.

Leader. Is the Spirit further likened to *rain?*

Class No. 8. Then shall we know, if we follow on to know the Lord: his going forth is prepared as the morning; and he shall come unto us as the rain, as the latter and former rain unto the earth. Hos. vi. 3.

He shall come down like rain upon the mown grass: as showers that water the earth. Psalms lxxii. 6.

>As when, in silence, vernal showers
>Descend, and cheer the fainting flowers,
>So, in the secrecy of love,
>Falls the sweet influence from above.

Leader. Is he anywhere likened to the *dew?*

Class No. 9. For so the Lord said unto me, I will take my rest, and I will consider in my dwelling-place like a clear heat upon herbs, and like a cloud of dew in the heat of harvest. Isa. xviii. 4.

I will be as the dew unto Israel: he shall grow as the lily, and cast forth his roots as Lebanon. Hos. xiv. 5.

>Like the dew thy peace distill,
>Guide, subdue our wayward will,
>Things of Christ, unfolding still,
>   Comforter, Divine.

Leader. In what passages is he spoken of as *fire?*

Class No. 10. I indeed baptize you with water unto repentance: but he that cometh after me is mightier than I, whose shoes I am not worthy to bear: he shall baptize you with the Holy Ghost, and with fire. Matt. iii. 11.

And there appeared unto them cloven tongues, like as of fire, and it sat upon each of them.

And they were all filled with the Holy Ghost. Acts ii. 3, 4.

>Eternal Spirit, source of light,
>   Enlivening, consecrating fire,
> Descend, and with celestial heat
>   Our dull and frozen hearts inspire,
> Our souls refine, our dross consume:
>   Come, condescending Spirit, come!

Leader. Where is he likened to *anointing oil?*

Class No. 11. The Spirit of the Lord God is upon me; because the Lord hath anointed me to preach good tidings unto the meek; he hath sent me to bind up the broken-hearted, to proclaim liberty to the captives, and the opening of the prison to them that are bound. Isa. lxi. 1.

But ye have an unction from the Holy One, and ye know all things.

But the anointing which ye have received of him abideth in you: and ye need not that any man teach you: but as the same anointing teacheth you of all things, and is truth, and is no lie, and even as it hath taught you, ye shall abide in him. I. John ii. 20, 27.

>Great Comforter! to thee we cry;
>O highest gift of God most high!
>O fount of life! O fire of love!
>Send sweet anointing from above!

Leader. Can you recite any texts in which the Spirit is referred to as a *seal?*

Class No. 12. In whom ye also trusted, after that ye heard the word of truth, the gospel of your salvation: in whom also, after that ye believed, ye were sealed with that Holy Spirit of promise. Eph. i. 13.

Now he which stablisheth us with you in Christ, and hath anointed us, is God;

Who hath also sealed us, and given the earnest of the Spirit in our hearts. II. Cor. i. 21, 22.

And grieve not the Holy Spirit of God, whereby ye are sealed unto the day of redemption. Eph. iv. 30.

> Dost thou not dwell in all the saints,
> And seal the heirs of heaven?
> When wilt thou banish my complaints,
> And show my sins forgiven?

Leader. Is the Spirit likened in any passage to a dove?

Class No. 13. And Jesus, when he was baptized, went up straightway out of the water: and, lo, the heavens were opened unto him, and he saw the Spirit of God descending like a dove, and lighting upon him. Matt. iii. 16.

> Come, gracious Spirit, heavenly Dove,
> With light and comfort from above.
> Be thou our guardian, thou our guide,
> O'er every thought and step preside.

Leader. Is any mention made of the Spirit as a voice?

Class No. 14. But when they deliver you up, take no thought how or what ye shall speak: for it shall be given you in that same hour what ye shall speak.

For it is not ye that speak, but the Spirit of your Father which speaketh in you. Matt. x. 19, 20.

David the son of Jesse said, and the man who was raised up on high, the anointed of the God of Jacob, and the sweet psalmist of Israel, said,

The Spirit of the Lord spake by me, and his word was in my tongue. II. Samuel xxiii. 1, 2.

Blest Comforter divine!
   Let rays of heavenly love
Amid our gloom and darkness shine,
   And guide our souls above.

Turn us, with gentle voice,
   From every sinful way,
And bid the mourning saint rejoice,
   Though earthly joys decay.

Leader. And now that we have heard of the titles and emblems of the Holy Spirit, let us inquire of his offices and work. Where is he named as inviting the sinner to Jesus?

Class No. 15. And the Spirit and the bride say, Come. And let him that heareth say, Come. And let him that is athirst come. And whosoever will, let him take the water of life freely. Rev. xxii. 17.

Leader. Where is he named as regenerating those who yield to his entreaties?

Class No. 16. Jesus answered, Verily, verily, I say unto thee Except a man be born of water and of the Spirit, he cannot enter into the kingdom of God.

That which is born of the flesh is flesh; and that which is born of the Spirit is spirit. John iii. 5, 6.

Not by works of righteousness which we have done, but according to his mercy he saved us, by the washing of regeneration, and renewing of the Holy Ghost. Titus iii. 5.

Leader. Where is he spoken of as the teacher of the saints?

Class No. 17. Now we have received, not the spirit of the world, but the Spirit which is of God; that we might know the things that are freely given to us of God.

Which things also we speak, not in the words which man's

wisdom teacheth, but which the Holy Ghost teacheth; comparing spiritual things with spiritual. I. Cor. ii. 12, 13.

For the Holy Ghost shall teach you in the same hour what you ought to say. Luke xii. 12.

Leader. Where is he spoken of as their guide?

Class No. 18. Howbeit when he, the Spirit of truth, is come, he will guide you into all truth: for he shall not speak of himself; but whatsoever ye shall hear, that shall he speak: and he will shew you things to come. John xvi. 13.

Leader. Where as their helper?

Class No. 19. Likewise the Spirit also helpeth our infirmities: for we know not what we should pray for as we ought: but the Spirit itself maketh intercession for us with groanings which cannot be uttered. Romans viii. 26.

Leader. Where as their comfort and joy?

Class No. 20. But when the Comforter is come, whom I will send unto you from the Father, even the Spirit of truth, which proceedeth from the Father, he shall testify of me. John xv. 26.

For the kingdom of God is not meat and drink; but righteousness, and peace, and joy in the Holy Ghost. Romans xiv. 17.

Leader. Is the Spirit named as sanctifying and making holy the children of God?

Class No. 21. And such were some of you: but ye are washed, but ye are sanctified, but ye are justified in the name of the Lord Jesus, and by the Spirit of our God. I. Cor. vi. 11.

But we all, with open face beholding as in a glass the glory of the Lord, are changed into the same image from glory to glory, even as by the Spirit of the Lord. II. Cor. iii. 18.

For if ye live after the flesh, ye shall die: but if ye through the Spirit do mortify the deeds of the body, ye shall live.

For as many as are led by the Spirit of God, they are the sons of God. Romans viii. 13, 14.

Leader. Is the Spirit also a witness to the saints that they are Christ's?

Class No. 22. And it is the Spirit that beareth witness, because the Spirit is truth. I. John v. 6.

The Spirit itself beareth witness with our spirit, that we are the children of God:

And if children, then heirs; heirs of God, and joint heirs with Christ. Romans viii. 16, 17.

The superintendent says:

But the fruit of the Spirit is love, joy, peace, long-suffering, gentleness, goodness, faith,

Meekness, temperance: against such there is no law.

And they that are Christ's have crucified the flesh with the affections and lusts. Gal. v. 22–24.

The assembly, in concert, recite:

If we live in the Spirit, let us also walk in the Spirit.

Let us not be desirous of vain-glory, provoking one another, envying one another. Gal. v. 25, 26.

The pastor may add:

Wherefore, I give you to understand, that no man speaking by the Spirit of God, calleth Jesus accursed: and that no man can say that Jesus is the Lord, but by the Holy Ghost. I. Cor. xii. 3.

Seek ye the Lord while he may be found, call ye upon him while he is near. Isaiah lv. 6.

A hymn is sung:

> The Spirit in our hearts
> Is whispering, sinner come.
>
> [*Song Flowers, p,* 89.

Leader. Will the Spirit of God always invite to salvation?

Class No. 23. And the Lord said, My Spirit shall not always strive with man. Gen. vi. 3.

Leader. What then is our duty towards the Spirit of God?

Class No. 24. Quench not the Spirit. I. Thess. v. 19.
Wherefore (as the Holy Ghost saith, To-day, if ye will hear his voice,
Harden not your hearts, as in the provocation, in the day of temptation in the wilderness.) Heb. iii. 7, 8.

Leader. In the first chapter of the Bible there is mention made of the Spirit of God. He is mentioned again in the closing chapter of the Book of God. The passage has already been recited. Let us now rise and recite it together. And God grant that each soul here may consider and heed the Spirit's invitation.

All rising, recite together:

I Jesus have sent mine angel to testify unto you these things in the churches. I am the root and the offspring of David, and the bright and morning star.
And the Spirit and the bride say, Come. And let him that heareth say, Come. And let him that is athirst come. And whosoever will, let him take the water of life freely. Rev. xxii. 16, 17.

The service closes with the singing of the hymn:

>Come, Holy Spirit, heavenly Dove!
>With all thy quickening powers.

LESSON V.

THE HOLY SCRIPTURES.

(Arranged by W. I. Fletcher, S. S. Missionary for Connecticut.)

For opening exercises, the schedules given on page 66 may be appropriately used.

GENERAL EXERCISES.

Leader. The Scriptures are mentioned by the sacred writers themselves under many different names or titles. What are some of these?

Class. No. 1. The word.

But be ye doers of the word, and not hearers only, deceiving your own selves. Jas. i. 22.

The word of God.

But he said, Yea rather, blessed are they that hear the word of God, and keep it. Luke xi. 28.

The word of Christ.

Let the word of Christ dwell in you richly in all wisdom; teaching and admonishing one another in psalms and hymns and spiritual songs, singing with grace in your hearts to the Lord. Col. iii. 16.

Leader. Can you give still others?

Class No. 2. The Holy Scriptures.

Which he had promised afore by his prophets in the Holy Scriptures. Rom. i. 2.

The Scripture of truth.

But I will shew thee that which is noted in the Scripture of truth. Dan. x. 21.

The law of the Lord.

But his delight is in the law of the Lord; and in his law doth he meditate day and night. Psalms i. 2.

Leader. What are some of the passages in which the word of God is represented under an emblem or figure?

Class No. 3. And take the helmet of salvation, and the sword of the Spirit, which is the word of God. Eph. vi. 17.

Is not my word like as a fire? saith the Lord; and like a hammer that breaketh the rock in pieces? Jer. xxiii. 29.

Thy word is a lamp unto my feet, and a light unto my path. Psalms cxix. 105.

As new-born babes, desire the sincere milk of the word, that ye may grow thereby. I. Pet. ii. 2.

RESPONSIVE RECITATION.

Class No. 4.

1. Wherewithal shall a young man cleanse his way? Psalms cxix. 9.

3. Thy word have I hid in mine heart. Psalms cxix. 11.

5. Sanctify them through thy truth. John xvii. 17.

7. The law of the Lord is perfect, converting the soul: the testimony of the Lord is sure, making wise the simple. Psalms xix. 7.

9. Do not my words do good to him that walketh uprightly? Micah ii. 7.

Class No. 5.

2. By taking heed thereto according to thy word. Psalms cxix. 9.

4. That I might not sin against thee. Psalms cxix. 11.

6. Thy word is truth. John xvii. 17.

8. The statutes of the Lord are right, rejoicing the heart: the commandment of the Lord is pure, enlightening the eyes. Psalms xix. 8.

10. Moreover by them is thy servant warned: and in keeping of them there is great reward. Psalms xix. 11.

Both classes recite in concert. More to be desired are they than gold, yea, than much fine gold: sweeter also than honey and the honey-comb. Psalms xix. 10.

Leader. All Scripture is given by inspiration of God, and is profitable for doctrine, for reproof, for correction, for instruction in righteousness. II. Timothy iii. 16.

HYMNS.

We won't give up the Bible,
God's holy book of truth.
[*Happy Voices, p.* 72.

Thank God for the Bible? 'tis here that we find
The story of Christ and his love.
[*Golden Chain, p.* 63.

Holy Bible! book divine!
Precious treasure! thou art mine!
[*Am. S. S. Hymn-Book, No.* 122.

Leader. What do we learn as to the character and work of the Bible; first, as a means of conviction of sin?

Class No. 6. For the word of God is quick, and powerful, and sharper than any two-edged sword, piercing even to the dividing asunder of soul and spirit, and of the joints and marrow, and is a discerner of the thoughts and intents of the heart. Heb. iv. 12.

For I was alive without the law once: but when the commandment came, sin revived, and I died. Rom. vii. 9.

Leader. Again, as tending to our faith and hope?

Class No. 7. But these are written, that ye might believe that Jesus is the Christ, the Son of God; and that believing, ye might have life through his name. John xx. 31.

For whatsoever things were written aforetime were written for our learning; that we through patience and comfort of the Scriptures might have hope. Rom. xv. 4.

Remember the word unto thy servant, upon which thou hast caused me to hope. Psalms cxix. 49.

So then faith cometh by hearing, and hearing by the word of God. Rom. x. 17.

Leader. In aiding to cleanse the heart and enlighten the mind?

Class No. 8. Now ye are clean through the word which I have spoken unto you. John xv. 3.

Through thy precepts I get understanding: therefore I hate every false way.

The entrance of thy words giveth light; it giveth understanding unto the simple. Psalms cxix. 104, 130.

Leader. In promoting growth in grace and sanctification?

Class No. 9. And now, brethren, I commend you to God, and to the word of his grace, which is able to build you up, and to give you an inheritance among all them which are sanctified. Acts xx. 32.

For this cause also thank we God without ceasing, because, when ye received the word of God which ye heard of us, ye received it not as the word of men, but, as it is in truth, the word of God, which effectually worketh also in you that believe. I. Thess. ii. 13.

Leader. What can the infant class [or department] tell us about the word of God?

[The first twenty lines may be assigned to as many scholars, or to ten, each repeating a couplet. The last four lines are to be repeated in concert by the whole class.]

Infant Class.
1. The Word of God to man—its praises sing!
   The Word of God to man good news doth bring.

2. The Word of God is mercy from above,
   The Word of God, glad token of his love!

3. The Word of God brings gracious news from Heaven,
   The Word of God reveals our sins forgiven.

4. The Word of God great comfort doth impart,
   The Word of God can heal the broken heart.

5. The Word of God—sweet music to our ears,
   The Word of God can banish all our fears.

6. The Word of God, that bright and shining light,
   The Word of God illumes affliction's night.

7. The Word of God gives cordial to the soul,
   The Word of God makes broken spirits whole.

8. The Word of God doth consolation bring,
   The Word of God can blunt death's sharpest sting.

9. The Word of God affords great consolation,
   The Word of God shows Christ our one salvation.

10. The Word of God can guide our souls to bliss,
    Where Jesus Christ our blessed Saviour is.

11. O, may this blessed word be our delight,
    Our meditation, morning, noon and night.
    May it refresh and cheer us on the road,
    Till we arrive at home, at peace with God.

HYMNS.

How gentle God's commands!
How kind his precepts are.
[*Song Flowers*, p. 29.

How precious is the story
Of our Redeemer's birth.
[*Happy Voices*, p. 24.

Blessed Bible! how I love it!
How it doth my spirit cheer.
[*Golden Censer*, p. 42.

THE CHILDREN'S BIBLE SERVICE.

Leader. In view of what we have heard, what is our duty towards the Holy Scriptures?

RESPONSIVE RECITATION.

Class No. 10.

1. This book of the law shall not depart out of thy mouth; but thou shalt meditate therein day and night, that thou mayest observe to do according to all that is written therein. Josh. i. 8.

3. And ye shall teach them your children, speaking of them when thou sittest in thine house, and when thou walkest by the way, when thou liest down, and when thou risest up. Deut. xi. 19.

5. Whoso despiseth the word shall be destroyed. Prov. xiii. 13.

7. Search the Scriptures; for in them ye think ye have eternal life. John v. 39.

9. For I testify unto every man that heareth the words of the prophecy of this book, If any man shall add unto these things, God shall add unto him the plagues that are written in this book. Rev. xxii. 18.

Class No. 11.

2. Therefore shall ye lay up these my words in your heart and in your soul, and bind them for a sign upon your hand, that they may be as frontlets between your eyes. Deut. xi. 18.

4. And thou shalt write them upon the door-posts of thine house, and upon thy gates. Deut. xi. 20.

6. But he that feareth the commandment shall be rewarded. Prov. xiii. 13.

8. And they are they which testify of me. John v. 39.

10. And if any man shall take away from the words of the book of this prophecy, God shall take away his part out of the book of life, and out of the holy city, and from the things which are written in this book. Rev. xxii. 19.

Both classes in concert. Continue thou in the things which thou hast learned, and hast been assured of, knowing of whom thou hast learned them;

And that from a child thou hast known the Holy Scriptures,

which are able to make thee wise unto salvation through faith which is in Christ Jesus. II. Tim. iii. 14, 15.

Leader. In reference to our duty towards the Scriptures as well as in all our duties, we may learn much from the example of our blessed Saviour. His frequent use of the Old Testament Scriptures shows a remarkable familiarity with them, his public teachings containing allusions to almost every part of them. Can you give any instance of his referring to the book of Genesis?

Class No. 12. And he answered and said unto them, Have ye not read, that he which made them at the beginning made them male and female. Matt. xix. 4.

But as the days of Noe were, so shall also the coming of the Son of man be. Matt. xxiv. 37.

Leader. Any instance of his referring to Exodus?

Class No. 13. Ye have heard that it was said by them of old time, Thou shalt not kill; and whosoever shall kill shall be in danger of the judgment.

Ye have heard that it hath been said, An eye for an eye, and a tooth for a tooth. Matt. v. 21, 38.

But as touching the resurrection of the dead, have ye not read that which was spoken unto you by God, saying,

I am the God of Abraham, and the God of Isaac, and the God of Jacob? God is not the God of the dead, but of the living. Matt. xxii. 31, 32.

Leader. To Leviticus?

Class No. 14. And saith unto him, See thou say nothing to any man: but go thy way, shew thyself to the priest, and offer for thy cleansing those things which Moses commanded, for a testimony unto them. Mark i. 44.

Leader. To Numbers?

Class No. 15. And as Moses lifted up the serpent in the wilderness, even so must the Son of man be lifted up;

That whosoever believeth in him should not perish, but have everlasting life. John iii. 14, 15.

Leader. To Deuteronomy?

Class No. 16. And when the tempter came to him, he said, If thou be the Son of God, command that these stones be made bread.

But he answered and said, It is written, Man shall not live by bread alone, but by every word that proceedeth out of the mouth of God.

Then the devil taketh him up into the holy city, and setteth him on a pinnacle of the temple,

And saith unto him, If thou be the Son of God, cast thyself down: for it is written, He shall give his angels charge concerning thee; and in their hands they shall bear thee up, lest at any time thou dash thy foot against a stone.

Jesus said unto him, It is written again, Thou shalt not tempt the Lord thy God.

Again, the devil taketh him up into an exceeding high mountain, and sheweth him all the kingdoms of the world, and the glory of them;

And saith unto him, All these things will I give thee, if thou wilt fall down und worship me.

Then saith Jesus unto him, Get thee hence, Satan: for it is written, Thou shalt worship the Lord thy God, and him only shalt thou serve. Matt. iv. 3-10.

Leader. To I. Samuel?

Class No. 17. But he said unto them, Have ye not read what David did, when he was an hungered, and they that were with him;

How he entered into the house of God, and did eat the shew-bread, which was not lawful for him to eat, neither for them which were with him, but only for the priests? Matt. xii. 3, 4.

Leader. To I. Kings?

Class No. 18. But I tell you of a truth, many widows were in Israel in the days of Elias, when the heaven was shut up three years and six months, when great famine was throughout all the land;

But unto none of them was Elias sent, save unto Sarepta, a city of Sidon, unto a woman that was a widow. Luke iv. 25, 26.

Leader. To II. Kings?

Class No. 19. And many lepers were in Israel in the time of Eliseus the prophet; and none of them was cleansed, saving Naaman the Syrian. Luke iv. 27.

Leader. To II. Chronicles?

Class No. 20. The queen of the south shall rise up in the judgment with this generation, and shall condemn it: for she came from the uttermost parts of the earth to hear the wisdom of Solomon; and, behold, a greater than Solomon is here. Matt. xii. 42.

That upon you may come all the righteous blood shed upon the earth, from the blood of righteous Abel unto the blood of Zacharias son of Barachias, whom ye slew between the temple and the altar. Matt. xxiii. 35.

Leader. To the Psalms?

Class No. 21. And when the chief priests and scribes saw the wonderful things that he did, and the children crying in the temple, and saying, Hosanna to the son of David; they were sore displeased,

And said unto him, Hearest thou what these say? And Jesus saith unto them, Yea; have ye never read, Out of the mouth of babes and sucklings thou hast perfected praise? Matt. xxi. 15, 16.

He saith unto them, How then doth David in spirit call him Lord, saying,

The Lord said unto my Lord, Sit thou on my right hand, till I make thine enemies thy footstool? Matt. xxii. 43, 44.

Leader. To Isaiah?

Class No. 22. For this is he, of whom it is written, Behold, I send my messenger before thy face, which shall prepare thy way before thee. Matt. xi. 10.

And in them is fulfilled the prophecy of Esaias, which saith, By hearing ye shall hear, and shall not understand; and seeing ye shall see, and shall not perceive:

For this people's heart is waxed gross, and their ears are dull of hearing, and their eyes they have closed; lest at any time they should see with their eyes, and hear with their ears, and should understand with their heart, and should be converted, and I should heal them. Matt. xiii. 14, 15.

Leader. To Daniel?

Class No. 23. When ye therefore shall see the abomination of desolation, spoken of by Daniel the prophet, stand in the holy place, (whoso readeth, let him understand,)

Then let them which be in Judea flee into the mountains. Matt. xxiv. 15, 16.

Leader. To Hosea?

Class No. 24. But go ye and learn what that meaneth, I will have mercy, and not sacrifice: for I am not come to call the righteous, but sinners to repentance. Matt. ix. 13.

Leader. To Jonah?

Class No. 25. But he answered and said unto them, An evil and adulterous generation seeketh after a sign; and there shall no sign be given to it, but the sign of the prophet Jonas:

For as Jonas was three days and three nights in the whale's belly, so shall the Son of man be three days and three nights in the heart of the earth. Matt. xii. 39, 40.

Leader. To Zechariah?

Class No. 26. And Jesus saith unto them, All ye shall be

offended because of me this night: for it is written, I will smite the Shepherd, and the sheep shall be scattered. Mark xiv. 27.

Leader. To Malachi?

Class No. 27. And if ye will receive it, this is Elias, which was for to come. Matt. xi. 14.

Leader. Now let us remember the word of the Lord:

If ye know these things, happy are ye if ye do them. John xiii. 17.

For not the hearers of the law are just before God, but the doers of the law shall be justified. Rom ii. 13.

Pastor. For if any be a hearer of the word, and not a doer, he is like unto a man beholding his natural face in a glass:

For he beholdeth himself, and goeth his way, and straightway forgetteth what manner of man he was.

But whoso looketh into the perfect law of liberty, and continueth therein, he being not a forgetful hearer, but a doer of the work, this man shall be blessed in his deed. James i. 23–25.

Prayer is offered.

HYMNS.

The heavens declare thy glory, Lord,
In every star thy wisdom shines.
[*Am. S. S. Hymn-Book, No.* 134.

Sinners, will you scorn the message
Sent from above?
[*Song Flowers, p,* 58.

The service is closed with the benediction, if a minister is present.

LESSON VI.

MAN.—HIS CONDITION BY NATURE AND BY GRACE.

OPENING HYMN.

We come with rejoicing, thanksgiving, and song,
The notes of our anthem let echo prolong.
To Him who redeemed us, and saved us from death,
We'll sing loudest praises, while He gives us breath.

[*Golden Shower, p.* 67.

SCRIPTURE READING.

To be read responsively:

Psalm li.

OPENING SENTENCES.

Pastor. What is man, that thou art mindful of him? and the son of man, that thou visitest him?

For thou hast made him a little lower than the angels, and hast crowned him with glory and honor. Ps. viii. 4, 5.

Assembly. Woe is me! for I am undone. Isa. vi. 5.

Superintendent. Thou hast destroyed thyself; but in ME is thine help. Hos. xiii. 9.

All. This is a faithful saying, and worthy of all acceptation, that Christ Jesus came into the world to save sinners; of whom I am chief. I. Tim. i. 15.

INFANT CLASS. RESPONSIVE RECITATION.

First Scholar. Jesus said Suffer little children, and forbid them not, to come unto me; for of such is the kingdom of heaven. Matt. xix. 14.

Second Scholar. O God, thou art my God; early will I seek thee. Psalms lxiii. 1.

THE CHILDREN'S BIBLE SERVICE.

RESPONSIVE RECITATION—CONTINUED.

Third Scholar. Then said Jesus unto them again, I am the good Shepherd, and know my sheep, and am known of mine. John x. 7, 14.

Fourth Scholar. The Lord is my shepherd, I shall not want. Psalms xxiii. 1.

Fifth Scholar. Remember now thy Creator in thy days of thy youth. Eccl. xii. 1.

Sixth Scholar. My Father thou art the guide of my youth. Jer. iii 4.

Seventh Scholar. I will feed my flock, and I will cause them to lie down, saith the Lord God. Ezek. xxxiv. 15.

Eighth Scholar. He shall gather the lambs with his arm, and carry them in his bosom. Isa. xl. 11.

Infant Class Teacher. Blessed be the Lord God of Israel; for he hath visited and redeemed his people. Luke i. 68.

Infant Class in Concert. Thanks be unto God for his unspeakable gift. II. Cor. ix. 15.

HYMN.

Just as I am, without one plea,
But that thy blood was shed for me. [*Song Flowers, p.* 23.

GENERAL EXERCISES.

Leader. How does the Bible describe the natural state of fallen man?

Class No. 1. The heart is deceitful above all things, and desperately wicked: who can know it? Jer. xvii. 9.

For the imagination of man's heart is evil from his youth. Gen. viii. 21.

The heart of the sons of men is fully set in them to do evil. Eccl. viii. 11.

Because the carnal mind is enmity against God: for it is not subject to the law of God, neither indeed can be. Rom. viii. 7.

Leader. What further description of the wickedness of man does the Bible give?

THE CHILDREN'S BIBLE SERVICE. 153

Class No. 2. For there is not a just man upon earth, that doeth good, and sinneth not. Eccl. vii. 20.
As it is written, There is none righteous, no, not one:
There is none that understandeth, there is none that seeketh after God.
They are all gone out of the way, they are together become unprofitable; there is none that doeth good, no, not one.
Their throat is an open sepulchre: with their tongues they have used deceit: the poison of asps is under their lips:
Whose mouth is full of cursing and bitterness:
Their feet are swift to shed blood:
Destruction and misery are in their ways;
And the way of peace have they not known:
There is no fear of God before their eyes. Rom. iii. 10-18.

Leader. Seeing that such is man's lost condition, is there any way of escape for him?

RESPONSIVE RECITATION.

Class No. 3.	*Class No.* 4.
1. Behold, I am vile; what shall I answer thee? Job. xl. 4.	2. Come now, and let us reason together, saith the Lord: Though your sins be as scarlet, they shall be as white as snow; though they be red like crimson, they shall be as wool. Isa. i. 18.
3. For mine iniquities are gone over mine head; as an heavy burden they are too heavy for me. Psalms xxxviii. 4.	4. Come unto me, all ye that labor and are heavy laden, and I will give you rest. Matt. xi. 28.
5. Oh that I knew where I might find him! that I might come even to his seat! Job. xxiii. 3.	6. Let us therefore come boldly unto the throne of grace, that we may obtain mercy, and find grace to help in time of need. Heb. iv. 16.

RESPONSIVE RECITATION—CONTINUED.

7. I have gone astray like a lost sheep. Psalms cxix. 176.

9. Have mercy upon me, O Lord; for I am weak: O Lord, heal me; for my bones are vexed. Psalms vi. 2.

8. For the Son of man is come to seek and to save that which was lost. Luke xix. 10.

10. My grace is sufficient for thee; for my strength is made perfect in weakness. II. Cor. xii. 9.

Class No. 5.

1. What must I do to be saved? Acts xvi. 30.

3. Lord, I believe; help thou mine unbelief. Mark ix. 24.

5. Hide not thy face far from me. Psalms xxvii. 9.

7. For thy name's sake lead me, and guide me. Psalms xxxi. 3.

9. I had fainted, unless I had believed to see the goodness of the Lord in the land of the living. Psalms xxvii 13.

Class No. 6.

2. Believe on the Lord Jesus Christ, and thou shalt be saved. Acts xvi. 31.

4. Thy faith hath saved thee; go in peace. Luke vii. 50.

6. In a little wrath I hid my face from thee for a moment; but with everlasting kindness will I have mercy on thee, saith the Lord thy Redeemer. Isa. liv. 8.

8. I will instruct thee, and teach thee in the way which thou shalt go: I will guide thee with mine eye. Psalms xxxii. 8.

10. He giveth power to the faint; and to them that have no might he increaseth strength. Isa. xl. 29.

Both Classes in concert. Blessed be the Lord, because he hath heard the voice of my supplications.

The Lord is my strength and my shield; my heart trusted in him, and I am helped: therefore my heart greatly rejoiceth; and with my song will I praise him. Psalms xxviii. 6, 7.

The infant class rises, and the scholars recite in concert, or one line or couplet each:

> I have an evil heart within,
> A heart that's often prone to sin:
> What can a feeble infant do,
> His naughty temper to subdue?
>
> This will I do, when first I find
> An evil thought within my mind,
> I'll go to Jesus, and I'll say,
> Lord, take this sinful heart away.
>
> Does not the name of Jesus mean,
> One that has power to save from sin?
> O Lamb of God, take mine away,
> And give me a new heart, I pray.
>
> <div style="text-align:right">[<i>Children's Friend</i>, 1862.]</div>

A hymn is sung:

> Depth of mercy, can there be,
> Mercy still reserved for me?
>
> <div style="text-align:right">[<i>Singing Pilgrim</i>, p. 14.]</div>

Or,

> Burdened with guilt, would'st thou be blest?
> Trust not the world; it gives no rest.
>
> <div style="text-align:right">[<i>Song Flowers</i>, p. 44.]</div>

Leader. Although such a free and full salvation is provided, many refuse to accept it. What does the Bible say as to the difference between such, and the righteous?

RESPONSIVE RECITATION.

Class No. 7.	Class No. 8.
1. There is no peace, saith my God, to the wicked. Isa. lvii. 21.	2. Great peace have they which love thy law: and nothing shall offend them. Psalms cxix. 165.

RESPONSIVE RECITATION—CONTINUED.

3. He shall never suffer the righteous to be moved. Ps. lv. 22.

4. But the wicked are like the troubled sea, when it cannot rest, whose waters cast up mire and dirt. Isa. lvii. 20.

5. Say ye to the righteous, that it shall be well with him; for they shall eat the fruit of their doings. Isa. iii. 10.

6. Woe unto the wicked! it shall be ill with him; for the reward of his hands shall be given him. Isa. iii. 11.

7. The light of the righteous rejoiceth. Prov. xiii. 9.

8. But the lamp of the wicked shall be put out. Proverbs xiii. 9.

9. The way of the wicked is as darkness; they know not at what they stumble. Prov. iv. 19.

10. But the path of the just is as the shining light, that shineth more and more unto the perfect day. Prov. iv. 18.

Both Classes in concert. And this is the condemnation, that light is come into the world, and men loved darkness rather than light, because their deeds were evil. John iii. 19.

Pastor. Yet a little while is the light with you. Walk while ye have the light, lest darkness come upon you : for he that walketh in darkness knoweth not whither he goeth.

While ye have light, believe in the light, that ye may be the children of light. John xii. 35, 36.

Leader. Can you give other similar passages?

Class No. 9.

1. The wicked flee when no man pursueth. Prov. xxviii. 1.

3. For thou, Lord, wilt bless the righteous; with favor wilt thou compass him as with a shield. Psalms v. 12.

Class No. 10.

2. But the righteous are bold as a lion. Prov. xxviii. 1.

4. But the wicked shall perish, and the enemies of the Lord shall be as the fat of lambs: they shall consume; into smoke shall they consume away. Ps. xxxvii. 20.

THE CHILDREN'S BIBLE SERVICE.

5. The mouth of the righteous speaketh wisdom, and his tongue talketh of judgment. Psalms xxxvii. 30.

7. The effectual fervent prayer of a righteous man availeth much. James v. 16.

9. The memory of the just is blessed. Prov. x. 7.

6. But the mouth of the wicked speaketh frowardness. Prov. x. 32.

8. He that turneth away his ear from hearing the law, even his prayer shall be abomination. Prov. xxviii. 9.

10. But the name of the wicked shall rot. Prov. x. 7.

Leader. How will this difference between the righteous and the wicked be manifest hereafter?

Class No. 11.

1. So shall it be at the end of the world: the angels shall come forth, and sever the wicked from among the just,

And shall cast them into the furnace of fire: there shall be wailing and gnashing of teeth. Matt. xiii. 49, 50.

3. Then shall the King say unto them on his right hand, Come, ye blessed of my Father, inherit the kingdom prepared for you from the foundation of the world. Matt. xxv. 34.

5. And these shall go away into everlasting punishment. Matt. xxv. 46.

7. He that is unjust, let him be unjust still: and he that is filthy, let him be filthy still. Rev. xxii. 11.

Class No. 12.

2. Then shall the righteous shine forth as the sun in the kingdom of their Father. Matt. xiii. 43.

4. Then shall he say also unto them on the left hand, Depart from me, ye cursed, into everlasting fire, prepared for the devil and his angels. Matt. xxv. 41.

6. But the righteous into life eternal. Matt. xxv. 46.

8. And he that is righteous, let him be righteous still: and he that is holy, let him be holy still. Rev. xxii. 11.

Leader. And, behold, I come quickly; and my reward is with me, to give every man according as his work shall be. Rev. xxii. 12.

Entire School. And the Spirit and the bride say, Come. And let him that heareth say, Come. And let him that is athirst come. And whosoever will, let him take the water of life freely. Rev. xxii. 17.

A hymn is sung:

>Come, ye sinners, poor and needy,
>Weak and wounded, sick and sore.
>
>[*Happy Voices, p.* 199.

Or,

>Come to Jesus, come to Jesus,
>Come to Jesus just now.
>
>[*Golden Censer, p.* 70.

The pastor closes the service, with the following as a benediction:

Now the God of peace, that brought again from the dead our Lord Jesus, that great Shepherd of the sheep, through the blood of the everlasting covenant,

Make you perfect in every good work to do his will, working in you that which is well pleasing in his sight, through Jesus Christ; to whom be glory for ever and ever. Amen. Heb. xiii. 20, 21.

LESSON VII.

THE PARABLE OF THE PRODIGAL SON,

EXPLAINED BY SCRIPTURE.

[Prepared originally for the Asylum Hill Church (Congregational), Sunday School, Hartford, Ct.]

The service opens with singing:

> Come, let us raise
> A song of praise,
> To him who rules on high.
>
> [*Am. S. S. Hymn Book, p.* 27.

The pastor says :

Hear, O heavens, and give ear, O earth: for the Lord hath spoken, I have nourished and brought up children, and they have rebelled against me. Isa. i. 2.

The assembly respond :

We acknowledge, O Lord, our wickedness, and the iniquity of our fathers; for we have sinned against thee. Jer. xiv. 20.

The pastor adds :

If we confess our sins, he is faithful and just to forgive us our sins, and to cleanse us from all unrighteousness. I. John i. 9.

The blood of Jesus Christ his son cleanseth us from all sin. I. John i. 7.

In concert, all say :

Blessed are they whose iniquities are forgiven, and whose sins are covered. Rom. iv. 7.

The pastor prays, all joining him in the Lord's prayer.

The superintendent reads a selection of Scripture from Matt. vii. 7-14.

All join in singing:

> I would love thee, Heavenly Father,
> My Redeemer, and my King.
> [*Golden Chain, p.* 47.]

The infant class recite Scripture passages as follows, each scholar giving one text:

1. I was my father's son, tender and only beloved in the sight of my mother. Prov. iv. 3.
2. He taught me also, and said unto me, Let thine heart retain my words. Prov. iv. 4.
3. I hated instruction, and my heart despised reproof. Prov. v. 12.
4. And have not obeyed the voice of my teachers, nor inclined mine ear to them that instructed me. Prov. v. 13.
5. I acknowledge my transgressions: and my sin is ever before me. Ps. li. 3.
6. I said, Lord be merciful unto me: heal my soul; for I have sinned against thee. Ps. xli. 4.
7. I sought the Lord, and he heard me, and delivered me from all my fears. Ps. xxxiv. 4.
8. Surely goodness and mercy shall follow me all the days of my life. Ps. xxiii. 6.
9. And I will dwell in the house of the Lord forever. Ps. xxiii. 6.

The Infant class recite in concert:

> God is so good that he will hear,
>   Whenever children humbly pray;
> He always lends a gracious ear
>   To what the youngest child can say.

His own most holy book declares
He loves good little children still,
And that he listens to their prayers,
Just as a tender father will.
[*Tract Primer, p.* 235.]

The pastor says:

O Lord our Lord, how excellent is thy name in all the earth! who hast set thy glory above the heavens. Out of the mouth of babes and sucklings hast thou ordained strength because of thine enemies, that thou mightest still the enemy and the avenger. Ps. viii. 1, 2.

The infant class sings:

I have a Father in the promised land.

GENERAL EXERCISES.

The superintendent announces as the subject for the day the parable of the prodigal son, in Luke xv. 11–32. He brings out by questions the fact that this parable was spoken by Jesus on his last journey to Jerusalem, before his crucifixion. He then asks:

To whom was this parable spoken?

Class No. 1 answers:

Then drew near unto him all the publicans and sinners for to hear him.... And he spake this parable unto them. Luke xv. 1, 3.

The superintendent reads: "A certain man had two sons," and adds the question:

Who is this Father?

Class No. 2 responds:

Doubtless thou art our Father, though Abraham be ignorant of us, and Israel acknowledge us not: thou, O Lord, art our Father, our Redeemer; thy name is from everlasting. Isa. lxiii. 16.

One God and Father of all, who is above all, and through all, and in you all. Eph. iv. 6.

Superintendent. "And the younger of them said to his father, Father, give me the portion of goods that falleth to me. And he divided unto them his living."

What does Solomon say of such a portion as this?

Class No. 3. He that loveth silver shall not be satisfied with silver; nor he that loveth abundance with increase. This is also vanity. Eccl. v. 10.

Superintendent. "And not many days after, the younger son gathered all together, and took his journey into a far country, and there wasted his substance with riotous living."

What are we told of those who thus go away from God?

Class No. 4. O Lord, the hope of Israel, all that forsake thee shall be ashamed, and they that depart from me shall be written in the earth, because they have forsaken the Lord, the fountain of living waters. Jer. xvii. 13.

Superintendent. "And when he had spent all, there arose a mighty famine in that land; and he began to be in want."

Does the soul hunger and thirst as truly as the body? and how is it satisfied?

Class No. 5. Therefore thus saith the Lord God, Behold, my servants shall eat, but ye shall be hungry: behold, my servants shall drink, but ye shall be thirsty: behold, my servants shall rejoice, but ye shall be ashamed. Isa. lxv. 13.

And Jesus said unto them, I am the bread of life: he that cometh to me shall never hunger; and he that believeth on me shall never thirst. John vi. 35.

Superintendent. "And he went and joined himself to a citizen of that country; and he sent him into his fields to feed swine."

How is every sinner, like this prodigal son, a servant?

Class No. 6. Jesus answered them, Verily, verily, I say unto you, Whosoever committeth sin is the servant of sin. John viii. 34.

Superintendent. "And he would fain have filled his belly with the husks that the swine did eat: and no man gave unto him."

What are the wages of sin? and do they satisfy?

Class No. 7. The wages of sin is death. Rom. vi. 23.

All the labor of man is for his mouth, and yet the appetite is not filled. Eccl. vi. 7.

Superintendent. "And when he came to himself, he said, How many hired servants of my father's have bread enough, and to spare, and I perish with hunger!"

How is this reflection of the prodigal like that of many a wanderer from God?

Class No. 8. I remember thee upon my bed, and meditate on thee in the night watches. Psalms lxiii. 6.

Blessed are they that dwell in thy house: they will be still praising thee. Psalms lxxxiv. 4.

My life is spent with grief, and my years with sighing: my strength faileth because of mine iniquity. Psalms xxxi. 10.

I thought on my ways, and turned my feet unto thy testimonies. Psalms cxix. 59.

Superintendent. "I will arise, and go to my father, and will say unto him, Father, I have sinned against Heaven, and before thee."

Is it enough to *think* of our Father's house? or must we *return* to God, and return *now ?*

Class No. 9. Return, ye backsliding children, and I will heal your backslidings. Behold, we come unto thee; for thou art the Lord our God. Jer. iii. 22.

Behold, now is the accepted time; behold, now is the day of salvation. II. Cor. vi. 2.

Superintendent. "And am no more worthy to be called thy son: make me as one of thy hired servants."

Must we confess our sins before they can be forgiven?

Class No. 10. He that covereth his sins shall not prosper; but whoso confesseth and forsaketh them shall have mercy. Prov. xxviii. 13.

Humble yourselves in the sight of the Lord, and he shall lift you up. James iv. 10.

The pastor recites:

Like as a father pitieth his children, so the Lord pitieth them that fear him. Psalms ciii. 13.

My son, give me thine heart. Prov. xxiii. 26.

Hearken, O daughter, and consider, and incline thine ear. Psalms xlv. 10.

All join in singing:

> Wanderer from God, return, return,
> And seek an injured Father's face.
>
> [*Golden Shower, p.* 10.

Superintendent. "And he arose and came to his father. But when he was yet a great way off, his father saw him, and had compassion, and ran, and fell on his neck, and kissed him."

How does this resemble God's dealings with his penitent children?

Class No. 11. If my people, which are called by my name, shall humble themselves, and pray, and seek my face, and turn from their wicked ways; then will I hear from heaven, and will forgive their sin. II. Chron. vii. 14.

Superintendent. "And the son said unto him, Father, I have sinned against Heaven, and in thy sight, and am no more worthy to be called thy son."

Does God's forgiving mercy increase our consciousness of sin?

Class No. 12. Have mercy upon me, O God, according to thy loving kindness: according unto the multitude of thy tender mercies blot out my transgressions.

For I acknowledge my transgressions: and my sin is ever before me.

Against thee, thee only, have I sinned, and done this evil in thy sight. Psalms li. 1, 3, 4.

Superintendent. "But the father said to his servants, Bring forth the best robe, and put it on him; and put a ring on his hand, and shoes on his feet."

How is righteousness mentioned in the Bible as the dress of the redeemed soul?

Class No. 13. I will greatly rejoice in the Lord, my soul shall be joyful in my God; for he hath clothed me with the garments of salvation, he hath covered me with the robe of righteousness, as a bridegroom decketh himself with ornaments, and as a bride adorneth herself with her jewels. Isa. lxi. 10.

Superintendent. "And bring hither the fatted calf, and kill it; and let us eat, and be merry."

Are the provisions of the Gospel compared to a feast?

Class No. 14. And in this mountain shall the Lord of hosts make unto all people a feast of fat things, a feast of wines on the lees, of fat things full of marrow, of wines on the lees well refined. Isa. xxv. 6.

Superintendent. " For this my son was dead, and is alive again; he was lost, and is found. And they began to be merry. "

What is said in the Bible, of sinners as being lost and dead, and as having hope of life again?

Class No. 15. For the Son of man is come to seek and to save that which was lost. Luke xix. 10.

He that hath the Son hath life; and he that hath not the Son of God hath not life. I. John v. 12.

A single verse is sung:

> No more a wandering sheep,
> I love to be controlled;
> I love my tender Shepherd's voice,
> I love the peaceful fold :
> No more a wayward child,
> I seek no more to roam;
> I love my heavenly Father's voice;
> I love, I love my home.
>
> [*Happy Voices, p.* 45.

Superintendent. " Now his elder son was in the field: and as he came and drew nigh to the house, he heard music and dancing."

What assurance is given to us that we shall find joy in coming back to our Father in heaven, in penitence and faith?

Class No. 16. And the ransomed of the Lord shall return, and come to Zion with songs and everlasting joy upon their heads: they shall obtain joy and gladness, and sorrow and sighing shall flee away. Isa. xxxv. 10.

In thy presence is fulness of joy; at thy right hand there are pleasures for evermore. Psalms xvi. 11.

Superintendent. "And he called one of the servants, and asked what these things meant."

Is God's reception of repenting sinners often a cause of wonder to the self-righteous?

Class No. 17. And the Pharisees and scribes murmured, saying, This man receiveth sinners, and eateth with them. Luke xv. 2.

O the depth of the riches both of the wisdom and knowledge of God! how unsearchable are his judgments, and his ways past finding out! Rom. 11. 33.

Superintendent. "And he said unto him, Thy brother is come; and thy father hath killed the fatted calf, because he hath received him safe and sound."

What does Christ say of the joy in heaven over the repentant sinner?

Class No. 18. I say unto you, That likewise joy shall be in heaven over one sinner that repenteth, more than over ninety and nine just persons, which need no repentance. Luke xv. 7.

Superintendent. "And he was angry, and would not go in: therefore came his father out, and entreated him."

We see here, in strong contrast, God's love and man's hardness of heart, toward the erring. Can you give a similar instance from another of Christ's parables?

Class No. 19. Then the lord of that servant was moved with compassion, and loosed him, and forgave him the debt.

But the same servant went out, and found one of his fellow-servants, which owed him an hundred pence; and he laid hands on him, and took him by the throat, saying, Pay me that thou owest. Matt. xviii. 27, 28.

Superintendent. "And he answering said to his father, Lo, these many years do I serve thee, neither transgressed I at any time thy commandment ; and yet thou never gavest me a kid, that I might make merry with my friends :

"But as soon as this thy son was come, which hath devoured thy living with harlots, thou hast killed for him the fatted calf."

A true son would not answer his father thus. How is this boasting and servile spirit elsewhere rebuked?

Class No. 20. Where is boasting then? It is excluded. By what law? of works? Nay; but by the law of faith.

Therefore we conclude, that a man is justified by faith without the deeds of the law. Rom. iii. 27, 28.

Superintendent. "And he said unto him, Son, thou art ever with me, and all that I have is thine."

Has God in his word given such an assurance as this to his children?

Class No. 21. And because ye are sons, God hath sent forth the Spirit of his Son into your hearts, crying, Abba, Father.

Wherefore thou art no more a servant, but a son ; and if a son, then an heir of God through Christ. Gal. iv. 6, 7.

Superintendent. "It was meet that we should make merry, and be glad: for this thy brother was dead, and is alive again; and was lost, and is found."

What is said by the prophet Isaiah of the fitness of universal rejoicing over God's redeeming grace?

Class No. 22. Sing, O ye heavens ; for the Lord hath done it : shout, ye lower parts of the earth : break forth into singing, ye mountains, O forest, and every tree therein : for the Lord hath redeemed Jacob, and glorified himself in Israel. Isa. xliv. 23.

THE CHILDREN'S BIBLE SERVICE.

Bless the Lord, ye his angels, that excel in strength, that do his commandments, hearkening unto the voice of his word.

Bless ye the Lord, all ye his hosts ; ye ministers of his, that do his pleasure.

Bless the Lord, all his works in all places of his dominion: bless the Lord, O my soul. Psalms ciii. 20–22.

The pastor recites :

Then shall the King say unto them on his right hand, Come, ye blessed of my Father, inherit the kingdom prepared for you from the foundation of the world. Matt. xxv. 34.

The assembly responds :

Eye hath not seen, nor ear heard, neither have entered into the heart of man, the things which God hath prepared for them that love him.

But God hath revealed them unto us by his Spirit. I. Cor. ii. 9, 10.

The pastor adds :

Let us therefore fear, lest, a promise being left us of entering into his rest, any of you should seem to come short of it. Heb. iv. 1.

A closing hymn is sung :

> A beautiful land by faith I see,
> A land of rest, from sorrow free.
>
> [*Golden Chain*, *p.* 124.

LESSON VIII.

PRAYER.

[Arranged by John B. Smith, East Hartford, Ct.]

In evergreen, or other letters, above the pulpit or desk, the words may appear:
MY HOUSE SHALL BE CALLED THE HOUSE OF PRAYER. Matt. xxi. 13.

Or this text may be shown on a banner, on the song-roll, or on the blackboard.

OPENING SENTENCES.

Leader. O thou that hearest prayer, unto thee shall all flesh come. Psalms lxv. 2.

Assembly. Lord, teach us to pray. Luke xi. 1.

Leader. Be not rash with thy mouth, and let not thine heart be hasty to utter anything before God: for God is in heaven, and thou upon earth; therefore let thy words be few. Eccl. v. 2.

Assembly. The Spirit also helpeth our infirmities: for we know not what we should pray for as we ought: but the Spirit itself maketh intercession for us with groanings which cannot be uttered. Rom. viii. 26.

Leader. Without faith it is impossible to please him: for he that cometh to God must believe that he is, and that he is a rewarder of them that diligently seek him. Heb. xi. 6.

Assembly. I will pray with the spirit, and I will pray with the understanding also. I. Cor. xiv. 15.

Leader. Jesus saith .... If ye shall ask anything in my name, I will do it. John xiv. 9, 14.

All, in concert. Let us therefore come boldly unto the throne of grace, that we may obtain mercy, and find grace to help in time of need. Heb. iv. 16.

SCRIPTURE READING.

Jesus at prayer while his disciples were on the water. Matt. xiv. 22-33.

HYMN.

Prayer is the soul's sincere desire,
Unuttered or expressed.

[*Am. S. S. Hymn Book, No.* 14.

GENERAL EXERCISES.

Leader. The subject of our lesson to-day is Prayer. It will be well for us to consider Who of us should pray; To whom we should pray; Why we should pray; Where we should pray; When we should pray; For what we should pray; and How we should pray. Will the members of the first class tell us Who should pray?

Class No. 1.—*First scholar.* Those who are in doubt.

If any of you lack wisdom, let him ask of God, that giveth to all men liberally, and upbraideth not; and it shall be given him. James i. 5.

Second scholar. Those who are in distress.

Is any among you afflicted? let him pray. James v. 13.

Third scholar. Those who are sore burdened.

Come unto me, all ye that labor and are heavy laden, and I will give you rest. Matt. xi. 28.

Fourth scholar. The children.

Jesus said, Suffer little children, and forbid them not, to come unto me; for of such is the kingdom of heaven. Matt. xix. 14.

Fifth scholar. Everybody.

Look unto me, and be ye saved, all the ends of the earth. Isa. xlv. 22.

Leader. Will the second class tell us
To whom we should pray?

Class No. 2.—First scholar. To the Lord.

Take with you words, and turn to the Lord. Hos. xiv. 2.

Second scholar. To our Creator.

O come, let us worship and bow down; let us kneel before the Lord our Maker. Psalms xcv. 6.

Third scholar. To our Heavenly Father.

Pray to thy Father which is in secret; and thy Father, which seeth in secret, shall reward thee openly. Matt. vi. 6.

Fourth scholar. To him whom we have offended.

Have mercy upon me, O God, according to thy loving-kindness. Against thee, thee only, have I sinned. Psalms li. 1, 4.

Fifth scholar. To him who died for us.

And they stoned Stephen, calling upon God, and saying, Lord Jesus, receive my spirit. Acts vii. 59.

All, rising, sing the hymn:

> From every stormy wind that blows,
> From every swelling tide of woes,
> There is a calm, a sure retreat—
> 'Tis found beneath the mercy-seat.
>
> [*Singing Pilgrim, p.* 68.

Leader. Will the third class tell us
Why we should pray?

Class No. 3.—First scholar. Because we are in want.

Bow down thine ear, O Lord, hear me; for I am poor and needy. Psalms lxxxvi. 1.

Second scholar. Because God alone can aid us.

Give us help from trouble: for vain is the help of man. Psalms lx. 11.

Third scholar. Because God gives blessings in response to prayer.

The hand of our God is upon all them for good that seek him. Ezra viii. 22.

Fourth scholar. Because the answers to prayer are rich and free.

For every one that asketh, receiveth; and he that seeketh, findeth; and to him that knocketh, it shall be opened. Matt. vii. 8.

Fifth scholar. Because of our danger from temptation.

Watch and pray, that ye enter not into temptation. Matt. xxvi. 41.

Leader. Will the fourth class tell us
Where we should pray?

Class No. 4.—First scholar. In secret.

But thou, when thou prayest, enter into thy closet. Matt. vi. 6.

Second scholar. In the family.

Pour out thy fury upon the heathen that know thee not, and upon the families that call not on thy name. Jer. x. 25.

Third scholar. At friendly interviews.

And they all brought us on our way, with wives and children, till we were out of the city: and we kneeled down on the shore, and prayed. Acts xxi. 5.

Fourth scholar. In the social praying circle.

He came to the house of Mary the mother of John, whose surname was Mark; where many were gathered together praying. Acts xii. 12.

Fifth scholar. In the house of worship.

Two men went up into the temple to pray; the one a Pharisee, and the other a publican. Luke xviii. 10.

Sixth scholar. Everywhere.

I will therefore that men pray everywhere, lifting up holy hands, without wrath and doubting. I. Tim. ii. 8.

A verse or two of a hymn is sung, as

> They who seek the throne of grace,
> Find that throne in every place ;
> If we live a life of prayer,
> God is present everywhere.

Leader. Will the fifth class tell us When we should pray?

Class No. 5.—First scholar. As often as David, who said:

Evening, and morning, and at noon, will I pray, and cry aloud; and he shall hear my voice. Ps. lv. 17.

Second scholar. As often as Daniel.

He kneeled upon his knees three times a day, and prayed, and gave thanks before his God. Dan. vi. 10.

Third scholar. In adversity.

And call upon me in the day of trouble: I will deliver thee, and thou shalt glorify me. Psalms l. 15.

Fourth scholar. In prosperity.

And one of them, when he saw that he was healed, turned back, and with a loud voice glorified God. Luke xvii. 15.

Fifth scholar. Always.

Pray without ceasing. I. Thess. v. 17.

The leader recites:

Seek ye the Lord while he may be found, call ye upon him while he is near. Isa. lv. 6.

The assembly responds:

When thou saidst, Seek ye my face; my heart said unto thee, Thy face, Lord, will I seek. Psalms xxvii. 8.

THE CHILDREN'S BIBLE SERVICE. 175

Leader. Will the sixth class tell us
For what we should pray?

Class No. 6.—First scholar. For whatever we need personally.

Cast thy burden upon the Lord, and he shall sustain thee. Psalms lv. 22.

Be careful for nothing; but in everything by prayer and supplication, with thanksgiving, let your requests be made known unto God. Phil. iv. 6.

Second scholar. For our friends.

Confess your faults one to another, and pray one for another. James v. 16.

Third scholar. For our enemies.

Pray for them which despitefully use you, and persecute you. Matt. v. 44.

Fourth scholar. For our country.

Pray for the peace of Jerusalem. Psalms cxxii. 6.

For kings, and for all that are in authority: that we may lead a quiet and peaceable life in all godliness and honesty. I. Tim. ii. 2.

Fifth scholar. For all men.

I exhort therefore, that, first of all, supplications, prayers, intercessions, and giving of thanks, be made for all men. I. Tim. ii. 1.

Leader. Will the seventh class tell us
How we should pray?

First scholar. In penitence.

I acknowledge my transgressions: and my sin is ever before me. Psalms li. 3.

Second scholar. In faith.

But let him ask in faith, nothing wavering. For he that

wavereth is like a wave of the sea driven with the wind and tossed. James i. 6.

Third scholar. With all the heart.

And ye shall seek me, and find me, when ye shall search for me with all your heart. Jer. xxix. 13.

Fourth scholar. Perseveringly.

And he spake a parable unto them to this end, that men ought always to pray, and not to faint. Luke xviii. 1.

Fifth scholar. In submissiveness, as Jesus prayed in Gethsemane.

And he went a little farther, and fell on his face, and prayed, saying, O my Father, if it be possible, let this cup pass from me: nevertheless not as I will, but as thou wilt. Matt. xxvi. 39.

Leader. Will the infant class give us an example of prayer from the lips of Jesus?

The infant class, rising, recites in concert the Lord's prayer, as given on page 53:

After this manner therefore pray ye:
Our Father which art in heaven, &c. Matt. vi. 9–13.

The entire assembly, rising, recites:

Hearken unto the voice of my cry, my King, and my God: for unto thee will I pray.

My voice shalt thou hear in the morning, O Lord; in the morning will I direct my prayer unto thee, and will look up. Psalms v. 2, 3.

I will bless the Lord at all times: his praise shall continually be in my mouth.

O magnify the Lord with me, and let us exalt his name together. Psalms xxxiv. 1, 3.

The exercises close with singing:

Sweet hour of prayer! sweet hour of prayer!

[*Golden Chain, p.* 10.

LESSON IX.

GIVING TO THE LORD.

A LESSON FOR MISSIONARY SUNDAY.

[Arranged from an Exercise of the Asylum Hill S. S., Hartford.]

Attention may be called, in connection with this lesson, to the facts that in all cases God's people, as described in the Bible, offered gifts of benevolence when coming to his worship; and that the Gospel of Christ clearly inculcates giving as essential to true religion.

The children should be taught that all can give something; that they should give that which costs them something — that which they have saved or earned; that they should give it cheerfully; that they should give it as unto the Lord—as an earnest of their grateful love for him who gave himself for them.

The service opens with a hymn, as:

>I will sing for Jesus,
>With his blood he bought me.
>[*Singing Pilgrim*, *p.* 89.

The pastor says:

God so loved the world, that he gave his only begotten Son, that whosoever believeth in him should not perish, but have everlasting life. John iii. 16.

The superintendent adds:

He that spared not his own Son, but delivered him up for us all, how shall he not with him also freely give us all things? Rom. viii. 32.

The assembly responds:

Every good gift and every perfect gift is from above, and cometh down from the Father of lights, with whom is no variableness, neither shadow of turning. James i. 17.

The pastor says:

The gift of God is eternal life through Jesus Christ our Lord. Rom. vi. 23.

The assembly responds:

Thanks be unto God for his unspeakable gift. II. Cor. ix. 15.

The superintendent says:

Freely ye have received, freely give. Matt. x. 8.

All, in concert, recite:

He which soweth sparingly shall reap also sparingly; and he which soweth bountifully shall reap also bountifully. II. Cor. ix. 6.

A hymn is sung, as:

Do good, do good, there is ever a way,
There's a way where there's ever a will.
[*Golden Censer*, p. 98.

The parable of the Good Samaritan (Luke x. 25-37) is read elliptically, as explained on pages 47, 48.

A hymn is sung, appropriate to the special work in which the Sunday-school or Missionary Association may be engaged, as, for instance:

Your Mission. If you cannot, on the ocean,
Sail among the swiftest fleet.
[*Singing Pilgrim*, p. 97

Or,
>Over the ocean wave, far, far away,
>There the poor heathen live, waiting for day.
>>[*Golden Chain, p.* 41.]

Or,
>Far out upon the prairie
>How many children dwell.
>>[*Golden Chain, p.* 20.]

GENERAL EXERCISES.

Each of the following questions may be answered by a single scholar, or in concert by an entire class, (or by the several members of a class, where more verses than one are in a text,) according to the size of the school, and by previous assignment.

Question. What was the first offering to the Lord of which we have an account?

Answer. And in process of time it came to pass, that Cain brought of the fruit of the ground an offering unto the Lord.

And Abel, he also brought of the firstlings of his flock, and of the fat thereof. And the Lord had respect unto Abel, and to his offering. Gen. iv. 3, 4.

Q. Why was Abel's offering acceptable to God?

A. By faith Abel offered unto God a more excellent sacrifice than Cain, by which he obtained witness that he was righteous, God testifying of his gifts; and by it he, being dead, yet speaketh. Heb. xi. 4.

Q. What was Jacob's promise, at Bethel, of offerings unto the Lord?

A. And Jacob vowed a vow, saying, If God will be with me, and will keep me in this way that I go, and will give me bread to eat, and raiment to put on,

So that I come again to my father's house in peace, then shall the Lord be my God:

And this stone, which I have set for a pillar, shall be God's house: and of all that thou shalt give me, I will surely give the tenth unto thee. Gen. xxviii. 20–22.

Q. When the tabernacle was to be builded, what offering did the Israelites make?

A. And they came, both men and women, as many as were willing-hearted, and brought bracelets, and ear-rings, and rings, and tablets, all jewels of gold: and every man that offered, offered an offering of gold unto the Lord.

And every man with whom was found blue, and purple, and scarlet, and fine linen, and goats' hair, and red skins of rams, and badgers' skins, brought them.

Every one that did offer an offering of silver and brass, brought the Lord's offering: and every man with whom was found shittim-wood, for any work of the service, brought it.

And all the women that were wise-hearted did spin with their hands, and brought that which they had spun, both of blue, and of purple, and of scarlet, and of fine linen.

And all the women, whose heart stirred them up in wisdom, spun goats' hair.

And the rulers brought onyx-stones, and stones to be set, for the ephod, and for the breastplate;

And spice, and oil for the light, and for the anointing oil, and for the sweet incense.

The children of Israel brought a willing offering unto the Lord, every man and woman, whose heart made them willing to bring, for all manner of work which the Lord had commanded to be made by the hand of Moses. Ex. xxxv. 22–29.

Q. What was King David's offering for the building of the first temple?

A. Moreover, because I have set my affection to the house of my God, I have of mine own proper good, of gold and silver, which I have given to the house of my God, over and above all that I have prepared for the holy house,

Even three thousand talents of gold, of the gold of Ophir, and seven thousand talents of refined silver. I. Chron. xxix. 3, 4.

Q. Incited by the king's example, what did others give for the same work?

A. Then the chief of the fathers and princes of the tribes of Israel, and the captains of thousands and of hundreds, with the rulers over the king's work, offered willingly.

And gave, for the service of the house of God, of gold, five thousand talents and ten thousand drams; and of silver, ten thousand talents; and of brass, eighteen thousand talents; and one hundred thousand talents of iron. I. Chron. xxix. 6, 7, 8.

Q. What was the spirit in which these gifts were made to the Lord, and which rendered them acceptable?

A. Then the people rejoiced, for that they offered willingly, because with perfect heart they offered willingly to the Lord: and David the king also rejoiced with great joy. I. Chron. xxix. 9.

Q. When the Lord had heard the prayer of Hannah and had given her a son—Samuel; what offering of gratitude did she bring?

A. For this child I prayed; and the Lord hath given me my petition which I asked of him:

Therefore also I have lent him to the Lord; as long as he liveth he shall be lent to the Lord. And he worshipped the Lord there. I. Sam. i. 27, 28.

Q. How may *we* lend to the Lord?

A. He that hath pity upon the poor lendeth unto the Lord; and that which he hath given will he pay him again. Prov. xix. 17.

Q. What instructions were given to the Jews, as to

their days of thanksgiving for deliverance from the designs of Haman?

A. That they should make them days of feasting and joy, and of sending portions one to another, and gifts to the poor. Esther ix. 22.

Leader. Our examples of giving to the Lord have thus far been from the Old Testament. After singing a hymn we will hear some similar examples from the New Testament.

HYMN.

Give, give, cheerfully give,
  As God has given to thee;
Do good to all is the great command,
And thine a crown shall be.

[*Worship in the School Room.*

Question. When the wise men came from the East to worship the infant Saviour, what offering did they bring?

Answer. And when they were come into the house, they saw the young child with Mary his mother, and fell down and worshipped him: and when they had opened their treasures, they presented unto him gifts; gold, and frankincense, and myrrh. Matt. ii. 11.

Q. What did Jesus observe of the giving at the temple treasury?

A. And Jesus sat over against the treasury, and beheld how the people cast money into the treasury: and many that were rich cast in much.

And there came a certain poor widow, and she threw in two mites, which make a farthing. Mark xii. 41, 42.

Q. What was his comment on this?

A. And he called unto him his disciples, and saith unto them,

Verily I say unto you, That this poor widow hath cast more in, than all they which have cast into the treasury:

For all they did cast in of their abundance; but she of her want did cast in all that she had, even all her living. Mark xii. 43, 44.

Q. What offering was made to Jesus by Mary at Bethany?

A. Then took Mary a pound of ointment of spikenard, very costly, and anointed the feet of Jesus, and wiped his feet with her hair: and the house was filled with the odor of the ointment. John xii. 3.

Q. What did Jesus say in approval of this costly gift?

A. She hath done what she could: she is come aforehand to anoint my body to the burying.

Verily I say unto you, Wheresoever this gospel shall be preached throughout the whole world, this also that she hath done shall be spoken of for a memorial of her. Mark xiv. 8, 9.

Q. How did the early Christians manifest a spirit of liberality for the cause of Christ?

A. And the multitude of them that believed were of one heart and of one soul: neither said any of them that aught of the things which he possessed was his own; but they had all things common. Acts iv. 32.

Q. How was an opposite spirit manifested by the young man of whom Jesus said he lacked one thing:

A. Jesus said unto him, If thou wilt be perfect, go and sell that thou hast, and give to the poor, and thou shalt have treasure in heaven; and come and follow me.

But when the young man heard that saying, he went away sorrowful: for he had great possessions. Matt. xix. 21, 22.

Leader. And now what has the infant class to say about giving to the Lord?

The infant class, rising, recites, scholar by scholar:

Remember the words of the Lord Jesus, how he said, It is more blessed to give than to receive. Acts xx. 35.
Sell that ye have, and give alms. Luke xii. 33.
Give, and it shall be given unto you. Luke vi. 38.
God loveth a cheerful giver. II. Cor. ix. 7.

Also the following stanzas, two lines to each scholar:

"Give," said the little stream,
    As it hurried down the hill:
"I am small, I know, but wherever I go,
    The fields grow greener still."

"Give," said the gentle rain,
    As it fell upon the flowers:
"I raise up the drooping heads again,
    And freshen the summer bowers."

"Give," said the violet sweet,
    In its soft and spring-like voice:
"From cottage and hall they will hear my call,
    They will find me and rejoice."

"Give," said they all; "for we
    Have much received from heaven;
And we fain would give, yes, would only live
    To give as God has given."

And you, dear children, too,
    Have something you can give;
Oh, do as the streams and the blossoms do,
    And for God and others live.

[Child's Companion.

The infant class sings:

> Little drops of water,
> Little grains of sand,
> Make the mighty ocean
> And the beauteous land. [*Happy Voices, p.* 91.

Leader. As we have thus far noted *examples*, from the Bible, of giving to the Lord, let us now look at the direct teachings of God's word on this theme.

Q. Who should give?

A. Every man according as he purposeth in his heart, so let him give. II. Cor. ix. 7.

Q. To whom should we give?

A. As we have therefore opportunity, let us do good unto all men, especially unto them who are of the household of faith. Gal. vi. 10.

Q. How should we give?

A. Quietly.

But when thou doest alms, let not thy left hand know what thy right hand doeth. Matt. vi. 3.

Systematically.

Upon the first day of the week let every one of you lay by him in store, as God hath prospered him. I. Cor. xvi. 2.

In faith.

Whatsoever ye do, do all to the glory of God. I. Cor. x. 31.
Without faith it is impossible to please him. Heb. xi. 6.
Whatsoever is not of faith is sin. Rom. xiv. 23.

Q. Is it safe to refrain from giving?

A. There is that withholdeth more than is meet, but it tendeth to poverty. Prov. xi. 24.

How hardly shall they that have riches enter into the kingdom of God! Mark x. 23.

If therefore ye have not been faithful in the unrighteous mammon, who will commit to your trust the true riches? Luke xvi. 11.

The pastor and the superintendent may recite (or read) in alternation, from Matt. xxv. 31–40, as follows:

Pastor. When the Son of man shall come in his glory, and all the holy angels with him, then shall he sit upon the throne of his glory:

And before him shall be gathered all nations: and he shall separate them one from another, as a shepherd divideth his sheep from the goats:

And he shall set the sheep on his right hand, but the goats on the left.

Superintendent. Then shall the king say unto them on his right hand, Come, ye blessed of my Father, inherit the kingdom prepared for you from the foundation of the world:

For I was an hungered, and ye gave me meat: I was thirsty, and ye gave me drink: I was a stranger, and ye took me in:

Naked, and ye clothed me: I was sick, and ye visited me: I was in prison, and ye came unto me.

Then shall the righteous answer him, saying, Lord, when saw we thee an hungered, and fed thee? or thirsty, and gave thee drink?

When saw we thee a stranger, and took thee in? or naked, and clothed thee?

Or when saw we thee sick, or in prison, and came unto thee?

Pastor. And the king shall answer and say unto them, Verily I say unto you, Inasmuch as ye have done it unto one of the least of these my brethren, ye have done it unto me.

The service closes with the singing of a hymn, as:

> What shall I for that kind Friend
> Who once for me so poor became?
>
> [*Golden Censer, p.* 23.

Or,

> As God has kindly blessed us,
> To others let us give. [*Singing Pilgrim, p.* 114.

LESSON X.

SCRIPTURAL HISTORY OF ABRAHAM.

For an opening exercise, schedule 1, on page 55, can be employed, with such variations as seem called for. For Scripture readings, the following are appropriate:

To be read by the Superintendent:

Now faith is the substance of things hoped for, the evidence of things not seen, &c. Heb. xi. 1–10.

To be read responsively by leader and assembly:

Blessed is the man that walketh not in the counsel of the ungodly, nor standeth in the way of sinners, nor sitteth in the seat of the scornful, &c. Psalm i.

Hymns on the subject of faith, or of a pilgrim life in promise of a better country, may be selected; such as:

>Rise, O my soul, pursue the path
>By ancient worthies trod;
>Aspiring, view those holy men
>Who lived and walked with God.
>[*Songs of Sanct.*, *p.* 190.

>A crown of glory bright
>By faith's clear eyes I see.
>[*Golden Shower*, *p.* 21.

How large the promise! how divine!
To Abraham and his seed.
[*Songs of Sanct.* p. 313.]

We're bound for the land of the pure and the holy.
[*Am. S. S. Hymn-Book,* p. 255.]

Joyfully, joyfully, onward we move.
[*Am. S. S. Hymn-Book,* p. 254.]

Courage, brother, do not stumble,
Though thy path be dark as night.
[*Singing Pilgrim,* p. 33.]

[This lesson may be used as an entire exercise, or as preliminary to a brief sermon or address on Abraham and the lessons of his life.]

GENERAL EXERCISES.

1. *Question.* By what name was Abraham first known?

Answer. Abram.

2. *Q.* What is the earliest mention of him in the Bible?

A. Now these are the generations of Terah: Terah begat Abram, Nahor, and Haran; and Haran begat Lot. Gen. xi. 27.

3. *Q.* Where seems to have been his birthplace?

A. And Haran died before his father Terah in the land of his nativity, in Ur of the Chaldees. Gen. xi. 28.

4. *Q.* Whither did Abram move from Ur?

A. And Abram took Sarai his wife, and Lot his brother's son, and all their substance that they had gathered, and the souls that they had gotten in Haran; and they went forth to go into the land of Canaan; and into the land of Canaan they came. Gen. xii. 5.

5. *Q.* Why did he make this move?

A. Now the Lord had said unto Abram, Get thee out of thy country, and from thy kindred, and from thy father's house, unto a land that I will show thee. Gen. xii. 1.

6. *Q.* What promise was given to him of temporal benefits?

A. And I will make of thee a great nation, and I will bless thee, and make thy name great; and thou shalt be a blessing. Gen. xii. 2.

7. *Q.* What was his promise of spiritual advantage?

A. And I will bless them that bless thee, and curse him that curseth thee: and in thee shall all families of the earth be blessed. Gen. xii. 3.

8. *Q.* What his promise of offspring?

A. And I will make thy seed as the dust of the earth: so that if a man can number the dust of the earth, then shall thy seed also be numbered. Gen. xiii. 16.

9. *Q.* What is the evidence that Abram worshiped the true God?

A. And he removed from thence unto a mountain on the east of Beth-el, and pitched his tent, having Beth-el on the west, and Hai on the east: and there he builded an altar unto the Lord, and called upon the name of the Lord. Gen. xii. 8.

10. *Q.* What is said of Abram's worldly prosperity?

A. And Abram was very rich in cattle, in silver, and in gold. Gen. xiii. 2.

11. *Q.* What is said of his spiritual life?

A. And he believed in the Lord; and he counted it to him for righteousness. Gen. xv. 6.

12. *Q.* What evidence of a love of peace is recorded of him?

A. And Abram said unto Lot, Let there be no strife, I pray thee, between me and thee, and between my herdmen and thy herdmen ; for we be brethren.

Is not the whole land before thee ? separate thyself, I pray thee, from me : if thou wilt take the left hand, then I will go to the right ; or if thou depart to the right hand, then I will go to the left. Gen. xiii. 8, 9.

13. *Q.* When was Abram's name changed, and why ?

A. And when Abram was ninety years old and nine, the Lord appeared to Abram, and said unto him, I am the Almighty God : walk before me, and be thou perfect.

Neither shall thy name any more be called Abram ; but thy name shall be Abraham : for a father of many nations have I made thee. Gen. xvii. 1, 5.

14. *Q.* What covenant did God then make with Abraham ?

A. And I will establish my covenant between me and thee, and thy seed after thee, in their generations, for an everlasting covenant, to be a God unto thee, and to thy seed after thee.

And I will give unto thee, and to thy seed after thee, the land wherein thou art a stranger, all the land of Canaan, for an everlasting possession ; and I will be their God. Gen. xvii. 7, 8.

15. *Q.* How old was Abraham when Isaac was born ?

A. And Abraham was a hundred years old, when his son Isaac was born unto him. Gen. xxi. 5.

16. *Q.* What demand did God make of Abraham, as to Isaac ?

A. And he said, Take now thy son, thine only son Isaac, whom thou lovest, and get thee into the land of Moriah ; and offer him there for a burnt-offering upon one of the mountains which I will tell thee of. Gen. xxii. 2.

17. *Q.* How did Abraham respond?

A. And Abraham rose up early in the morning, and saddled his ass, and took two of his young men with him, and Isaac his son, and clave the wood for the burnt-offering, and rose up, and went unto the place of which God had told him. Gen. xxii. 3.

18. *Q.* What did the Lord's angel say to Abraham when he had made ready for the sacrifice?

A. And he said, Lay not thine hand upon the lad, neither do thou anything unto him: for now I know that thou fearest God, seeing thou hast not withheld thy son, thine only son, from me. Gen. xxii. 12.

19. *Q.* Why was Abraham willing to comply with God's command?

A. Accounting that God was able to raise him up, even from the dead; from whence also he received him in a figure. Heb. xi. 19.

20. *Q* What kind of a dwelling was Abraham's?

A. And the Lord appeared unto him in the plains of Mamre: and he sat in the tent-door in the heat of the day. Gen. xviii. 1.

21. *Q.* What evidence is furnished of Abraham's hospitality?

A. And he lifted up his eyes and looked, and, lo, three men stood by him: and when he saw them, he ran to meet them from the tent door, and bowed himself toward the ground,

And said, My Lord, if now I have found favor in thy sight, pass not away, I pray thee, from thy servant:

Let a little water, I pray you, be fetched, and wash your feet, and rest yourselves under the tree:

And I will fetch a morsel of bread, and comfort ye your hearts; after that ye shall pass on: for therefore are ye come to your servant. And they said, So do, as thou hast said. Gen. xviii. 2-5.

22. *Q.* To whom did Abraham bequeath his possessions?

A. And Abraham gave all that he had unto Isaac. Gen. xxv. 5.

23. *Q.* At what age did Abraham die?

A. And these are the days of the years of Abraham's life which he lived, a hundred threescore and fifteen years. Gen. xxv. 7.

24. *Q.* What is the record of him at his death?

A. Then Abraham gave up the ghost, and died in a good old age, an old man, and full of years; and was gathered to his people. Gen. xxv. 8.

25. *Q.* What was ever the greatest pride of ancestry of the Jewish people?

A. We be Abraham's seed, and were never in bondage to any man.

Abraham is our father. John viii. 33, 39.

26. *Q.* How did Jesus make reference to the Jewish figure of Abraham's bosom as the final abode of the blessed?

A. And it came to pass, that the beggar died, and was carried by the angels into Abraham's bosom: the rich man also died, and was buried. Luke xvi. 22.

27. *Q.* What did Jesus say of Abraham's faith in Him?

A. Your father Abraham rejoiced to see my day; and he saw it, and was glad. John viii. 56.

28. *Q.* How may we be children of Abraham?

A. Know ye therefore, that they which are of faith, the same are the children of Abraham. Gal. iii. 7.

29. *Q.* What benefits are secured to those who by faith are thus Abraham's children?

A. So then they which be of faith are blessed with faithful Abraham.

Christ hath redeemed us from the curse of the law, being made a curse for us: for it is written, Cursed is every one that hangeth on a tree:

That the blessing of Abraham might come on the Gentiles through Jesus Christ; that we might receive the promise of the Spirit through faith. Gal. iii. 9, 13, 14.

A closing hymn is sung:

>Children of the Heavenly King,
>As ye journey, sweetly sing;
>Sing your Saviour's worthy praise,
>Glorious in his works and ways.
>
>[*S. S. Hosanna, p.* 37.

LESSON XI.

BIBLE MOUNTAINS, AND THEIR LESSONS.

[Arranged from a lesson by Mrs. S. J. McCall, Saybrook, Ct.]

Portions of the opening exercises of Lesson I. on pages 86–89, may be appropriately used with this lesson.

Psalm xlvi. is a fitting one to be read as a Scripture selection.

For hymns, either of the following named will answer:

    Zion stands with hills surrounded—
    Zion, kept by power divine.
          [*Songs for the Sanct.* p. 349.

    Oh, give me a harp on the bright hills of glory—
    A home when life's sorrows are o'er.
          [*Golden Shower*, p. 72.

GENERAL EXERCISES.

1. *Question.* On what mountain did the ark rest after the deluge?

Answer. And the ark rested in the seventh month, on the seventeenth day of the month, upon the mountains of Ararat. Gen. viii. 4.

2. *Q.* What mountain was the scene of Abraham's trial of faith?

A. Take now thy son, thine only son Isaac, whom thou lovest, and get thee into the land of Moriah; and offer him there for a burnt offering upon one of the mountains which I will tell thee of. Gen. xxii. 2.

3. *Q.* At what mountain did God appear in the burning bush to Moses?

A. Now Moses kept the flock of Jethro his father-in-law, the priest of Midian: and he led the flock to the back side of the desert, and came to the mountain of God, even to Horeb.

And the Angel of the Lord appeared unto him in a flame of fire out of the midst of a bush: and he looked, and, behold, the bush burned with fire, and the bush was not consumed. Ex. iii. 1, 2.

4. *Q.* What other miracle was performed at Horeb?

A. Behold, I will stand before thee there upon the rock in Horeb; and thou shalt smite the rock, and there shall come water out of it, that the people may drink. And Moses did so in the sight of the elders of Israel. Ex. xvii. 6.

5. *Q.* Where were the commandments delivered to Moses?

A. And the Lord came down upon Mount Sinai, on the top of the mount: and the Lord called Moses up to the top of the mount; and Moses went up. Ex. xix. 20.

And he gave unto Moses, when he had made an end of communing with him upon Mount Sinai, two tables of testimony, tables of stone, written with the finger of God. Ex. xxxi. 18.

6. *Q.* Where is Mount Sinai referred to as a type of the Law, by which no man is justified?

A. For ye are not come unto the mount that might be touched, and that burned with fire, nor unto blackness, and darkness, and tempest,

And the sound of a trumpet, and the voice of words; which voice they that heard entreated that the word should not be spoken to them any more. Heb. xii. 18, 19.

7. *Q.* On what mountain did Aaron die?

A. And Moses did as the Lord commanded: and they went up into Mount Hor in the sight of all the congregation.

And Moses stripped Aaron of his garments, and put them upon Eleazar his son; and Aaron died there in the top of the mount: and Moses and Eleazar came down from the mount. Num. xx. 27, 28.

8. *Q.* On what mountain did Moses die?

A. And Moses went up from the plains of Moab unto the mountain of Nebo, to the top of Pisgah, that is over against Jericho; and the Lord shewed him all the land of Gilead, unto Dan.

So Moses, the servant of the Lord, died there, in the land of Moab, according to the word of the Lord. Deut. xxxiv. 1, 5.

9. *Q.* What mountain of the promised land did Moses long to see before his death?

A. I pray thee, let me go over, and see the good land that is beyond Jordan, that goodly mountain, and Lebanon. Deut. iii. 25.

10. *Q.* For what trees was Mount Lebanon noted?

A. I am come up to the height of the mountains, to the sides of Lebanon, and will cut down the tall cedar trees thereof, and the choice fir trees thereof. II. Kings xix. 23.

11. *Q.* What was Solomon's message to the king of Tyre concerning these trees, for the temple building?

A. Send me also cedar trees, fir trees, and algum trees, out of Lebanon: for I know that thy servants can skill to cut timber in Lebanon; and, behold, my servants shall be with thy servants.

Even to prepare me timber in abundance: for the house which I am about to build shall be wonderful great. II. Chron. ii. 8, 9.

12. *Q.* How is the fruitfulness of this mountain used in a figure as a promise to God's people?

A. The righteous shall flourish like the palm tree: he shall grow like a cedar in Lebanon. Psalms xcii. 12.

13. *Q.* What two mountains were designated to Israel as those of blessing and cursing?

A. Behold, I set before you this day a blessing and a curse:

And it shall come to pass, when the Lord thy God hath brought thee in unto the land whither thou goest to possess it, that thou shalt put the blessing upon Mount Gerizim, and the curse upon Mount Ebal. Deut. xi. 26, 29.

14. *Q.* Was this command obeyed when Joshua entered Canaan with Israel?

A. And all Israel, and their elders, and officers, and their judges, stood on this side the ark and on that side before the priests the Levites, which bare the ark of the covenant of the Lord, as well the stranger, as he that was born among them; half of them over against Mount Gerizim, and half of them over against Mount Ebal; as Moses the servant of the Lord had commanded before, that they should bless the people of Israel. Josh. viii. 33.

15. *Q.* Do you recall an occasion when God's people and their enemies were actually over against each other on opposite mountains?

A. Yes. When David went out to meet Goliath of Gath.

And the Philistines stood on a mountain on the one side, and Israel stood on a mountain on the other side: and there was a valley between them. I. Sam. xvii. 3.

16. *Q.* On which of the two mountains named did Joshua build an altar?

A. Then Joshua built an altar unto the Lord God of Israel in Mount Ebal. Josh. viii. 30.

17. *Q.* What gave subsequent prominence to Gerizim?

A. The temple of the Samaritans was built there.

18. *Q.* On what occasion was reference made to this fact, and how?

A. When Jesus talked with the woman at Jacob's well, near the foot of Mount Gerizim.

The woman saith unto him, Sir, I perceive that thou art a prophet.

Our fathers worshiped in this mountain; and ye say, that in Jerusalem is the place where men ought to worship. John iv. 19, 20.

19. *Q.* On what mountain was Joshua buried?

A. And it came to pass after these things, that Joshua the son of Nun, the servant of the Lord, died, being a hundred and ten years old

And they buried him in the border of his inheritance in Timnath-serah, which is in Mount Ephraim, on the north side of the hill of Gaash. Josh. xxiv. 29, 30.

20. *Q.* On what mountain were Saul and his three sons slain?

A. And it came to pass on the morrow, when the Philistines came to strip the slain, that they found Saul and his three sons fallen in Mount Gilboa. I. Sam. xxxi. 8.

21. *Q.* On what mountain did Elijah meet and confound the prophets of Baal?

A. Now therefore send, and gather to me all Israel unto Mount Carmel, and the prophets of Baal four hundred and fifty, and the prophets of the groves four hundred, which eat at Jezebel's table.

So Ahab sent unto all the children of Israel, and gathered the prophets together unto Mount Carmel. I. Kings xviii. 19, 20.

22. *Q.* On what mountain was the temple built by Solomon?

A. Then Solomon began to build the house of the Lord at Jerusalem in Mount Moriah, where the Lord appeared unto David his father, in the place that David had prepared in the threshing-floor of Ornan the Jebusite. II. Chron. iii. 1.

23. *Q.* What incident have we already noted as occurring at Mount Moriah?

A. The attempted sacrifice of Isaac by Abraham.

24. *Q.* What mountain near Mount Moriah was the home of David, and an accepted type of the Church of God?

A. Beautiful for situation, the joy of the whole earth, is Mount Zion, on the sides of the north, the city of the great King. Psalms xlviii. 2.

25. *Q.* As Mount Sinai was referred to as a type of the Law, how is Mount Zion named as a type of Christ?

A. But ye are come unto Mount Sion, and unto the city of the living God, the heavenly Jerusalem, and to an innumerable company of angels,

To the general assembly and church of the firstborn, which are written in heaven, and to God the Judge of all, and to the spirits of just men made perfect,

And to Jesus the mediator of the new covenant, and to the blood of sprinkling, that speaketh better things than that of Abel. Heb. xii. 22-24.

26. *Q.* Against what mountain was Ezekiel called to prophesy evil?

A. Son of man, set thy face against Mount Seir, and prophesy against it,

And say unto it, Thus saith the Lord God ; Behold, O Mount Seir, I am against thee, and I will stretch out mine hand against thee, and I will make thee most desolate. Ezek. xxxv. 2, 3.

27. *Q.* What comfort was spoken, at the same time, by Ezekiel, to the mountains of Israel ?

A. But ye, O mountains of Israel, ye shall shoot forth your branches, and yield your fruit to my people of Israel; for they are at hand to come. Ezek. xxxvi. 8.

28. *Q.* What mountain was a favorite resort of Jesus with his disciples ?

A. And he came out, and went, as he was wont, to the Mount of Olives ; and his disciples also followed him. Luke xxii. 39.

29. *Q.* Did Jesus ever visit this mountain alone ?

A. And when he had sent the multitudes away, he went up into a mountain apart to pray : and when the evening was come, he was there alone. Matt. xiv. 23.

30. *Q.* What was the place of the transfiguration of Jesus ?

A. And after six days Jesus taketh with him Peter, and James, and John, and leadeth them up into a high mountain apart by themselves : and he was transfigured before them. Mark ix. 2.

31. *Q.* What mountain is this supposed to have been ?

A. It has been generally called Tabor. Some have deemed it Hermon. Yet others have supposed it one of the mountains near Gennesareth.

32. *Q.* On what mount was Jesus crucified ?

A. And when they were come to the place which is called Calvary, there they crucified him, and the malefactors ; one on the right hand, and the other on the left. Luke xxiii. 33.

33. *Q.* From which of these mountains did Jesus ascend to Heaven?

A. And when he had spoken these things, while they beheld, he was taken up; and a cloud received him out of their sight.

Then returned they unto Jerusalem from the mount called Olivet, which is from Jerusalem a sabbath day's journey. Acts i. 9, 12.

34. *Q.* As the mountains were chosen places for the worship of God by his children, were they ever used for idolatrous worship by the heathen?

A. Ye shall utterly destroy all the places, wherein the nations which ye shall possess served their gods, upon the high mountains, and upon the hills, and under every green tree. Deut. xii. 2.

35. *Q.* Did the Israelites ever follow the heathen in this evil worship?

A. And Judah did evil in the sight of the Lord, and they provoked him to jealousy with their sins which they had committed, above all that their fathers had done.

For they also built them high places, and images, and groves, on every high hill, and under every green tree. I. Kings xiv. 22, 23.

36. *Q.* How are the mountains named as a symbol of protection?

A. As the mountains are round about Jerusalem, so the Lord is round about his people from henceforth even for ever. Psalms cxxv. 2.

37. *Q.* How as a symbol of stability?

A. They that trust in the Lord shall be as Mount Zion, which cannot be removed, but abideth forever. Psalms cxxv. 1.

38. *Q.* How as a symbol of magnitude?

A. Thy righteousness is like the great mountains; thy judgments are a great deep: O Lord, thou preservest man and beast. Psalms xxxvi. 6.

39. *Q.* How are they named as a source of hope and help?

A. I will lift up mine eyes unto the hills, from whence cometh my help.

My help cometh from the Lord, which made heaven and earth. Psalms cxxi. 1, 2.

How beautiful upon the mountains are the feet of him that bringeth good tidings, that publisheth peace; that bringeth good tidings of good, that publisheth salvation; that saith unto Zion, Thy God reigneth! Isa. lii. 7.

The superintendent reads or recites:

And it shall come to pass in the last days, that the mountain of the Lord's house shall be established in the top of the mountains, and shall be exalted above the hills; and all nations shall flow unto it.

And many people shall go and say, Come ye, and let us go up to the mountain of the Lord, to the house of the God of Jacob; and he will teach us of his ways, and we will walk in his paths: for out of Zion shall go forth the law, and the word of the Lord from Jerusalem. Isa. ii. 2, 3.

The pastor adds:

Truly in vain is salvation hoped for from the hills, and from the multitude of mountains: truly in the Lord our God is the salvation of Israel. Jer. iii. 23.

Yet have I set my King upon my holy hill of Zion.

I will declare the decree: the Lord hath said unto me, Thou art my Son; this day have I begotten thee. Psalms ii. 6, 7.

The assembly responds:

God hath fulfilled the same unto us their children, in that he hath raised up Jesus again; as it is also written in the second psalm, Thou art my Son, this day have I begotten thee. Acts xiii. 33.

All join in a closing hymn :
> I'm trying to climb up Zion's Hill,
> For the Saviour whispers, "Love me."
>
> [*Singing Pilgrim*, *p.* 27.

It will be well to have a map of Palestine before the assembly, on which the leader shall point out the several mountains as they are named. Or he can sketch rudely the outlines of the Holy Land on the blackboard, filling in the mountains in their proper places as they are mentioned. In doing this he can question the assembly as to the locality of the several mountains, to bring out the scholars' knowledge of Bible geography.

LESSON XII.

MUSIC AND MUSICAL INSTRUMENTS OF THE BIBLE.

[Arranged from a lesson by Mrs. McCall.]

An appropriate opening passage is Psalms cxlviii., to be read responsively.

For hymns, either of the following will answer:

> Who shall sing if not the children?
> Did not Jesus die for them?
> [*Golden Chain, p.* 14.
>
> Awake, my soul, in joyful lays,
> And sing thy great Redeemer's praise.
> [*Am. S. S. Hymn Book, p.* 49.

The leader should call attention to the fact that, the Bible references to these instruments being brief and merely incidental, it is not easy to ascertain just what instrument was meant by a particular Hebrew word; hence there are various opinions as to the style and form of a number of these. He may call out by questions the fact that these instruments are divided into three classes: 1. Stringed instruments; 2. Wind instruments; 3. Instruments of percussion. The blackboard may aid him in showing differences in these.

GENERAL EXERCISES.

1. *Question.* Where did music have its origin?

Answer. When the morning-stars sang together, and all the sons of God shouted for joy. Job. xxxviii. 7.

2. *Q.* Who was the inventor of musical instruments?

A. Jubal: he was the father of all such as handle the harp and organ. Gen. iv. 21.

3. *Q.* Will you name any stringed instruments mentioned in the Bible?

A. I will also praise thee with the *psaltery*, even thy truth, O my God: unto thee will I sing with the *harp*, O thou Holy One of Israel. Psalms lxxi. 22.

4. *Q.* Can you name another of this class?

A. Take thou away from me the noise of thy songs; for I will not hear the melody of thy *viols*. Amos v. 23.

5. *Q.* Do you recall another?

A. The sackbut.

Thou, O king, hast made a decree, that every man that shall hear the sound of the cornet, flute, harp, *sackbut*, psaltery, and dulcimer, and all kinds of music, shall fall down and worship the golden image. Dan. iii. 10.

6. *Q.* What wind instrument can you name?

A. And the sons of Aaron, the priests, shall blow with the *trumpets:* and they shall be to you for an ordinance for ever throughout your generations. Num. x. 8.

7. *Q.* What other of this class do you recall?

A. With trumpets, and sound of *cornet*, make a joyful noise before the Lord the King. Psalms xcviii. 6.

8. *Q.* Do you remember another?

A. My harp also is turned to mourning, and my *organ* into the voice of them that weep. Job xxx. 31.

9. *Q.* Yet another?

A. Ye shall have a song, as in the night, when a holy solemnity is kept; and gladness of heart, as when one goeth with a *pipe* to come into the mountain of the Lord, to the mighty One of Israel. Isa. xxx. 29.

10. *Q.* Do you remember yet others of this class?

A. Flute and dulcimer.

Now, if ye be ready, that at what time ye hear the sound of the cornet, *flute*, harp, sackbut, psaltery, and *dulcimer*, and all kinds of music, ye fall down and worship the image which I have made, well. Dan. iii. 15.

11. *Q.* What instrument of percussion can you mention?

A. Asaph made a sound with *cymbals*. I. Chron. xvi. v.

12. *Q.* What other?

A. And Jephthah came to Mizpeh unto his house, and, behold, his daughter came out to meet him with *timbrels* and with dances. Judges xi. 34.

13. *Q.* What other?

A. He hath made me also a by-word of the people; and aforetime I was as a *tabret.* Job xvii. 6.

14. *Q.* Yet another?

A. In that day shall there be upon the *bells* of the horses, Holiness unto the Lord. Zech. xiv. 20.

15. *Q.* Of what wood were these instruments made?

A. And David, and all the house of Israel, played before the Lord on all manner of instruments made of fir-wood, even on harps, and on psalteries, and on timbrels, and on cornets, and on cymbals. II. Sam. vi. 5.

And the king made of the almug-trees pillars for the house of the Lord, and for the king's house, harps also and psalteries for singers: there came no such almug-trees, nor were seen unto this day. I. Kings x. 12.

16. *Q.* Of what metals?

A. And the Lord spake unto Moses, saying, Make thee two trumpets of silver; of a whole piece shalt thou make them; that thou mayest use them for the calling of the assembly, and for the journeying of the camps. Numb. x. 1, 2.

So the singers, Heman, Asaph, and Ethan, were appointed to sound with cymbals of brass. I. Chron. xv. 19.

17. *Q.* Were they ever made of other material?

A. And seven priests shall bear before the ark seven trumpets of rams' horns; and the seventh day ye shall compass the city seven times, and the priests shall blow with the trumpets. Josh. vi. 4.

18. *Q.* What is the evidence that music formed an important part in the religious worship of the Jews?

A. And David and all Israel played before God with all their might, and with singing, and with harps, and with psalteries, and with timbrels, and with cymbals, and with trumpets. I. Chron. xiii. 8.

And Hezekiah commanded to offer the burnt-offering upon the altar: and when the burnt-offering began, the song of the Lord began also with the trumpets, and with the instruments ordained by David king of Israel.

And all the congregation worshiped, and the singers sang, and the trumpeters sounded: and all this continued until the burnt-offering was finished. II. Chron. xxix. 27, 28.

19. *Q.* Is there any evidence that music had also a place in idolatrous worship?

A. Therefore at that time, when all the people heard the sound of the cornet, flute, harp, sackbut, psaltery, and all kinds of music, all the people, the nations, and the languages, fell down and worshiped the golden image that Nebuchadnezzar the king had set up. Dan. iii. 7.

20. *Q.* Was music employed at seasons of general or national rejoicing?

A. And Miriam the prophetess, the sister of Aaron, took a timbrel in her hand; and all the women went out after her with timbrels and with dances.

And Miriam answered them, Sing ye to the Lord, for he hath triumphed gloriously; the horse and his rider hath he thrown into the sea. Ex. xv. 20, 21.

21. *Q.* Is there mention of its use in welcoming victorious chieftains?

A. And it came to pass as they came, when David was returned from the slaughter of the Philistine, that the women came out of all cities of Israel, singing and dancing, to meet king Saul, with tabrets, with joy, and with instruments of music.

And the women answered one another as they played, and said, Saul hath slain his thousands, and David his ten thousands. I. Sam. xviii. 6, 7.

22. *Q.* Had it a place on the occasion of the departure of friends?

A. Wherefore didst thou flee away secretly, and steal away from me, and didst not tell me, that I might have sent thee away with mirth, and with songs, with tabret, and with harp? Gen. xxxi. 27.

23. *Q.* Was it employed in rejoicing over the return of friends?

A. Now his elder son was in the field: and as he came and drew nigh to the house, he heard music and dancing. Luke xv. 25.

24. *Q.* What mention is made of its use at the coronation of a king?

A. And Zadok the priest took an horn of oil out of the tabernacle, and anointed Solomon: and they blew the trumpet; and all the people said, God save king Solomon.

And all the people came up after him; and the people piped with pipes, and rejoiced with great joy, so that the earth rent with the sound of them. I. Kings i. 39, 40.

25. *Q.* What passages go to prove that refraining from music indicated sorrow and sadness?

A. By the rivers of Babylon, there we sat down; yea, we wept, when we remembered Zion.

We hanged our harps upon the willows in the midst thereof.

For there they that carried us away captive required of us a song; and they that wasted us required of us mirth, saying, Sing us one of the songs of Zion.

How shall we sing the Lord's song in a strange land? Psalms cxxxvii. 1-4.

The new wine mourneth, the vine languisheth, all the merry-hearted do sigh.

The mirth of tabrets ceaseth, the noise of them that rejoice endeth, the joy of the harp ceaseth. Isa. xxiv. 7, 8.

26. *Q.* What mention is made of the calming power of music over the disturbed spirit?

A. And it came to pass, when the evil spirit from God was upon Saul, that David took an harp, and played with his hand: so Saul was refreshed, and was well, and the evil spirit departed from him. I. Sam. xvi. 23.

27. *Q.* What instance is given of Elisha's desiring the aid of music when he sought inspiration of God?

A. And Elisha said, As the Lord of hosts liveth, before whom I stand, surely, were it not that I regard the presence of Jehoshaphat the king of Judah, I would not look toward thee, nor see thee.

But now bring me a minstrel. And it came to pass, when the minstrel played, that the hand of the Lord came upon him. II. Kings iii. 14, 15.

28. *Q.* Is music named as an appropriate mode of expressing Christian joy?

A. Is any merry? let him sing psalms. James v. 13.

Speaking to yourselves in psalms, and hymns, and spiritual songs, singing and making melody in your heart to the Lord ;

Giving thanks always for all things unto God and the Father in the name of our Lord Jesus Christ. Eph. v. 19, 20.

29. *Q.* What reason have we for believing that Jesus joined in singing?

A. And when they had sung an hymn, they went out into the Mount of Olives. Matt. xxvi. 30.

30. *Q.* What is the evidence that there will be music in Heaven?

A. As well the singers as the players on instruments shall be there. Psalms lxxxvii. 7.

And I saw as it were a sea of glass mingled with fire; and them that had gotten the victory over the beast, and over his image, and over his mark, and over the number of his name, stand on the sea of glass, having the harps of God.

And they sing the song of Moses the servant of God, and the song of the Lamb, saying, Great and marvellous are thy works, Lord God Almighty; just and true are thy ways, thou King of saints. Rev. xv. 2, 3.

31. *Q.* Who are to join in the "new song" in Heaven?

A. And I heard a voice from heaven, as the voice of many waters, and as the voice of a great thunder: and I heard the voice of harpers harping with their harps :

And they sung as it were a new song before the throne, and before the four beasts, and the elders : and no man could learn that song but the hundred and forty and four thousand, which were redeemed from the earth. Rev. xiv. 2, 3.

The entire assembly, rising, join in reciting Psalm cl.

Praise ye the Lord. Praise God in his sanctuary: praise him in the firmament of his power.
Praise him for his mighty acts: praise him according to his excellent greatness.
Praise him with the sound of the trumpet: praise him with the psaltery and harp.
Praise him with the timbrel and dance: praise him with stringed instruments and organs.
Praise him upon the loud cymbals: praise him upon the high-sounding cymbals.
Let every thing that hath breath praise the Lord. Praise ye the Lord.

The exercises close with singing:

> Shall we sing in heaven for ever—
> Shall we sing? shall we sing?
> [*Golden Chain*, p. 34.

SERMONS IN BIBLE LANGUAGE.

Another approved style of general biblical exercises for the children's service is a sermon exclusively in Bible language. The skeleton, or plan, of a sermon is prepared in advance—the text and general heads or divisions of its treatment being announced to the school. These heads are then assigned to particular classes, or to individual scholars, for Bible illustration or enforcement. On the concert Sabbath, after ordinary opening exercises, the pastor or superintendent announces the text, the general heads are then stated by the teachers, in course, and the proofs or illustrations are recited consecutively by the scholars. Thus an important Bible truth is presented, and an elaborate sermon preached, all in the words of inspired wisdom, with the attractiveness and variety of different children's voices, and with the impressiveness and authority of Holy Writ.

The text may be shown stenciled on the "song-roll," or illuminated on a muslin banner, or it may be displayed on the blackboard, with the sermon synopsis added, point by point, as the recitation progresses. The exercise may be broken by the occasional singing of a verse or two of an appropriate hymn, and enlivened by illustrations or explanations, according to the judgment of the leader.

The idea of this exercise is capable of indefinite expansion, and by an ingenious Bible student and lover of the truth can be made uniformly pleasing and profitable. It furnishes every opportunity for preaching the great doctrines of the Gospel afforded by the ordinary uninspired sermon, while divine precept, parable, narrative, promise and poem, may be brought out separately in their beauty and power, or introduced as aids in unfolding and enforcing other great truths.

The following lessons are kindly furnished as specimens of this class of exercise, by Rev. J. Aspinwall Hodge, pastor of the Presbyterian Church, Hartford, Ct., who has been peculiarly successful in its use with the children of his parish, and has accumulated in such labor a large variety of sermons of this peculiar character.

LESSON XIII.

THE GOOD SHEPHERD.

As an appropriate Scripture reading with this lesson, I. Samuel xvi. 1–13 is named.

For hymns, either of the following may be used:

> The Lord my Shepherd is;
> I shall be well supplied.
> [*Am. S S Hymn Book, p.* 75.

> See Israel's gentle Shepherd stand,
> With all engaging charms.
> [*New Golden Chain, p.* 97.

> Saviour, like a shepherd, lead us;
> Much we need thy tender care.
> [*Song Flowers, p.* 5.

I AM THE GOOD SHEPHERD. THE GOOD SHEPHERD GIVETH HIS LIFE FOR THE SHEEP. John x. 11.

I. *Who is this Shepherd?*

1. Jesus is our Shepherd.

The Lord is my shepherd; I shall not want. Psalms xxiii. 1.

Give ear, O Shepherd of Israel, thou that leadest Joseph like a flock; thou that dwellest between the cherubim, shine forth. Psalms lxxx. 1.

And I will set up one Shepherd over them, and he shall feed them, even my servant David. Ezek. xxxiv. 23.

And David my servant shall be king over them: and they all shall have one shepherd. Ezek. xxxvii. 24.

I Jesus have sent mine angel to testify unto you these things in the churches. I am the root and the offspring of David. Rev. xxii. 16.

For ye were as sheep going astray; but are now returned unto the Shepherd and Bishop of your souls. I. Pet. ii. 25.

The God of peace, that brought again from the dead our Lord Jesus, that great Shepherd of the sheep, through the blood of the everlasting covenant. Heb. xiii. 20.

2. Jesus is our good Shepherd.

I am the good shepherd. John x. 14.

O taste and see that the Lord is good: blessed is the man that trusteth in him. Ps. xxxiv. 8.

Truly God is good to Israel, even to such as are of a clean heart. Ps. lxxiii. 1.

And Jesus said unto him, Why callest thou me good? none is good, save one, that is, God. Luke xviii. 19.

II. *How does Jesus behave towards his sheep?*

3. Jesus knows his sheep.

I am the good shepherd, and know my sheep, and am known of mine, John x. 14.

Nevertheless the foundation of God standeth sure, having this seal, The Lord knoweth them that are his. II. Tim. ii. 19.

To him the porter openeth : and the sheep hear his voice: and he calleth his own sheep by name, and leadeth them out. John x. 3.

4. Jesus loves his sheep.

He shall gather the lambs with his arm, and carry them in his bosom, and shall gently lead those that are with young. Isa. xl. 11.

The Lord hath appeared of old unto me, saying, Yea, I have loved thee with an everlasting love ; therefore with loving-kindness have I drawn thee. Jer. xxxi. 3.

A new commandment I give unto you, That ye love one another ; as I have loved you, that ye also love one another. John xiii. 34.

Now, before the feast of the passover, when Jesus knew that

his hour was come that he should depart out of this world unto the Father, having loved his own which were in the world, he loved them unto the end. John xiii. 1.

5. Jesus feeds his sheep.

I will feed my flock, and I will cause them to lie down, saith the Lord God. Ezek. xxxiv. 15.

He shall feed his flock like a shepherd. Isa. xl. 11.

He shall feed them, and he shall be their shepherd. Ezek. xxxiv. 23.

He maketh me to lie down in green pastures: he leadeth me beside the still waters. Psalms xxiii. 2.

6. Jesus protects his sheep.

Hear the word of the Lord, O ye nations, and declare it in the isles afar off, and say, He that scattered Israel will gather him, and keep him, as a shepherd doth his flock. Jer. xxxi. 10.

As a shepherd seeketh out his flock in the day that he is among his sheep that are scattered; so will I seek out my sheep, and will deliver them out of all places where they have been scattered in the cloudy and dark day. Ezek. xxxiv. 12.

And they shall never perish, neither shall any pluck them out of my hand. John x. 28.

7. Jesus giveth his life for the sheep.

As the Father knoweth me, even so know I the Father: and I lay down my life for the sheep. John x. 15.

But he was wounded for our transgressions, he was bruised for our iniquities: the chastisement of our peace was upon him; and with his stripes we are healed. Isa. liii. 5.

Greater love hath no man than this, that a man lay down his life for his friends. John xv. 13.

III. *How do the sheep behave towards Jesus?*

8. The sheep belong to Jesus.

I have manifested thy name unto the men which thou gavest

me out of the world : thine they were, and thou gavest them me. John xvii. 6.

And they shall be mine, saith the Lord of hosts, in that day when I make up my jewels ; and I will spare them, as a man spareth his own son that serveth him. Mal. iii. 17.

My beloved is mine, and I am his ; he feedeth among the lilies. Cant. ii. 16.

9. The sheep know Jesus' voice.

I am the good shepherd, and know my sheep, and am known of mine. John x. 14.

For they know his voice. John x. 4.

Behold, I stand at the door, and knock : if any man hear my voice, and open the door, I will come in to him, and will sup with him, and he with me. Rev. iii. 20.

10. The sheep love Jesus.

Yea, though I walk through the valley of the shadow of death, I will fear no evil : for thou art with me ; thy rod and thy staff they comfort me. Psalms xxiii. 4.

Whom have I in heaven but thee ? and there is none upon earth that I desire besides thee. Psalms lxxiii. 25.

Tell me, O thou whom my soul loveth, where thou feedest, where thou makest thy flock to rest at noon : for why should I be as one that turneth aside by the flocks of thy companions ? Cant. i. 7.

11. The sheep follow Jesus.

My sheep hear my voice, and I know them, and they follow me. John x. 27.

And when he putteth forth his own sheep, he goeth before them, and the sheep follow him. John x. 4.

These are they which follow the Lamb whithersoever he goeth. These were redeemed from among men, being the first-fruits unto God and to the Lamb. Rev. xiv. 4.

IV. *How do the sheep behave towards others ?*

12. They do not know others.

All that ever came before me are thieves and robbers : but the sheep did not hear them. John x. 8.

A froward heart shall depart from me : I will not know a wicked person. Psalms ci. 4.

13. They will not follow others.

And a stranger will they not follow, but will flee from him; for they know not the voice of strangers. John x. 5.

Then Simon Peter answered him, Lord, to whom shall we go? Thou hast the words of eternal life. John vi. 68.

V. *How do others behave towards the sheep?*

14. They hate the sheep.

I have given them thy word; and the world hath hated them, because they are not of the world, even as I am not of the world. John xvii. 14.

Marvel not, my brethren, if the world hate you. I. John iii. 13.

If ye were of the world, the world would love his own; but because ye are not of the world, but I have chosen you out of the world, therefore the world hateth you. John xv. 19.

15. They tempt the sheep to wander from Jesus.

For among my people are found wicked men : they lay wait, as he that setteth snares; they set a trap, they catch men. Jer. v. 26.

For they sleep not, except they have done mischief; and their sleep is taken away, unless they cause some to fall. Prov. iv. 16.

16. They seek to destroy the sheep.

The thief cometh not, but for to steal, and to kill, and to destroy. John x. 10.

Their feet run to evil, and they make haste to shed innocent blood; their thoughts are thoughts of iniquity; wasting and destruction are in their paths. Isa. lix. 7.

Be sober, be vigilant; because your adversary the devil, as a roaring lion, walketh about, seeking whom he may devour. I. Pet. v. 8.

VI. *What results from these efforts of others?*

17. The sheep sometimes wander from Jesus.

And they were scattered, because there is no shepherd: and they became meat to all the beasts of the field, when they were scattered.

My sheep wandered through all the mountains, and upon every high hill: yea, my flock was scattered upon all the face of the earth, and none did search or seek after them. Ezek. xxxiv. 5, 6.

All we, like sheep, have gone astray; we have turned every one to his own way; and the Lord hath laid on him the iniquity of us all. Isa. liii. 6.

18. The sheep sometimes are wounded.

But he that is a hireling, and not the shepherd, whose own the sheep are not, seeth the wolf coming, and leaveth the sheep, and fleeth; and the wolf catcheth them, and scattereth the sheep. John x. 12.

For she hath cast down many wounded; yea, many strong men have been slain by her. Prov. vii. 26.

My flock became a prey, and my flock became meat to every beast of the field, because there was no shepherd, neither did my shepherds search for my flock, but the shepherds fed themselves, and fed not my flock. Ezek. xxxiv. 8.

VII. *What results from the love of Jesus for his sheep?*

19. Jesus seeks and brings back the wanderers.

For thus saith the Lord God: Behold, I, even I, will both search my sheep, and seek them out.

I will seek that which was lost, and bring again that which was driven away. Ezek. xxxiv. 11, 16.

And I will gather the remnant of my flock out of all countries whither I have driven them, and will bring them again to their folds; and they shall be fruitful and increase. Jer. xxiii. 3.

20. Jesus heals the wounded sheep.

I will heal their backsliding, I will love them freely. Hos. xiv. 4.

And will bind up that which was broken, and will strengthen that which was sick. Ezek. xxxiv. 16.

The Spirit of the Lord is upon me, because he hath anointed me to preach the gospel to the poor; he hath sent me to heal the broken-hearted, to preach deliverance to the captives, and recovering of sight to the blind, to set at liberty them that are bruised. Luke iv. 18.

21. Jesus brings all the sheep at last to a safe and happy fold.

I give unto them eternal life; and they shall never perish, neither shall any man pluck them out of my hand. John x. 28.

I will feed them in a good pasture, and upon the high mountains of Israel shall their fold be: there shall they lie in a good fold, and in a fat pasture shall they feed upon the mountains of Israel. Ezek. xxxiv. 14.

They shall be abundantly satisfied with the fatness of thy house; and thou shalt make them drink of the river of thy pleasures. Psalms xxxvi. 8.

For the Lamb, which is in the midst of the throne, shall feed them, and shall lead them unto living fountains of waters; and God shall wipe away all tears from their eyes. Rev. vii. 17.

In the two following lessons only the plan of the sermons is given. The scholars and teachers may be left to select appropriate texts in proof or illustration of the subdivisions assigned to them; or the leader can find fitting Scripture passages, and give out their references in advance.

LESSON XIV.

GOD'S LOVE.

God commendeth his love toward us, in that while we were yet sinners, Christ died for us. Rom. v. 8.

I. *The strength of God's love for us.*
1. God's love is greater than that of friend for friend.
2. Bible illustration of the love of friends.
3. God's love is greater than that of parents for children.
4. Bible illustration of parental love.
5. God's love is greater than the love of a brother.
6. Bible illustration of a brother's love.

II. *The character of God's love.*
7. God's love provides for us.
8. God's love defends us.
9. God's love is unchangeable.
10. God's love is undeserved by us.
11. God's love is unwilling that we should perish.
12. God loved us while we were yet sinners.
13. God's love sent Christ to die for us.

III. *Our duty in view of God's love.*
14. We ought to love God.

IV. *The proof of our love for him.*
15. If we love God we shall serve him.

LESSON XV.

JESUS OUR EXEMPLAR.

Let this mind be in you which was also in Christ Jesus. Phil. ii. 5.

I. *Jesus furnishes an example unto us.*

1. How did Jesus behave towards God?
2. How did Jesus behave towards his parents?
3. How did Jesus behave towards children?
4. How did Jesus behave towards the poor?
5. How did Jesus behave towards the ignorant?
6. How did Jesus behave towards the suffering?
7. How did Jesus behave towards his friends?
8. How did Jesus behave towards his enemies?
9. How did Jesus behave towards sinners?
10. How did Jesus behave towards his disciples?
11. How did Jesus behave towards those who would not believe?
12. How did Jesus behave when tempted?
13. How did Jesus behave when afflicted?
14. How did Jesus behave when insulted?
15. How did Jesus behave when dying?

II. *How we can follow the example set us.*

16. How can we have this mind which was in Christ Jesus?

ILLUSTRATIONS OF CLASS MOTTOES.

It is quite common for Sunday-school classes to adopt special names, with appropriate Scripture texts as mottoes. By these names the classes are often known as auxiliary branches of the Missionary Association of the entire school. Sometimes the classes have banners on which are inscribed these names and mottoes, or illuminated cards giving the texts and titles are suspended on the school-room walls, above the class-seats.

The following are named as specimens of this style of class names and mottoes:

CROWN SEEKERS.

Blessed is the man that endureth temptation: for when he is tried, he shall receive the crown of life, which the Lord hath promised to them that love him. James i. 12.

CHEERFUL GIVERS.

Every man according as he purposeth in his heart, so let him give; not grudgingly, or of necessity: for God loveth a cheerful giver. II. Cor. ix. 7.

SOLDIERS OF THE CROSS.

Thou therefore endure hardness, as a good soldier of Jesus Christ. II. Tim. ii. 3.

CASKET OF JEWELS.

And they shall be mine, saith the Lord of hosts, in that day when I make up my jewels; and I will spare them, as a man spareth his own son that serveth him. Mal. iii. 17.

THE CHILDREN'S BIBLE SERVICE.

THE UNITED BAND.

Two are better than one; because they have a good reward for their labor. Eccl. iv. 9.

YOUTHFUL DISCIPLES.

We love him, because he first loved us. I. John iv. 19.

A profitable exercise is the illustration of these class mottoes by Scripture texts. Two or three of them may be thus illustrated as an entire exercise for a concert Sabbath, or one of them may be thus presented at the close of an ordinary school session, or in connection with a sermon or address to the children on any special occasion.

John B. Smith, superintendent of the Congregational church Sunday-school, at East Hartford, Conn., has arranged many of these exercises. Specimens of his work are given in the next two lessons.

LESSON XVI.

BIBLE LOVERS.

Class Motto. Search the Scriptures; for in them ye think ye have eternal life: and they are they which testify of me. John v. 39.

The motto is first recited by the entire class.
The superintendent asks:
Why search the Scriptures?
The class replies:

The law of the Lord is perfect, converting the soul: the testimony of the Lord is sure, making wise the simple.

The statutes of the Lord are right, rejoicing the heart: the commandment of the Lord is pure, enlightening the eyes.

The fear of the Lord is clean, enduring forever: the judgments of the Lord are true and righteous altogether. Psalms xix. 7-9.

Superintendent. Will you give some illustration of this Scripture searching?

Class. It is said of the Jews in Berea:

These were more noble than those in Thessalonica, in that they received the word with all readiness of mind, and searched the Scriptures daily, whether those things were so. Acts xvii. 11.

Superintendent. What came of this?

Class. Therefore many of them believed; also of honorable women which were Greeks, and of men, not a few. Acts xvii. 12.

Superintendent. Has the teacher anything to say of this searching for Scripture truths?

Teacher. More to be desired are they than gold, yea, than much fine gold: sweeter also than honey and the honeycomb.

Moreover by them is thy servant warned: and in keeping of them there is great reward. Psalms xix. 10, 11.

Superintendent. He that hath an ear, let him hear what the Spirit saith unto the churches. Rev. ii. 7.

Therefore shall ye lay up these my words in your heart and in your soul, and bind them for a sign upon your hand, that they may be as frontlets between your eyes.

And ye shall teach them your children, speaking of them when thou sittest in thine house, and when thou walkest by the way, when thou liest down, and when thou risest up.

And thou shalt write them upon the door-posts of thine house, and upon thy gates:

That your days may be multiplied, and the days of your children, in the land which the Lord sware unto your fathers to give them, as the days of heaven upon the earth. Deut. xi. 18-21.

The pastor adds:

But be ye doers of the word, and not hearers only, deceiving your own selves.

For if any be a hearer of the word, and not a doer, he is like unto a man beholding his natural face in a glass: For he beholdeth himself, and goeth his way, and straightway forgetteth what manner of man he was. James i. 22-24.

The school joins in singing:

 Thank God for the Bible! 'tis there that we find
 The story of Christ and his love.
     [*Am. S. S. Hymn-Book, p.* 98.

LESSON XVII.

WORKERS FOR JESUS.

Class Motto. He that winneth souls is wise. Prov. xi. 30.

Superintendent. How are souls to be won?

Answer No. 1. By having in us the life and light of Christ.

That ye may be blameless and harmless, the sons of God, without rebuke, in the midst of a crooked and perverse nation, among whom ye shine as lights in the world. Phil. ii. 15.

Answer No. 2. By earnest entreaty.

Now then we are ambassadors for Christ, as though God did beseech you by us: we pray you in Christ's stead, be ye reconciled to God. II. Cor. v. 20.

Answer No. 3. By faithful, consistent living.

Take heed unto thyself, and unto the doctrine; continue in them: for in doing this thou shalt both save thyself, and them that hear thee. I. Tim. iv. 16.

Answer No. 4. By united prayer.

Again I say unto you, That if two of you shall agree on earth as touching any thing that they shall ask, it shall be done for them of my Father which is in heaven. Matt. xviii. 19.

Superintendent. What are the motives to, or rewards for, this work for souls?

Teacher. Let him know, that he which converteth the sinner from the error of his way shall save a soul from death, and shall hide a multitude of sins. Jas. v. 20.

Superintendent. And they that be wise shall shine as the

brightness of the firmament; and they that turn many to righteousness as the stars for ever and ever. Dan. xii. 3.

All join in singing:

Brother, you may work for Jesus. [*Singing Pilgrim, p.* 91.

SUGGESTIONS TO THE LEADER.

All the foregoing lessons are published originally in this volume, none of them having previously appeared in print. Quite a number of similar exercises suitable for the children's Bible service have, however, been published from time to time in the various Sunday-school periodicals in our land. An interesting series on the natural history of the Bible, with rhymed questions and opening and closing stanzas, from the pen of Mrs. Mary B. C. Slade, has appeared in the Sunday-school Teacher, of Chicago. Recitations arranged for a given number of voices, on themes like the Holy Land and the Holy City, with texts and hymns appropriately interchanged, have been presented in the Sunday-School Journal, of the Methodist Episcopal Church. A number of topical lessons, coming fairly within the limits suggested in this work have been published in the Sunday-School Times, and some of them reprinted separately; but no collection of such Bible lessons has, it is believed, been given until now to the public.

It is not supposed that schools will be alike pleased with all the exercises given herewith; but enough can perhaps be found by each school to complete a monthly series for a year,—at the end of which time another such collection is likely to follow this.

These lessons are generally quite long, yet not too long for a full service in a large and well conducted school. All can, however, be easily shortened by the judicious omission of proofs or points of the respective themes, and some can be divided to make two or three lessons for small schools, or for partial services.

Illustrations may be freely used in connection with any of these lessons—in some of them to decided advantage. It has not been deemed necessary to insert these in their places, since so much depends in this department on the taste of the leader and the peculiar circumstances of the school. References are, however, repeatedly made to such volumes as will supply appropriate material of this kind.

The selections for Bible readings and the hymns given with each lesson are only to indicate the proper character of such portions of the service: it is not supposed that they will in all cases be adopted. The hymns are taken from various books in more or less general use, to show that in almost any approved collection fitting selections may be found.

In many instances a portion of a Bible verse is used as a better response to the question asked than the whole verse would prove. In such cases, where this book is not available to the scholar, the teacher should be careful to designate in advance the precise portion to be committed to memory. This will necessitate a preliminary examination by the teacher of each part assigned to his or her class for recitation.

PART IV.

SERMONS AND ADDRESSES

TO CHILDREN.

CHILDREN'S PREACHING SERVICE.

BIBLE RECITATIONS NOT A SUBSTITUTE FOR SERMONS.

THE systematized recitations from Scripture presented in the preceding portions of this work are by no means intended to supersede sermons and other formal addresses to children. Children as well as adults are entitled to instruction from the pulpit; and to perform this service for them wisely, "decently and in order," requires special preparation on the part of him who is their minister. This department of effort for the children should not be overlooked in a volume which treats of public religious services for their benefit.

RARITY OF CHILDREN'S PREACHERS.

Until recently, few sermons to children have been preached. No longer ago than 1855, in the preface to a collection of sermons to youth chiefly from English ministers, published by Carlton and Porter, under the title of "The Child's Preacher," the editor remarked, in explanation of the fact that but little of the material was supplied by American ministers, "That we have not similar contributions from other American preachers is not because we have failed to solicit them. The truth is that American ministers have as yet written but few sermons to children; and, indeed, have preached quite too few."

Even at the present time it is not uncommon for a pastor to refer to his inability to preach fittingly to children, as though it were after all a matter of no serious moment. "I confess I cannot preach to children," or "I have no tact in that line," is uttered much as would be the statement "I have never studied Italian," or "I have no special fondness for chemistry, or mechanics." Says a recent writer on this theme,* "I once asked a reverend doctor of divinity, who was present in my Sunday-school, to talk to the children...... 'I never talk to children!' That was my answer, with an expressive shake of the head, and a matter-of-surprise-and-of-course sort of tone, that sent me away humbled and sorry for my offending. I felt as though I ought to apologize." Is not such a treatment of this matter more common than excusable?

THE CLAIMS OF CHILDREN ON THE MINISTRY.

Cannot children be saved? If they are to be saved, is it in exception to the rule that it hath "pleased God by the foolishness of preaching to save them that believe?"† "How shall they believe in him of whom they have not heard? and how shall they hear without

---

* Rev. H. C. McCook, in the S. S. Times. † I. Cor. i. 21.

THE CHILDREN'S PREACHING SERVICE.

a preacher?"* Parents may neglect their duty towards their children, "yea, they may forget:" "a woman [may] forget her sucking child, that she should not have compassion on the son of her womb,"† yet would not God leave such home-neglected little ones without hope, nor cause that their teeth should be set on edge because of the sour grapes which their fathers have eaten.‡ Hence it is that he has sent ambassadors with a message as to the right, to "every creature" out of the way, and has declared that "the priest's lips should keep knowledge, and they should seek the law at his mouth, for he is the messenger of the Lord of hosts."§ Are not all who are old enough to be lost without the knowledge of Jesus, entitled to hear of him at the lips of his messenger?

"Shall he [the minister,] only teach the adult mind and heart?" says an eloquent advocate of the children's claims.‖ "Shall he say, 'Ho! ye men and women who can understand introduction, proposition, head and points, peroration and application, come *ye* and have the truth?' Shall he say to the simple-minded 'I cannot come down to you.!' shall he say to the little children, 'I have no crumbs for you! I will preach only here, [in the pulpit,] and in order to preach here I will gauge the average power of mind and susceptibility of heart before me, and preach at the average man and woman?' or shall he care for *all* his flock? There was a Good Shepherd once, who was foretold in

---

* Rom. x. 14. † Isa. xlix 15. ‡ Ezek. xviii. 2. § Mal. ii. 7.
‖ Rev. Dr. J. T. Duryea, in the New York S. S. Institute.

prophecy, who was to feed his flock like a shepherd, and gather the lambs with his arm, and carry them in his bosom, and gently lead those that were with young."

The relative numbers of children in every community entitle them to a full share of pastoral labor, and their needs are as great as their numbers.

"As many as one-half of our parishioners are under the age of sixteen years, and one-third, according to my bills for forty-eight years, die under ten," is the testimony of a venerable New England pastor;* doubtless in accordance with the exhibit of most parish registers. Says Dr. Kirk, in pleading the cause of Christian education: "Christian families have but a small portion of the youthful population within their circle. We must then look mainly to the pastor and the Sunday-school teacher for this important result." "Nor," adds a recent clerical writer,† "can he whose commission requires him to feed the lambs as well as the sheep, *afford* to give up the instruction of the young to other hands." By every consideration of duty, the pastors are called on to give the children their portion in due season.

INDUCEMENTS TO PREACH TO CHILDREN.

And it is well for ministers to recognize the children's claims. Work for them is a good pastoral investment. "If we would retain the young under our instructions in after life, we must interest them now,"

---

* Rev. Dr. Cooley.   † Rev. E. W. Gilman, in New Englander.

says a well-known English preacher to children.* "The pulpit will not be honored and beloved by them in future days, if they now associate it only with thoughts of weariness and impatience. At the best the chances of keeping them when free to act for themselves, will be small and perilous." Not only have the results of labor for children by such special preachers to them as E. P. Hammond, E. M. Long, and others of their class, indicated the value of efforts in that direction, but the ordinary children's sermons of pastors who preach often to their little ones, have been so blessed in soul fruits as to give the highest encouragement to all who are engaged in this work.

Rev. Dr. Tyng, reporting, in 1860, his habit of preaching *weekly* sermons to children, for then eleven years, testified: "I have considered no part of my work more valuable and important than this; and certainly no portion of it has seemed so popular and acceptable to others."† And he added, as the expression of his conviction: "If every pastor would give one sermon on every Sunday especially addressed to the young, and designed and prepared to teach them, he would find himself enlarging his direct usefulness in this particular work, and equally advancing the value and benefit of every other class of his public and private labors in religious instruction also. The parents and adults of his flock will learn as much, and love as much the teaching for themselves, when he speaks to

---

* Rev. S. G. Green in the Introduction to Addresses to Children.
† Forty Years' Experience in S. S., p. 25.

the youth directly and simply, as when he addresses them in a deeper and more mature discourse."*

In a recent note to the author of this volume, this veteran pastor says: "I still abide in my habit of preaching, in series of sermons, to the young on every Sunday afternoon." Surely, his success as a minister of Christ, with a church numbering now fourteen hundred communicants, and Sunday-schools comprising one hundred and fifty teachers and eighteen hundred and fifty scholars; the similar success of Rev. Dr. Newton in Philadelphia, and like results in the parishes of the sons of both divines, (all these pastors giving efforts for the children marked prominence in pulpit labors,) would seem to justify the expressed opinion of Dr. T., as well as to indicate something of what may be expected in other fields when ministers generally follow the example of these workers for Jesus, and of their blessed Master, who never neglected the little ones. Neither of these ministers seems to have lessened his hold on adults by his labors for the young.

The Rev. Dr. Robert Boyd testifies similarly of his work in the West: "During the several years of my pastorate in Chicago it was my habit to address the children on the first Sabbath evening of each month. The attendance was always large, and great interest was shown not only by the little ones, but also by their parents and teachers."† Says Dr. Newton: "I have

---

* Forty Years' Experience in S. S., p. 210.
† Preface to Food for the Lambs. Church and Goodman, Chicago.

found my children's sermons encouragingly rich in their results, so far as regards the spiritual interests of the young for whom they were prepared, and at the same time of frequently acknowledged profit to the adult portion of the congregation. I am thoroughly satisfied that labor, *properly bestowed*, in this department of ministerial work, *pays* better than any other in promoting the great interests of our Master's cause."*

It is pleasanter, as well as more profitable, to preach to children than to adults. "I would rather be an apostle to the children than an 'apostle to the Gentiles,'" says a lover of this work. † And an impulsive and whole-souled pastor has said in heartiness: "I find but little pleasure, comparatively, in preaching to old gospel-hardened sinners. I preach to them, to be sure; preach right at them; preach Christ to them, in love and earnestness, Sabbath after Sabbath; but, oh! they straighten up and grin and take it so easy, I have to pray the Lord to give me patience that I may bear with them as he does. But when I talk to the *children* about Jesus, they hear me; and as I look down into their eyes with my heart full of love for them, they see me and feel with me. There is a beauty, a loveliness in this work I can find in no other." ‡ Dr. Tyng, speaking of the pastor's "sweet solace of the children's relation to him, a comfort to his wearied spirit," says

---

* This testimony, and all that follows from Dr. Newton on the subject of sermons to children, is from a personal letter recently received by the author of this volume.

† Rev C. Greenwood in The Child and the Man, p. 262.

‡ See S. S. Times, Nov. 1859.

truly: "The minister deprived of this loses one of the most precious of the pleasures of his work."*

PREACHING TO CHILDREN NOT AN EASY MATTER.

"That children are a difficult part of the flock to feed, the experience of every one who has ever tried to do his duty to them will testify," says Dr. Todd,† while evidencing his own success in that direction, and he adds the testimony of Cecil; "Nothing is easier than to *talk* to children; but to talk to them as they ought to be talked to, is the very last effort of ability. It requires great genius to throw the mind into the habits of children's minds. I aim at this, but I find it the utmost effort of ability. No sermon ever put my mind half so much on the stretch." "It is no easy thing to speak effectively to children," says a foremost English preacher,‡ to the little ones; and Dr. Newton adds: "I began talking to children when I was sixteen years old, which is forty years ago, and have cultivated the habit industriously ever since. My children's sermons cost me more time and labor than any that I preach." Thus agree those who best succeed in this department of ministerial effort, while of the frequency of failures, many can speak in sympathy with a vigorous writer already quoted:§ "How few there are of our clergy who can hold the attention of youth on any subject; and above all, how few who can handle a religious

---
* Forty Years' Experience in S. S., p. 211.   † Preface to Lectures to Children.
‡ Rev. S. G. Green.   § Rev. H. C. McCook.

truth so as at once to interest and instruct! Let those be my witnesses who have vainly sought such service; or who have twisted in nervous torment under malapropos harangues which pass for religious addresses, but which might with equal truth be labeled hotch-potch of irrelevant or irreverent stories, strained illustration, stilted declamation, wild exhortation, dreary platitudes, inflated beatitudes, incomprehensible magnitudes, and so on through the long, sad list of *styles* that run the round of Sunday-school, anniversary, and monthly-concert speeches, only here and there relieved by an address that reaches the true standard of sound religious truth made pleasant and plain to the minds of children! Have I stated the fact too strongly? think a moment and I am sure you will answer, Nay."

'WHERE THERE'S A WILL THERE'S A WAY.'

But when it is understood that children *must* be preached to,—when the command "Feed my lambs" is recognized as equally binding and imperative on the under shepherds, with that other direction from the same divine lips, "This do in remembrance of me," no man will venture to call himself fitted for the gospel ministry, until he has learned how to preach to children. He will not announce himself as a candidate for the pastorate, without full preparation for that part of his mission. In the spirit of Douglass Jerrold's advice to the young writer in haste to appear in print, he will "not take down the shutters until there is something in the window." If he cannot secure needful instruction in this direction in an existing seminary, he will join in the outcry which will soon become general, against such ministerial training schools as ignore the interests of a vast and needy multitude to be preached to. He will not only believe that "this theme is certainly one to which the attention of candidates for the ministry should be turned during their seminary course;"* but he will be inclined to say of that culture for the ministry which leaves children out of account in preaching, as a distinguished theological professor† has recently expressed himself concerning that which fails to make one a preacher to the common people, "I would abandon the whole of it. I would drop it as I would a viper."

"Jesus would not have imposed upon his ministers a duty which he had not given them the ability to perform," says Rev. Dr. John Cotton Smith.‡ "For the pastor it is only necessary that he have the interest which our Saviour himself had in the young, in order to interest them and do them good. . . . . It will be impossible for them to escape the attractions of a warm heart earnestly enlisted in seeking their good." The human mind is capable of great expansion under culture, and the man who can preach well to educated adults can by yet more of prayerful study attain to the capacity to preach well to children; and when there is sufficient pressure on him, from his instructed conscience and the demands of the church, he will be likely to strive untiringly, and

---

* Rev. E. W. Gilman.   † Rev. Dr. Austin Phelps, of Andover.
‡ See New York S. S. Institute Report, p. 112.

THE CHILDREN'S PREACHING SERVICE. 241

with success, for this high and important attainment. Indeed there are those who think that it is easier to learn how to preach to children than to adults. Mr. Pardee says:* "If you would only take one quarter the pains to learn how to preach to children that you have [taken] to learn how to preach to adults, you would generally succeed to so great an extent as to astonish yourself and all your friends."

It is doubtless true that "success in this department of public speaking is to be attained by the selfsame means that win success in others;"† and it may be confidently hoped that ere long it will be as exceptional and absurd for ministers to admit their inability to preach to children, as for them to confess their incapacity to lead in public prayer, or to speak in such tones as may be heard half-way down the church aisle. Already it is very clear that "if they have no love for children, and no desire especially to bless them, they are manifestly wanting in a most important characteristic of the Saviour's example, and an indispensable qualification for a useful and successful ministry."‡

PREPARATION FOR THE WORK.

"The one great requisite for effectively addressing *any* congregation," says a standard writer on this theme,§ "is sympathy with the audience..... He must think not in his own accustomed train, but in theirs..... In striving to interest the children, let us

---
* S. S. Index, p. 209.   † Introduction to Green's Addresses.
‡ Rev. Dr. Tyng in Forty Years' Experience in S. S.   § Rev. S. G. Green.

understand their minds. If any minister is deficient in this, let him study them; the materials are ample. Let him listen to the merry voices of little ones at their play: let him talk to children, as often and as familiarly as they will allow him: let him even not be above reading the books of those who have shown extraordinary aptness to understand and interest the young. By these, and similar means, he will gain an amount of knowledge, a degree of readiness, aye, and an intenseness of affection, too, which will surprise himself."

Says a more recent and equally reliable writer* on this point: "Dean Swift, so the story goes, was wont to read his sermons to his cook before their delivery, to find out whether all the words in them could be easily understood by plain people. If those who desire to interest and instruct children would remember how they talk to their own or neighbor's boys and girls around the family hearth-stone, they would have success where now they have failure."

Doubtless, an immediate connection with the Sunday-school of his parish will aid any pastor in his preparation to preach to children. Dr. Tyng says of this pastoral Sunday-school labor: "It is the very manufacture which the raw material of a multitude of ministers requires to transform them into useful, appropriate and practical agents in the Lord's house. It mortalizes their ministry, by bringing them down to a practical shape, and compelling the cultivation of a

---

* Rev. E. House in S. S. Hand-Book, p. 130.

common-sense habit of teaching and address. It converts their abstractions into realities, and, by making them the 'teachers of babes,' makes them the more intelligible and useful teachers for all."*

NO STEREOTYPED PLAN.

The question, How shall children be preached to? is no more to be answered dogmatically than is the question, What style of preaching is uniformly best for adults? The command of God to his ministers to feed his lambs is positive; so is the direction to employ as their food "the sincere milk of the Word;" but as to how, and when, and in what portions, that food is to be given out, there are ever likely to be varying opinions. All that can be done in such a volume as this, is to indicate the views of those who have had most experience in the practice of preaching to children, or who have written judiciously on the subject, and to name certain essential elements of success, and certain common errors, or causes of failure.

FREQUENCY OF SERMONS.

There are ministers who, like Dr. Tyng, preach to the children each Lord's day. Their number is increasing, and it would be larger if the public sentiment of the church permitted. Others, like Dr. Newton, preach thus each month. This includes, probably, the greater portion of all preachers to children. Yet, again, some preach bi-monthly or quarterly; and there

---

* Forty Years' Experience in S. S., p. 199.

are even those who preach a single sermon to children in the year; thus admitting the claim of this class on their ministerial labors, while making prominent by such an exceptional service their usual neglect of them. These occasional sermons to children were in vogue even in the earlier days of New England, before the young had as large a share as now in the labors of the church; but *then* one such sermon was ponderous enough to furnish material for a multitude of modern services. For example, a published sermon to children, preached by Rev. Samuel Phillips, of Andover, Mass., in 1739, occupies nearly one hundred close printed pages of an 18mo. volume. It could hardly be expected or desired that sermons of that length be now-a-days preached oftener than once a year. As an illustration of the style of preaching to children in the last century, an extract from this sermon may prove of interest. Its title is, "The Children's Hosannahs Highly Pleasing to our Great Saviour." The text is Matt. xxi. 15, 16.

—" And the children crying in the temple, and saying, Hosanna to the Son of David; they were sore displeased;... And Jesus saith unto them: Yea; have ye never read, Out of the mouth of babes and sucklings thou hast perfected praise?"

The following is one of the opening paragraphs:

In *this Chapter*, we have an Account of Christ's riding in Triumph into *Jerusalem*.

The *Beast* which he rode upon, is said to be *an Ass, and a Colt the Fole of an Ass*. The Words do *not* intend that he sat on *both*; sometimes on one, and then on the other, as some have imagin'd: It plainly appears by the other *Evangelists*,* that

---

* Mark 11, and Luke 19.

Christ rode on the *Colt* only. *Matthew* names two for one, by a *Synecdoche;* or, after the familiar Use of the *Hebrew* Tongue, he rehearseth one thing twice;* or, both are mention'd, because the Dam might probably follow after her Colt †—And this was done, that the *Scripture* might be *fulfilled;* see Zech. ix. 9. The Beast which *Christ* improv'd, is called a *Colt;* and is said to be one, *on which never Man sat.* Mark xi. 2. But notwithstanding, he was fit for Man's Use, and, without Doubt, the Owner intended him for speedy Service; for we read that the Disciples found him *tied:* And it was no unusual Thing for young Asses to be called Colts, even, *after* they were used for Riding, as may be seen in *Judg.* x. 4. and xii. 14.——The Ass being sent for, and by the Owner's Leave, bro't, for he was borrowed; the *Disciples put on him* some of their *Garments*, and then they *set Jesus thereon:* Which plainly teacheth us, to part with our very *Cloathing* for *Christ's* Sake, and that freely, when called thereunto; and when we have an Opportunity to serve him, and advance his Glory, by our so doing.

CHILDREN FED WITH CRUMBS FROM THE ADULTS' TABLE.

There are those, again, who, preaching no special sermons to children, have a "children's corner" in many of their discourses to adults, addressing to the little ones words of explanation of the truth taught their parents; telling them in simple language what is the substance of the sermon, (frequently to the enlightenment of children of a larger growth), making a point for their especial benefit, or illustrating one already made, by an incident suited to their comprehension. This plan is warmly approved by some who

---

* Calvin.
† Non utrique insedit, sed pulle vehebatur, sequente, illius matre.—*Liv.*

are as yet unwilling to give an entire service to children. It is certainly practicable where what is better cannot yet be secured. "Almost any doctrinal, exegetical or practical discourse has room for words and thoughts that any child will relish. No difficulty in feeding the sheep and lambs together:

> 'I have heard my father say,
> And well my father knew,
> In it was meat for full-grown men,
> And milk for children too.'"*

A good illustration of this style of digression for the children's benefit is found in a sermon of Dr. Doddridge on the Religious Education of Children. After addressing the parents at some length, he turns to the little ones, saying:

"II. I would address myself to children. To you, the dear lambs of the flock, whom I look upon as no contemptible part of my charge; I have been speaking for you a great while, and now give me leave to speak to you; and pray do you endeavor, for a few minutes, to mind every word that I say.

"You see, it is your parents' duty to bring you up for God. The great God of Heaven and earth has been pleased to give his express command, that you be trained up in the way in which you should go, even in the nurture and admonition of the Lord. It is wonderful goodness in God to give such a charge; and you should be affected with it, and should be inquiring what you should do in return.

"Now there are three things, which I would ask of every one of you in return for this gracious notice which the great God has taken of you, children; and I am sure, if you love your own souls, you will not deny me any of them. Be willing to learn the

---

* House's S. S. Hand-Book, p. 103.

things of God; pray for them that teach you; and see to it, you do not learn them in vain. Listen diligently, that you may understand and remember each of these."

[Then follows the exposition and improvement of each of the three points named.]

It is well urged as an argument for this plan that "'The time of the service, which often appears so long to children, will appear the shorter if they are noticed and interested in the way indicated;" and that "in expectation of what is coming for them, they will pay greater attention to what is addressed to adults."

"Papa, are you going to say anything to-day that I can understand?" asked a little girl of her father—a Massachusetts pastor—as he was setting out for church on a Sabbath morning. This tender appeal touched the loving father's heart, and he could not answer his daughter nay; he could not say to his child that she must sit in penance through all the long service with never a word designed for her instruction or cheer. So, as he preached, he said, "And now, children, I will say something to you about this." At once the face of every child in that audience brightened. Sleepy little ones started up; tired ones took fresh heart. Looking first at the minister, then at each other, again back to him, they were all eagerness for his message, as though now there was something else for them than to nod and yawn and ache uncared for; and although the pastor's following sentences to them were few and simple, doubtless many felt as did the child who had pleaded for this attention, when, on her return at noon, she said contentedly, "Papa, I understood all that you said this morning." Dear children! who wouldn't do as much as this for them in every sermon?—they are gratified so easily.

In the instance quoted, no adult listener seemed the loser by the added words of counsel to the young. Indeed, the testimony of those who have tried or noted this plan of ministering to children, tends to show that its results as a means of grace to both young and old are every way encouraging. The truth re-stated for children acquires often a new hold on parents, and the coldest hearts are quite as likely to be touched by loving appeals to the little ones about them as by arguments addressed directly to their maturer judgments.

ELEMENTS OF SUCCESS.

But whether children are preached to frequently or seldom, in separate services or at the ordinary exercises of worship, the same elements of success enter into all hopeful efforts to instruct them by public address.

In preaching to children, or to adults, a man can hope to interest others only in that in which he is himself interested. "Out of the Heart" is the suggestive title of one of Hans Christian Andersen's collections of stories to children, furnishing as it does one reason why that writer's tales of fiction have reached the hearts of so many children of all growths. Sanctified earnestness is an essential quality for every useful preacher to the little ones; not "that a preacher must aim at *earnestness*, but that he must aim at *his object*, which is to do some spiritual good to his hearers, and which will at once *make* him earnest."*

And only in reliance on the Holy Ghost can any preach in proper hope of a blessing. Successful preaching is ever, as was Paul's, "in demonstration of the Spirit and of power,"† "neither he that planteth [being] anything, neither he that watereth, but God that giveth the increase."‡

But while in this condition of heart towards God and towards those whom he addresses, the preacher must have a care to use advantageously all the talents wherewith God has blessed him; and it is to point out some of the truths he must bear in mind in his work that the following suggestions are presented.

HAVE SOMETHING TO TEACH.

Every preacher to children should have clearly in his own mind at the outset a well defined idea which he intends that his hearers shall have in theirs at the close. It may seem superfluous to name this point; yet it is true that children are often addressed in religious assemblies by those who have never a thought beyond interesting them or exciting their emotions. A formal sermon is hardly likely to be preached without some thought in it; but what is here written is intended equally for all who publicly address children, be they ministers or laymen. A minister may freely use anecdote and illustration, and loving words and tones, to

---
* Rev. Newman Hall.   † I. Cor. ii. 4.   ‡ I. Cor. iii. 7.

11*

attract the children's attention and excite their interest; but this must be solely for the purpose of conveying some valuable instruction to those whose attention and interest are thus secured. His business is to *feed* the lambs; not merely to gather them about himself with open mouths and pleading looks. It matters less to the hungry soul whether the dinner call is made by the noisy gong or the tinkling bell, than that the food supplied is abundant and nourishing. Let then every man who has addressed children ask himself, as he leaves the desk or platform, What new or important thought have I communicated to, or impressed on, these children's minds? How would they be likely to re-state it, if questioned? If he cannot define his idea, they surely cannot, and the time he has taken has been worse than lost.

The very statement of the subject of a sermon or address to children may be a means of attracting attention to what is said, and of fastening in the mind the truth taught. Thus the titles of many of the published sermons to children, taken in connection with the texts preached from, are suggestive and instructive. For example:

In Todd's " Lectures to Children."
GREAT EVENTS HANG ON LITTLE THINGS.
A certain man drew a bow at a venture. I. Kings xxii. 24.

FRAGMENTS ALL TO BE SAVED.
Gather up the fragments that remain, that nothing be lost. John vi. 12.

In McLean's " Food for the Lambs."*

THE LITTLE FOXES, AND HOW TO CATCH THEM.

Take us the foxes, the little foxes that spoil the vines; for our vines have tender grapes. Song xi. 15.

THE SNOW SERMON.

"*Wash me, and I shall be whiter than snow.*"

In Green's " Addresses to Children."

THE LITTLE SLAVE GIRL.

Now the Syrians had gone out by companies, and had brought away captive out of the land of Israel a little maid; and she waited on Naaman's wife. II. Kings v. 2.

A SERMON FOR SPRING-TIME.

Consider the lilies of the field. Matt. vi. 28.

In Peabody's Sermons for Children. †

USE AND ABUSE OF THE TONGUE.

Keep thy tongue from evil, and thy lips from speaking guile. Ps. xxxiv. 13.

FALSE SHAME.

I am not ashamed of the gospel of Christ. Rom. i. 16.

HAVE A PLAN OF TEACHING.

And when a man knows what he wants to teach, he should have a plan of teaching it. Even if he is to make but a five-minutes talk to children, he should have a system in presenting the thought he seeks to impart. John Bright has said that he never speaks without knowing beforehand just how he is to *begin* and how he is to *close*, whatever freedom he may allow

---

*By Rev. A. McLean, Buffalo, N. Y. N. Tibbals & Co., N. Y.
† Published by Am. Unit. Assoc., Boston.

himself in the body of his speech. More speakers would approach him in effectiveness if all were thus careful in their plan of discourse. Above all, a *sermon* to children should have a well arranged design, a skeleton to give strength and symmetry to the entire body. Says Dr. Newton, "In preparing a sermon for children, I regard it of the first importance to make clear, natural, distinct points. My plan is always to begin with an outline, the several points of which can be stated in language as simple as possible. If each point can be made to turn on a single word, so much the better. When these points are before me, I range through my scrap-books, and all the material at hand, in search of illustrations. I have sometimes spent as much as two days in seeking illustrations for a single sermon. When this is done, I go carefully over what has thus been gleaned and cull out such illustrations as seem best adapted to the several points before me."

Any of Dr. Newton's published sermons will illustrate his plan of arrangement. For instance:

"THE BEST WORKERS.*

My Father worketh hitherto, and I work. John v. 17.

The Heavenly Workers are the Best Workers, because they work so *extensively;* so *quietly;* so *powerfully;* so *carefully;* and so *wisely.*

We may learn two things from this subject. In the first place it teaches us that *Work is an honorable thing.* . . . We may also learn from the subject *How we should try to do our work.*"

---

* The Best Things, p. 65.

"THE TENTH COMMANDMENT.*

Thou shalt not covet. . . . Ex. xx. 17.

We have considered four reasons why we should not covet. Because it is *unsatisfying;* because it is *disgraceful;* because it is *injurious;* and because it is *sinful.*"

The sermons of Rev. John Edmond, of London, published,† in two series, under the title of "The Children's Church at Home," are admirable models in design, and are well worth the study of those who would preach wisely to children. The outlines of a few of them are subjoined.

"SHINING LAMPS.

And said unto me, What seest thou? And I said, I have looked, and behold a candlestick all of gold, with a bowl upon the top of it, and his seven lamps thereon, and seven pipes to the seven lamps, which are upon the top thereof:

And two olive trees by it, one upon the right side of the bowl, and the other upon the left side thereof. Zech. iv. 2, 3.

Every one of us should have a lamp, or rather be a lamp, to shine out into the darkness of the world. . . . .

Now there are four things necessary to a lamp's giving light properly. It must be—

I. Lighted.
II. Set.
III. Fed.
IV. Trimmed."

"THE FAREWELL PROMISE.

He which testifieth these things saith, Surely I come quickly: Amen. Even so, come, Lord Jesus. Rev. xxii. 20.

"Take the different parts of this verse as they stand, and you have three things for consideration:

I. *A description of Jesus*: 'He which testifieth these things.'

---

* The King's Highway, p. 338. † By T. Nelson & Sons.

254 THE CHILDREN'S PREACHING SERVICE.

II. *A saying of Jesus:* 'Surely I come quickly, Amen.'
III. *A prayer to Jesus:* 'Even so, come, Lord Jesus.'"

Similar skill in sermon outlines is shown by the Rev. Dr. W. P. Breed, of Philadelphia, in his collections of discourses to children known as " Under the Oak," and " Grapes from the Great Vine."* For instance, he has one called

"THE FIVE WONDERS.

Behold, I stand at the door and knock: if any man hear my voice, and open the door, I will come in to him, and will sup with him, and he with me. Rev. iii. 20.

At least five several wonders in one short text of Scripture !

The First wonder is found in—*The Person mentioned in that little word 'I.'*

The Second wonder is—*His object in knocking there.*

The Third wonder is—*That Jesus is permitted to stand, without being admitted.*

The Fourth of the five wonders is—*The patience of Jesus in standing so long at the sinner's heart.*

The Fifth and last of these wonders is—*Christ supping with the sinner.*"

Another choice collection of sermons to children is from the pen of Rev. Joseph A. Collier, Kingston, N. Y., under the title of " Little Crowns and How to Win them."†

The plan of the first of these is as follows:

"Josiah was eight years old when he began to reign. II. Chron. xxiv. 1.

" What boy has not sometimes wished that he might become a king, and live in a splendid palace, all shining with gold and

---

* Published by Presb. Board of Publication.
† By R. Carter & Bros., New York.

gems? . . . Now I am going to tell you . . . how you may all wear crowns, if you will only take the pains to win them. . . .

    I. One of these crowns is *Self-Government*. . . .
    II. Another crown is *Wisdom*. . . .
    III. Another crown is *Obedience to God*. . . .
    IV. Another crown, beautiful and bright as if it had come straight down from heaven, is that of *Love*. . . .
    V. I must tell you of one more crown: and it is as bright as all the others melted into one can make it—'*The crown of glory that fadeth not away.*'"

USE SIMPLE LANGUAGE.

Equally important with the having something to teach, and a plan in presenting it, is the use of simple language, in addresses to children.

"Be plain in speech. Give a clear view of what you teach. Let your teaching be understood," says Dr. Robert Steel in his admirable work on Sunday-school teaching;* and he quotes Dr. South as saying: "He is the powerfulest preacher, and the best orator who can make himself best understood." But Mr. Green forcibly suggests that it is not by using words of one syllable that language is made simple. "We never talk to children in monosyllables. . . . . Let us be plain and Saxon as possible in our speech; but let us not imagine that we have simplified our language when we have only reduced the size of our words. The measure of simplicity is not linear measure."† And Dr. Waterbury adds:‡ "Children comprehend more readily than you imagine. You need not insult their understanding by descending to a

---

* The Christian Teacher in Sunday-schools, p. 216. T. Nelson & Sons.
† Preface to Addresses to Children.   ‡ Children Led to the Saviour.

style of babyish simplicity. How do you make your own children of eight, ten and twelve years understand you? Does it require a studied simplicity? By no means. You talk to them in plain Saxon language, just such as you use in your intercourse with ordinary grown people. Do they not understand you? Why should you adopt any different style in *preaching* to them?"

A strong thought loses none of its force by being expressed in familiar speech. A feeble idea gains no power by being rendered in high-sounding phrase. Yet it requires more of ability to grasp a great truth and then to give it simple expression, than to use swelling words without full appreciation of their meaning; and care is always necessary, in talking to children, not to employ words above their possible comprehension. In evidence of the truth that simplicity in style and language is compatible with intellectual breadth and culture, it is only necessary to refer to some of the published sermons or writings for children from men of strong thought and high attainment who have had marked success in this direction.

Rev. W. S. Plumer, D.D., LL.D., has written massive volumes of theologic lore, and also an attractive collection of " Short Sermons to Little Children."* It would be difficult to find lessons to the young presented in simpler terms than in some portions of this latter volume. For instance:

"THERE IS A GOD.
He that cometh to God must believe that he is. Heb. xi. 6.

---

* Published by Am. S. S. Union.

THE CHILDREN'S PREACHING SERVICE. 257

I believe there is a God; but I do not believe so because I ever saw him. 'No man hath seen God at any time.' God says, 'No man shall see me and live.' But we may all believe in some things which we never saw. We never saw the wind, and yet we know it blows..... Therefore it is as foolish as it is wicked to doubt whether there be a God, simply because we never saw him. But I will tell you why I believe there is a God.

Not long ago, I went with four little children into a watchmaker's shop, and there a man brought out a little box, and put a key into a small hole in the side of it, and wound it up. He then set down the box, and touched a spring, and the top flew open, and a little bird, not as large as a humming-bird, hopped out, and flapped its wings, and sang, or seemed to sing, a pretty tune..... It was very small and very beautiful. The little boys and girls that were with me were much pleased..... Mary said, 'I wish I had it. I would give a dollar for it.' She was told the price of it was six hundred dollars. Jane asked, 'Who made it?' Mr. Smith, the watchmaker, told her it was made by a man in Geneva, in Switzerland. We all left the store in good spirits and went out to a grove. Here were many living birds..... Every one of them could hop from branch to branch, and from tree to tree. They could all make some noise. The notes of most of them were very sweet..... We all walked through the grove, and found some pretty flowers. We then came to a cool spring, and took a drink of water..... I thought it was a good time to talk. So I said, 'If a man in Geneva made the bird in the box, how came all the living birds here? Did they make themselves?' Charles said, 'How could they make themselves? I saw in my book the other day that nothing can make nothing.' 'Well,' said I, 'did the man in Geneva make them?' Jane answered, 'No! he never saw them. He could not make such birds as these......' I then said, 'Did they just grow without any one making them?' Charles replied 'How could they?' Mary said, 'I can tell you how they came here, God made them...... I know there is a God, because there are so many pretty birds.' I added, 'You are all right, my children.

There is a God.... He has made everything good, and we ought to believe that he is. His works are all around us. They are many, and great, and wise. Let us never doubt that there is a God.'

REMARKS.

If there be a God, we ought to believe in him, and think of him. We ought to love him, and fear him, and obey him, and not sin against him. We ought also to trust in him. Little birds do his will, and praise him *in their way*. We ought to praise him in our pretty hymns, and in our hearts. And we ought to pray to him, as he has taught us:

'Our Father,' etc."

FEW ESSENTIALS TO HOPEFUL SPEECH.

The three points thus named will doubtless be conceded as indispensable to every proper address to children. Without something to say, a plan of saying it, and saying it simply, no man can hope to address children profitably. With these qualifications, he may always hope to be heard and understood, and to edify his hearers, for children love to be talked to, and their minds are ever open to bright and fresh ideas. Of course it must not be forgotten, that to really benefit children by any address, the speaker must employ God's truth, in reliance on God's Spirit; but the suggestions herein made are rather as to the manner of preaching, than as to its spirit and substance.

In addition to these essential elements, there are others scarcely less important in successful preaching to the little ones, foremost among which is

QUESTIONING ON THE TRUTH TAUGHT.

To state a truth to a child does not teach it to him.

He may or may not receive and understand it. But if, on being questioned concerning it, he returns correct answers, he not only indicates his apprehension of its meaning, but, by the very act of re-stating its substance, acquires to it a new right of mental ownership. It is doubtless true that a man hardly makes any thought his own until he has in some way given it expression; hence it is doing much for a child to induce him to shape or repeat any statement made to him in public address, as the text or main divisions of a sermon, or the points of an address, or to draw out from him by skilful questioning his own ideas on the theme considered, that they may be approved or corrected.

In the early Church, the young were always taught catechetically,—indeed the younger classes of catechumens were not even permitted to attend on pulpit preaching; and the superiority of that mode, for purposes of *teaching*, is admitted almost universally by educators. "More knowledge," says Dr. Owen, "is ordinarily diffused, especially among the young and ignorant, by one hour's catechetical exercise than by many hours' continued discourse." Says Bridges,* "The catechetical mode is decidedly the most effective to maintain attention, elicit intelligence, convey information, and, most of all, apply the instructions to the heart;" and George Herbert adds:† "This practice exceeds even sermons in teaching." "It is more fitted to communicate truth to the youthful mind," says Dr.

---

* Christian Ministry, p. 404.
† Country Parson, Chap. xxi.

Steel, in quoting the foregoing authorities. "The knowledge is riveted by catechising."* Do all preachers bear this truth in mind in their efforts to teach the young? Is it not true, as Dr. Duryea suggests,† that "The pulpit has turned away utterly from that which philosophy has used with such tremendous power from the beginning until now?" and that "The pulpit must sit at her feet and learn the simple lesson?" It is true that the didactic form of address is most effective as a means of inspiration, and best suited to hortatory and illustrative instruction; hence, sermons cannot—should not—be exclusively, or even chiefly, catechetical; but the two modes can be employed together, to the increase of the value of each. As Dr. Steel says of the use of exhortation and illustration in teaching: "We do not despise, or wish to dispense with, these means. We are only anxious to keep them in their place; and the strict attention to, and exercise of the catechetical, afford ample room for their introduction."

Some of the most successful preachers to children make ample use of the power of questioning. Says Rev. Dr. Todd:‡ "I have tried to talk in such a manner, that, on pausing several times, and asking my little bright audience what point had just been stated and illustrated, the child who could only lisp should usually be able to throw his voice in with the rest in answering." Whoever has heard Rev. Dr. Newton, knows that much of his effectiveness as a preacher to

---

* The Christian Teacher in Sunday-schools, p. 128.
† New York S. S. Institute, p. 137.   ‡ Preface to Lectures to Children.

children comes of his skill and tact as a questioner. He asks the children to repeat aloud the text he announces; he calls on them to re-state each division of his discourse; he questions them as to the meaning of words used by him; and before he states a new head he asks them to remind him of those which preceded it. At the close of the sermon, he has his young hearers give, in response to his well-timed questions, the entire synopsis of his discourse, so that it is then as much theirs as it was his. They and he have preached it together. They are likely never to forget its lessons or substance. Ralph Wells, as a lay-preacher to children, questions yet more freely, and with like success. The same may be said of many others.

Dr. Wilberforce, Lord Bishop of Oxford, has published some of his Sunday stories to his own children,* and at the close of a number of these he has given questions and answers as indicative of what is desirable in impressing such truths on the young. His children were from five to nine years old when these stories were told to them, and some of the answers "are the very answers he received from his children."

For example, he tells an allegory, under the title of "The Tent on the Plain." A king has his headquarters in a shining tent. Soldiers are coming to enlist in his army, and he receives even those who have been in rebellion against him, giving to each a ring, containing a stone that sparkles as long as the

---

* The Children and the Lion. Carlton & Porter.

wearer is trustful of him, but grows dull when he doubts. Even the youngest are received by this king, and may fight for him. A powerful glass given to the dreamer who tells the allegory, shows the air about the young soldiers of the king to be "full of ugly and venomous creatures who were the king's enemies," and they are continually provoking trouble among the little ones; but if the king's name is mentioned, or trust in him expressed, the vile creatures flee away. Again, in a child's sick room the powerful glass shows "beautiful forms of heavenly creatures which the king had sent to watch over him;" and as the boy dies, a golden door is shown to open above him, and as he passes in happy music sounds out, and a crown is offered him. The questions and answers at the close of this allegory are as follows:

"*Q.* Who is the King who takes rebels as soldiers?
A. The Lord our God; who says, 'Am not I a great King?'
Q. Who are these rebels?
A. All mankind: for it is written, 'All have sinned and come short of the glory of God.' Rom. iii. 23. And again: 'We were by nature the children of wrath, even as others.' Eph. ii. 3.
Q. What is the ring of adoption?
A. Our being taken to be God's own children.
Q. What is the sparkling stone?
A. The faith by which we must ourselves believe in Christ, if we would be saved.
Q. What is the meaning of the stone becoming dull?
A. A child of God growing unfaithful, or forgetful of him.
Q. How soon may we begin to fight the good fight of faith?
A. As soon as we know anything.
Q. What are the dreadful forms which the glass showed?

A. Temptations to sin.
Q. Then are little children tempted to sin?
A. Yes; that they are, very often.
Q. And how must they resist?
A. By remembering whose children they are; and that God the Father sees them; and that he for Christ's sake will help them if they pray, and so be asking always for his help.
Q. What are the good forms the glass showed?
A. The helps God will give to those who pray to him.
Q. What are we to learn from the dying boy?
A. That God will take holy children to dwell with him forever in his heavenly glory."

THE USE OF ILLUSTRATION.

Next in prominence, certainly comes the use of illustration in preaching to children. Indeed it is usually given a higher place, sometimes the first.

"The popularity of great preachers is largely attributable to their powers of illustration," says Groser.[*] "On the other hand, it is chiefly the absence of illustration which renders a style heavy and uninteresting, and imparts that peculiar and well known quality denominated 'prosiness.'" Dr. Dowling adds:[†] "The power of illustration, while it is an eminently useful qualification to the instructor of men, is absolutely indispensable to the successful instructor of youth." Says Freeman,[‡] "The importance of illustration in the instruction of children can hardly be overestimated." "Mere didactic abstract instruction will not meet their

---
[*] Illustrative Teaching, p. 7. By. W. H. Groser.
[†] The Power of Illustration, p. 19. Rev. J. Dowling, D.D.
[‡] The Use of Illustration, in S. S. Teaching, p. 5. Rev. Jas. M. Freeman.

wants," says Dr. Tyng.* "This is only to be done by a system of illustration from every variety of source accessible to the teacher, and adapted to the minds of children." Cecil declares of the children's preacher, that "He must have extensive knowledge, to call in illustration from the four corners of the earth; for he will make but little progress but by illustration." "Illustrations of divine truths are," says Pardee, † "in fact indispensable."

The Great Teacher was an example in this regard. "He was illustrative in his teaching, and knew that great secret of popular oratory, the art of using familiar objects as figures of spiritual truth. He was always telling what the kingdom of heaven was like,"‡ and "without a parable spake he not" unto his followers. This was because "he knew what was in man," his tastes and his needs; and man is now much as then. "Childhood loves parables. The word must be made flesh to dwell among them. A good illustration will fasten a truth, with God's blessing forever upon the memory and heart;"§ or as Brace puts it, concerning his Short Sermons to News Boys. "The street-boy, [and other boys are not unlike him in this,] cannot listen to abstract truth: he must have concrete. Facts and realities are what he needs, and especially the teaching of parables, or dramatic and illustrative modes of teaching." With all classes and ages, the truth is

---

* Forty Years' Experience in S. S., p. 237.
† S. S. Index, p. 87.
‡ Christian Teacher in S. S., p. 217.
§ Stories from Life. Rev. B. K. Peirce, D. D. Henry Hoyt.

best impressed on the memory through illustrative incidents. "The story, like a float, keeps it from sinking; like a nail, fastens it on the mind; like the feathers of an arrow, makes it strike, and like the barb, makes it stick."*

Most of the effective preachers to children use illustrations freely in their sermons. So do the foremost lay-speakers to the little ones in their addresses. The best writers on the children's cause press the advantages of this mode of enforcing truth on the young mind; and it is given large prominence in nearly all of the Sunday-school teachers' institutes and conventions of the day. Having divine sanction, in the example of the Model Teacher, it may not be lightly passed over as unworthy of full consideration. It demands the earnest attention of him who would religiously instruct the young, and especially should the children's preacher faithfully consider the entire subject of Illustration, and prepare himself for his work by gathering material in this line. Freeman recommends† to the Sunday-school teacher (and the advice is equally good to the preacher) the keeping of "a memorandum book in which to jot down from time to time such illustrations of various kinds as may occur to the mind either in reading, or conversation, or hearing a public speaker, or meditation;" and as a good way of rendering these available, to "mark on the margin of the Bible, opposite the text illustrated, the

---

* Dr. Guthrie on The Parables.
† Use of Illustrations, p. 27.

number of the page of the blank book on which the illustration is found." He adds, that "a scrap-book will also be o very great assistance. In this may be pasted such scraps illustrative of Bible truth as may be gathered from the papers. Anecdotes, narratives, allusions to biblical customs or history, may in this way be preserved for future use. The page of the scrap-book may be noted in the margin of the Bible, opposite the passage illustrated, as in the case of the memorandum book." An index to the memorandum or scrap-book will also prove of value for purposes of reference.

But there seems less danger just now that illustrations will be undervalued, than that they will be made too much of by speakers to children. Sure it is that "the children too often are glutted with anecdotes;"[*] and that "some speakers, unable to interest their juvenile auditory in any legitimate way, endeavor to stimulate attention by a succession of stories;"[†] but "the stories seem to be without point, and the 'illustrations' not brought in for the sake of illustrating anything in particular."[‡] "The practice of *illustrating nothing* is too common in Sunday-schools to be overlooked," says Groser;[§] and he adds the important suggestion: "It is not enough that there be doctrine and illustration; the latter must be made subordinate to the former. An illustration misses its mark whenever it withdraws the attention of the hearer from the truth

---

[*] Children Led to the Saviour, p. 118. Waterbury.
[†] Preface to Addresses to Children. Green.
[‡] Sunday-school Photographs, p. 163. Taylor.
[§] Illustrative Teaching, p. 21.

THE CHILDREN'S PREACHING SERVICE. 267

which it illustrates." "The great aim of the lesson," says Steel,* "may be lost by the interest of the story. The Spanish artist obliterated certain vases which he had introduced into a painting of the Lord's Supper, because he observed that every spectator was at once affected by the exquisite finish of these ornaments, instead of being interested in the great subject of his art." It can hardly be questioned that some successful preachers and talkers to children use anecdote and illustration too freely, and are successful in spite of, rather than through, their much story-telling.

So much being said, and with truth, of the value of illustration to the children's preacher, there is a possibility of its relative importance being exaggerated, to the discouragement of those who have least skill in that department. Hence it is well to have it understood that good sermons are often preached to children with no help from anecdote and little from illustration. Rev. S. G. Green of England, so successful as a children's preacher, and so competent a judge as to the wants of the little ones, says, in the introduction to his "Addresses," in commendation of "a little volume of Sermons to Children, by the late Dr. Greenwood of America:" "In most qualities of thought and style they surpass, to my mind, any collection of children's sermons I ever saw." Turning to the volume of sermons so highly praised,† it is seen that their author thus speaks of his view of anecdotic illustration: "I re-

---

* The Christian Teacher in S. S., p. 219.
† Sermons to Children, by F. W. P. Greenwood, D.D. Am. Unit. Asso.

solved also to dispense with the advantage which might be derived from the introduction of illustrative stories, as I thought that children were already in possession of abundance of that species of instruction, and that I would rather trust to the ideas presented in a plain, didactic form, to fix their attention."

The sermons of the well known English preacher to children, Rev. Dr. Alexander Fletcher, show comparatively few illustrations, and a published sermon by the Rev. J. C. Ryle * is almost if not entirely devoid of illustration, but by no means devoid of interest or suitableness for the young. A specimen of its style is appended:

"CHILDREN WALKING IN TRUTH.

I rejoiced greatly, that I found of thy children walking in truth. II. John iv.

Beloved Children.—The book from which my text is taken is the shortest in the Bible. Look at it when you go home, and you will find it so. It has only thirteen verses; but, short as it is, it is full of important things, and I think the verse I have just read is one of them.

This book is an epistle, or letter, written by the apostle John. He wrote it to a good Christian lady whom he knew. This lady had children, and some of them were the children spoken of in the text.

It seems that John found some of this good lady's children at a place where he happened to go; and you see how well he found them behaving. He was able to write a good report of them to their mother, and that is the report of our text: 'I rejoiced greatly, that I found of thy children walking in truth.'

Now, dear children, there are only two things I want to tell you about out of this text. Some of you, perhaps, are thinking

---

* In Child's Preacher.

this very minute 'What does walking in truth mean?' Others, perhaps, are thinking, 'Why did John rejoice so greatly?' I shall try to answer these two questions.

I. Firstly, I shall try to show you *when it can be said that children walk in truth.*

II. Secondly, I shall try to show you *what were the reasons that made the apostle John rejoice so greatly.*

Dear children, let me ask you all one favor,—let me ask you all to try to *attend.* I shall not keep you long. Come, then, and listen to what I have to tell you. May the Holy Spirit open all your hearts, and bless what I say!

. . . .

And now I have finished what I have to say about our text. I have done what I promised. I have told you *what it is to walk in truth.* This is one thing. I have told you *why John rejoiced so much* to find this lady's children walking in truth. That is another. Let me now wind up all by saying something which, by God's help, may fasten this sermon in your minds. Alas! how many sermons are forgotten! I want this sermon to abide in your hearts and do good.

Ask yourselves, then, every one, 'Would John, if he knew me at this time, rejoice over me? Would John be pleased if he saw my ways and my behavior, or would he look sorrowful and grave?'

O children, children, do not neglect this question. This is no light matter. It may be your life. No wise man will ever rejoice over bad children. They may be clean and pretty, and have fine clothes, and look well *outwardly;* but a wise man will feel sad when he sees them; he will feel they are wrong *inwardly.* They have not new hearts—they are not going to heaven. Believe me, it is far better to be good than to be pretty. It is far better to have grace in your hearts than to have much money in your pockets, or fine clothes on your backs. None but children who love Christ are the children who rejoice a wise man's heart.

Beloved children, hear the last words I have to say to you. I give you all an invitation from Christ, my Master. I say to you in his name, *Come and walk in truth.*"

It is thus manifest that the free use of illustration is by no means the foremost requisite in preaching to children. Yet it has an important place, and one that is not likely to be overlooked.

PREACH SCRIPTURALLY.

In choosing illustrations, the Bible should be held as the choicest treasury of supply. Its imagery and incident are of never failing variety and interest, and children cannot be better instructed or pleased than through those things which God has written for their benefit. No other topics are of equal importance with those found in the Bible; nor are their like to be found in freshness and uniform attractiveness. The children hear enough else in other places. In God's house, on his day, nothing is better for them than what is furnished in his Word.

Charles Dickens, in commenting on Preaching in London Theatres, some years since, said on this point:

"In the New Testament there is the most beautiful and affecting history conceivable by man, and there are the terse models for all prayer and all preaching. As to the models, imitate them, Sunday preachers; else, why are they there? consider. As to the history, tell it. Some people cannot read; some people will not read; many people (this especially holds among the young and ignorant) find it hard to pursue the verse form in which the book is presented to them, and imagine that those breaks imply gaps and want of continuity. Help them over that first stumbling-block, by setting forth the history in narrative, with no fear of exhausting it. You will never preach so well; you will never move them so profoundly; you will never send them away with half so much to think of."

Jesus, the Model Preacher, used Scripture freely in his discourses, and his most useful ministers have imitated him in this. "Christ made much of the written Word. It was his appeal at all times. It dropped from his lips as honey from the honeycomb. He quoted the oracles of God to confirm his own sayings. .... There is scarcely a book from which he did not directly quote, and the words of the great singer of Israel trembled on his dying lips. Herein the apostles followed their Master. They were Scriptural teachers. St. Peter was so most strikingly on the day of Pentecost..... The historian of [Paul's] labors says of him, again and again that 'Paul, *as his manner was*, ... reasoned with them out of the Scriptures.' Luther rejoiced when he received his degree in Divinity, that he was a Biblical doctor."*

TREAT SACRED THEMES REVERENTLY.

In all the use of Scripture themes and terms, there should be sincere reverence displayed by the children's preacher. There is a certain flippancy of speech common among talkers to children, even in the mention of the holy names of the Trinity, or of the most sacred topics of religion, which should be shunned conscientiously. Reverence for God, and for all that in any sense

---
* The Christian Teacher in S. S., p. 213.

represents him, must be taught by example as well as by precept to the young.

"'Put off thy shoes from off thy feet; for the place whereon thou standest is holy ground.' This should be, from the first, the temper carefully wrought into our children's minds, if we would have them approach God with acceptance. To teach them to think boldly of mysteries, in the vain hope of explaining to their childish minds what, in the fulness of their highest understanding, they can never truly comprehend, may make them shrewd and forward questioners, but cannot make them meek and teachable disciples."*

It is better to have children seriously *impressed* with an important truth, in their Sabbath service, than to have them thoroughly *amused*, so as to laugh with or at the speaker, or connect ludicrous associations with a passage of Scripture, albeit not all who address them seem to think so.

VARIETY DESIRABLE.

Monotony is no pleasanter to children than to adults. They love variety, and to the children's preacher, versatility is an important qualification. An examination of the best published sermons to children will show what diversity of themes is attainable within due bounds. Says Mr. Edmond, of his first volume,† "The subjects of discourse have been selected and arranged so as to present as much variety as possible. Some are

---

* Preface to The Children and the Lion, by Dr. Wilberforce.
† In Preface to The Children's Church at Home.

connected with Scripture characters of note,—some are on the essential doctrines of the gospel,—some on special but important views of duty,—some are anecdotical,—some more didactic,—some have threads of allegory. All it is hoped will be found simple, instructive and pleasing." Of his second volume, he says, " Diversity alike in the subjects treated, and in the mode of treating them, has again been aimed at; and the readers of the first series will find, amid the 'old stories,' that must always recur, not a few topics different from any there introduced," and this may be made true of all preaching of this class.

Yet the desire for mere variety may be carried too far. The same truth must often be several times restated to give it proper force, and a single theme may gain greatly by being newly presented in varying form, yet ever similar in substance. Rev. Dr. Tyng, who has doubtless preached more children's sermons than any other pastor in this country—perhaps in the world —and this with uniform success, is in the "habit of preaching in *series* of sermons to the young," often giving a number of sermons on one text. Thus he has (somewhat paradoxically) "ten on the text, 'There is one and there is not a second;' fourteen on 'A three-fold cord is not easily broken,'" and nine on "Ye are come unto Mount Sion," &c. Yet Dr. Tyng's sermons would never be called monotonous; nor are any of his texts yet worn out.

KEEP CHILDREN'S MINDS ACTIVE.

Even in the efforts to present subjects and to employ language suited to the comprehension of children, the speaker to them must not expect, nor should he endeavor, to say nothing but what they will fully understand. He should keep ahead of them, that their minds may be on the stretch. They would gain but little, if they never heard that which was not clear to them. While the subject should be within their mental reach, and presented in clear and simple terms, it cannot be expected that it will prove wholly intelligible to them at the outset. They should be able to learn enough from it for encouragement, while having yet other attainment in its lessons to strive after. Says the Lord Bishop of Oxford in cômmending allegories: "The minds of children may be fatally dwarfed by never having presented to them anything but that which they can understand without effort." *

And Mr. Green condemns the practice of those speakers to children who "attenuate the matter to the last degree of feebleness, as if simplicity and babyism were identical. 'He talked to us just as if we were all little children,' was a Sunday scholar's scornful comment on a sermon of this class." †

MANNER OF ADDRESS.

There is scarcely a limit to the suggestions that may be made to the children's speaker. Everything that

---

* Preface to The Children and the Lion.
† Introduction to Addresses to Children.

goes to render the preacher to adults effective is of service to him who addresses the young. His very manner of speech is potent. His tones of voice may attract, enliven and thrill his young hearers, or may chill and repel them. "Children will respond to every gleam of the eye, to every throb of the heart; but as by intuition they will detect and repudiate a lukewarm earnestness or a counterfeit enthusiasm. . . . . Tears will call for tears, love for love, tenderness for tenderness."* The speaker may so invest the truth he utters with his personal qualities of attractiveness, that for *his* sake, the children will believe and love it.

A certain vivacity, a quickness and life in speech and manner, is called for by children, which is less important in addressing adults. The children's preacher should think and speak and move with somewhat of their promptness and "snap," if he would carry along their sympathies.

And he should be as natural and unconstrained as possible. He should *talk* to the little ones, rather than read an essay or deliver an address to them. "I can understand your *talkin' talk*, but I can't much understand your *preachin' talk*,"† was the remark of a German hearer to an American minister; and the same could be said by many a child to those who essay to address him. "Naturalness implies simplicity in language, in manner, and in illustration. The beauty of childhood is its guileless simplicity, and he who learns again, or

---

* House's S. S. Hand-Book, p. 130.
† See Congregationalist and Recorder for Oct. 29, 1868.

who never loses, this freshness of heart, will become the best recipient and the most successful teacher of divine truth."*

SEATING OF THE CHILDREN.

The location of the children in the house of worship, when they are being preached to, is a matter of not a little moment. They are sometimes put in the galleries, to be talked to over the heads of their parents. The folly of such an arrangement for reaching children without displacing adults below, is much like the sportsman's attempt to shoot around a corner by curving his gun-barrel. The charge will be lost, and the gun may burst, but the object aimed at will not be hit. The only way to speak to children, or to shoot, is straightforward. Tortuous or indirect addresses to them are useless. They should be in front of the speaker, where he can look into their eyes, and they into his; otherwise, any aid of magnetic influence is out of the question; there can be no direct personal intercourse between him and them, in his discourse. Yet the children should be brought together, where they can have an atmosphere of mutual sympathy and encouragement. If they are scattered throughout the congregation, they are likely to be overawed by the adults under whose shadow they are placed. They cannot answer questions freely, nor feel that the meeting is their own; nor is the preacher as likely to remember that he is addressing only them; and this is

---

* London S. S. Times, Aug. 21, 1863.

an important item in his effort. "The temptation to please the adult portion of the audience, rather than to edify the children, will sometimes be strong, but yielding to it must ordinarily be disastrous."*

Says Dr. Todd: "The *best* way of preaching to children is to have them *entirely* alone,—not an adult in the house. You can then come down to them, and can interest them. The next best way is to have all the children in the centre of the house, and the congretion above and around them; and then let the speaker *forget*, if he can, that any body is present besides the children." †

"At all such public meetings of children," says Rev. Edward Eggleston, ‡ "one of the most important points is to have the children seated in a body in the centre and front of the room." And Mr. House adds, wisely: "Have the youngest nearest you, and often direct your remarks to them; varying your tone by an occasional word to some one who may be less attentive than others. As long as you have the eyes of the youngest, you are pretty sure of the eyes and ears of the older ones."§

If the children are worth preaching to at all, they are entitled to the best place in the sanctuary,—the place where they can best hear, and will be most likely to receive profit.

---

* House's S. S Hand-Book, p. 129.
† Preface to Lectures to Children.
‡ In appendix to House's S. S. Hand-Book.
§ House's S. S. Hand-Book, p. 130.

278 THE CHILDREN'S PREACHING SERVICE.

And now it only remains to further illustrate the style and modes of successful preaching to children, by examples from the sermons and addresses of those peculiarly skilled in this department of Christian labor.

SPECIMEN DISCOURSES TO CHILDREN.

The sermons and addresses here given have been kindly furnished, by the several authors, at the request of the compiler of this volume. They are not put forward by their writers as in any sense models, but are specimens of their ordinary discourses to the children of their charge. None of them have before been furnished for publication. Only one or two of them have ever been reported partially by others, for the public.

———•••———

The first sermon is one of Dr. Tyng's latest series, of nine sermons in all, on The Privileges of the Youthful Christian, from Hebrews xii. 22–24.

THE RULING POWER OF AN EXALTED SAVIOUR.

BY THE REV. STEPHEN H. TYNG, D.D.,
Rector of St. George's (Episcopal) Church, New York.

But ye are come unto Mount Sion, and unto the city of the living God, the heavenly Jerusalem, and to an innumerable company of angels.

To the general assembly and church of the first-born, which are written in heaven, and to God the Judge of all, and to the spirits of just men made perfect. And to Jesus the mediator of the new covenant, and to the blood of sprinkling, that speaketh better things than that of Abel. Heb. xii. 22-24.

These beautiful descriptions illustrate the present actual privileges of the children of God in Christ Jesus. Have you, in the renewing of your heart by the Holy Ghost, by a new and living faith, embraced the promises of Jesus, and yielded to his commands? Then these are the inestimable privileges bestowed upon you. And you may thankfully say, "I have come to Mount Zion." Here is the catalogue of the blessings which have been bestowed upon you by the infinite grace of God in the gospel. I wish you to contemplate them separately with me. Great and precious instructions are presented to you in the illustrations here arranged. The first is *the Mount Zion.* "Ye are come unto Mount Zion."

I. *Its historical meaning.* Two separate hills made up the southern part of the city of Jerusalem,—Moriah on the east, Zion on the west. When David selected Jerusalem, then called Jebus, as the seat of his kingdom over Israel, Zion was in possession of the natives of the land. They called it the Castle of Zion. It was so fortified that they boasted that even the lame and the blind who were within it could defend it against assault. Its name of Zion meant a high monument of stones,—a walled fortress. This stronghold of Zion, David took, and called it the City of David,—the royal town, and so it remains. From that time, Zion became the seat of David's throne, the title which described his royal power. Thus, in the language of succeeding Scripture, it is called: "I have set my king upon my holy hill of Zion."

But David and his temporal throne were but typical of that great Son of David, the glorious Redeemer of mankind. And Mount Zion, in all the language of prophecy, and in all the descriptions of the gospel history, is the royal power of Jesus, the dominion of the Son of God. "The Redeemer shall come out of Zion." "The ransomed of the Lord shall return unto Zion." "The Lord shall reign in Mount Zion." "I looked, and lo, a Lamb stood on the Mount Zion." The Lamb is Lord of lords, and King of kings.

II. *Its practical* meaning. This is the *first* privilege of the child of God, the member of Christ, in this passage, "Ye are come unto Mount Zion"—that is, you are brought to the *royal power of Jesus*,—to Jesus as your exalted king and ruler, by the power of the Holy Ghost. "The joy of the whole earth is Mount Zion." "Let Mount Zion rejoice." "Walk about Zion, and go round about her: tell the towers thereof." "This God is our God for ever and ever."

This is the privilege here described. Every true believer in Jesus has come unto Mount Zion;—is made a partaker of the royal power of Jesus. His Saviour is a triumphant, ruling Saviour,—God over all, blessed forever! "Ye are come unto Mount Zion." You have a royal, ruling Saviour. Your salvation is in his hands, accomplished by his power; your safety in his truth, secure and unchangeable in him. If you love him, it is because he first loved you. You are in him, and he in you.

Think of this precious privilege with thankfulness. How secure and perfect is your condition in this ruling Saviour. They who love him, are like the "Mount Zion, which cannot be removed," but standeth fast forever and ever. This great privilege the gospel brings to you,—security in a ruling, almighty Saviour. Because he lives, you shall live also. When you accept, in your heart, the invitation of the gospel, when you receive, in your heart, the Saviour whom it brings to you,—this gospel gives you all the triumphant blessings which are laid up in him. It begs you to consider them and your own blessedness in having them. It says to you, "Ye are not come to the mount that burned with fire"—"Ye are come unto Mount Zion." Crowned with salvation, you are not to fight your way to peace through impassable difficulties; you are to accept peace as a divine gift. You are not to find salvation in your own works or by your own power; you are to receive it all as the work of a glorious Saviour,—as a gift of boundless grace, made yours through the divine power and the divine love. You are not brought to a dominion of fear and contest, but to a dominion of peace and triumph and rest. You "are come unto Mount Zion,"—to a royal, ruling Saviour.

III. *In its actual purpose.*

1. This is Jesus in *the triumphs of his redemption.* On earth, as man, he labored, suffered and died, for you. Then, he was a contending, struggling Saviour. He had a baptism of unspeakable suffering, a death accursed and outcast. He "endured the cross and despised the shame." But he arose in triumph. He ascended in glory. God raised him up by his own right hand, and "set his king upon his holy hill of Zion." And there he is, —a triumphant Saviour. Redemption has triumphed in him. Divine acceptance has been gained for you, in his perfect obedience. And the Lamb that was slain is in the midst of the throne, and ruleth forevermore.

And when, with a grateful, trusting heart, you believe him, submit to him, accept him, follow him, you come to no uncertain gospel, no yea and nay gospel, but to a glorious Saviour, to an everlasting salvation, to a throne of triumphant power, to a crown of endless glory. "Ye are come unto Mount Zion."

2. This is Jesus in *his earthly dominion.* The government over all things is upon his shoulder. He maketh "all things work together for good to them that love him." When you come to Jesus as your Saviour, you come to an earthly life ruled by his wisdom and his love. All things here are subject to his will. As for him, his work is perfect. Go round about Zion, mark her bulwarks. Tell it to those who come after, "This God is our God. We have a goodly heritage. He lays out our path, he orders all our ways. He leads us according to his good pleasure. He never fails, and never forsakes us. The Lord is our helper. He provides. He directs. He prospers. He bestows. The Lord himself is our inheritance even here. We have our portion in him. We 'are come unto Mount Zion.'"

3. This is Jesus *in his spiritual power.* He rules within us, as well as *for* us in heaven, and around and over us on the earth. We have within us a ruling Saviour. A thousand enemies are there. A thousand contests are there. Difficulties unceasingly arising are there. We often fall,—we are often cast down. But the house of Saul waxes weaker and weaker, and the house of

David stronger and stronger. Christ will give us the victory, and makes us more than conquerors through his power. Tempers, lusts, habits, he will subdue by his Spirit. Virtues, love, obedience, he will create within us; by his power he will cause us to triumph in all things. And we are never to fear. We are to trust and not be afraid; to realize the power, the truth, the loving-kindness of our Lord, and not to dishonor him by unbelief. "Rejoice not against me, O mine enemy; though I fall, I will rise again; though I sit in darkness, the Lord will be a light unto me; these things will he do unto me and not forsake me." Ye "are come unto Mount Zion." Lift up your heads, and rejoice with exceeding joy. "Your redemption draweth nigh."

4. It is Jesus in *his heavenly presence*. He dwells in light inaccessible,—the brightness of the Father's glory. But where he is, there shall also his servants be. This is his sure promise, "I go to prepare a place for you; . . . . I will come again and receive you unto myself, that where I am, there ye may be also." We are saved by this hope, upheld by it, encouraged by it, made partakers of it. It is "an anchor to our souls, both sure and steadfast." In the light of it we walk; with the joy of it upon us, we press onward. Rejoicing in it, we hold on unto the end, "more than conquerors through him who hath loved us, and given himself for us." To this glorious hope we are begotten again by the Spirit whom he hath given to us. Our glorious head is in heaven; and all his members, chosen and beloved, shall be there also. This is our unspeakable privilege. We "are come unto Mount Zion."

This is the ruling power of Jesus.

In a *redemption complete in heaven*.
In a *providence governing on earth*.
In a *Spirit in the hearts of his people*.
In a *glorious hope which he has laid up*.

These all, the gospel brings us. To these the Holy Spirit leads us in conversion, when we embrace this gospel.

In living, trusting faith we may sit down at a Saviour's feet, and say with thankfulness, "We are come unto Mount Zion;" to an almighty, ruling Saviour, who will never leave us nor suffer us to leave him. He will hold us by his right hand. He will guide us by his counsel, he will afterwards receive us to his glory.

This is your privilege in the gospel. Take it as your own. Make it the basis of believing prayer. We "are come to Mount Zion." Make it the foundation of thankful praise. Make it the fountain of strength and peace. Make it the element of your Christian walk and warfare. Live and walk as becomes it;—the children of a King. "Ye are come unto Mount Zion," to the royal, triumphant, glorious power of a ruling Saviour. Thy God, O Zion, reigneth forever in love.

The following is the outline of the second of Dr. Tyng's recent series. In successive sermons of this kind, the truth of the whole passage is brought out with rare power and beauty, and the repeated presentation of the great theme, in ever-varying form, tends to impress it durably on the children's minds. The privileges of the youthful Christian are shown under the successive types of the text: 1. Mount Zion. 2. The city of the living God. 3. The heavenly Jerusalem. 4. The innumerable company of angels. 5. The general assembly and church of the first-born, which are written in heaven. 6. God the Judge of all. 7. The spirits of just men made perfect. 8. Jesus, the mediator of the new covenant. 9. The blood of sprinkling, that speaketh better things than that of Abel.

Ye are come . . . unto the city of the living God.

. . . The divine illustrations are as precise as they are full. And when the Spirit describes your Christian privileges as coming to the *city* of the living God, we may consider what the special points of illustration are which are intended by this figure. .... It is that aspect of the present church of God, which the analogy of a city so clearly displays.

I. The church of God on earth is a scene of *great activity*. An earthly city bustles with labor. ..... Everybody must be at work. ..... The church of Jesus, the association of his redeemed, is no place for idleness.

II. ... It is a scene and relation of constant *temptation*. Such is the earthly city always. ..... " Ye are come to the city of the living God." But your present life is yet more completely a life of contest. ..... " Let him that thinketh he standeth take heed lest he fall."

III. A city life is .... also a life of *peculiar usefulness*. .... The objects of personal effort are multiplied .... and the ability of every agent is as much enhanced as the opportunities which call upon him are multiplied. ..... Jesus has called you in his church to a life of positive usefulness.

IV. A city life demands the *most intense effort*. ..... Every profession, living, trade, is on the stretch. ..... No man has a rightful hope of success, but by personal, patient, intelligent efforts. ..... Thus are you called to the city of God ....

V. But a city life is also a life of *great results*. All the great things of earth are accomplished by its cities. ..... And you are brought into the city of the living God, to be a partaker of unspeakable triumphs.

SAMSON'S RIDDLE, OR THE SLAYER SLAIN.

BY THE REV. A. J. GORDON,
Pastor of the Baptist Church, Jamaica Plain, Mass.

Out of the eater came forth meat: and out of the strong came forth sweetness. Judges xiv. 14.

Samson, the strong man of Israel, is journeying to Timnath, and as he is passing a certain vineyard a young lion comes out against him, roaring and gnashing his teeth and saying to himself, no doubt—" What a splendid meal this big man will make me." Samson is unarmed. But he has what is mightier than any human weapon—" The Spirit of the Lord "—resting upon him; and so seizing the lion with his hands, he tears him open as easily as you could tear a sheet of paper : and having done this he goes on his way as if nothing had happened. Passing this way again not long after, he thought he would turn aside and take a look at the carcass of his old enemy; and while he is looking at it he discovers to his surprise that a swarm of bees has taken up its abode inside the body, and that already quite a little store of honey has been collected. So, taking out the honey and eating it, it turns out singularly enough that Samson makes a meal out of the lion, instead of the lion making a meal out of Samson.

Afterwards, when Samson had made his wedding feast, and a large number of friends were present, he made this story of his experience into a riddle, and offered a large prize to any one who would guess it. And this was the riddle : " Out of the eater came forth meat ; and out of the strong came forth sweetness." Now I cannot stop to tell you, children, how the riddle was guessed; you will find this described in the chapter in which the text occurs. I only wish to call your attention to the lessons to be derived from this story.

I. First—*There is a lion lying in wait for all of you.* Wherever you go, he is sure to come out against you. The apostle Peter tells you who he is, and warns you against him. " Your adversary, the *Devil*, as a roaring lion walketh about seeking whom he may devour."

But, children, you will say, " I have never seen this lion or heard him roar; how do I know that he is seeking to destroy me ? " Ah ! but you have seen him : you have heard him roar. For you must remember that he comes to you in a great many different forms.

1. *Anger* is one form he takes. Look at that boy who is fighting. Don't you see the lion rising up within him ? See how he scratches with his finger nails. Isn't that the lion's claws ? See how he grates his teeth. Isn't that the lion's gnashing ? Hear

how he swears, rages, and threatens. Isn't that the lion's roaring? Surely the devil has got this boy completely in his power now. He is "tearing his soul like a lion; he is rending it in pieces."

2. *Falsehood* is another form this lion takes. Here is a boy who is tempted to deceive—to lie to his father. He knows that it is wicked, and that God will be displeased with him; but something seems to rise up within him to make him do it in spite of himself. That is that old lion the Devil. The Bible tells us that "he is a liar and the father of it;" and whenever you are tempted to tell a falsehood, you may be sure that it is the Devil that has come upon you to destroy you.

3. *Dishonesty* is another form that this lion assumes. Have you ever seen a boy trying to steal? How he sneaks and skulks about; how he stealthily watches his chance; how he will lie and deceive and swear in order to accomplish his ends. Is not it very strange that he should do so? Oh, it is that cursed lion—that devil of dishonesty—that does it. David described him long ago—the thief—"He lieth in wait secretly as a lion in his den; he croucheth and humbleth himself; his mouth is full of cursing and fraud." These are only *some* of the forms he assumes to injure and destroy men.

II. The second lesson drawn from this history is this:

You must slay the lion of temptation, or he will slay you. If the lion that besets you more fiercely is *anger*, you must conquer it. When it attacks you, instead of letting it overcome you, you must rend it, and trample it beneath your feet:

Illustration. Looking from my window one day, I saw two boys meet, each of them having a basket of candies and fruit. One was a stout rough looking boy: the other a pale inoffensive lad. As they met, I heard the large boy say, "I'm going to give you a thrashing; you have no business selling apples on my territory," and suiting the action to the word, he struck him a blow that almost felled him to the ground. The pale boy dropped his basket; the fire flashed from his eyes; he grated his teeth and doubled up his fist. "Now," said I to myself, "poor boy the lion is upon you. He is going to overcome you, and make you do the wicked thing of striking back." But no. A moment's struggle, a moment's suspense, and our hero turns about and walks away with not so much as an angry word in reply to his assailant. "Thank God," said I, "he has slain the lion; he has got the victory over his anger."

How often have you felt the temptation to *falsehood* rising within you, when it seemed that something desirable might be attained or something disagreeable avoided by deceiving. Have you always conquered it, or has it many times made you its prey? Have not you sometimes said to yourselves, "Oh it is only a *little lie*. It is not so very bad?" It was only a *young* lion that came out against Samson. But it had teeth, and little lies have teeth. They bite the conscience and devour the soul. The temptation to *dishonesty* is a lion that has destroyed many a young soul. And though you think that he could never harm you, you cannot tell how hard it might be to slay him if he should come upon you suddenly.

Illustration.—Newsboy, walking along the streets of Boston and saying to himself, "Oh, how I wish I was only rich; then I could help my poor sick mother," Finds a pocket-book containing a large sum of money, and the owner's name and residence marked upon it. His struggle with the lion of dishonesty, and his final victory, etc.

III. The third lesson.

Temptation overcome, a source of strength and happiness. "Out of the eater came forth *meat;* and out of the strong came forth *sweetness.*"

The *strength* which one acquires by constant and successful conflict with temptation, illustrated by Van Amburgh's great power, and ability to handle his lions with perfect ease. The *sweetness* extracted from a conquered temptation—the joy of a good conscience, and the sense of God's approval, which are "sweeter than honey and the honeycomb."

CONCLUSION.

How can we successfully overcome temptations?

1. *We must dispatch them immediately,* as soon as they appear

to us. Had Samson stopped long to think about the matter, the lion would probably have killed him. *If we stop to reason with sin it will get the better of us.*

Illustration.—An English gentleman had a tame young lion, which seemed to have become a lamb in gentleness, and was a favorite pet in moments of leisure.

One day falling asleep, his hand hung over the side of his couch. The lion came to his side, and commenced licking the hand. Soon the file-like surface of the animal's tongue wore off the cuticle and brought blood to the surface. The sleeper was disturbed, and moved his hand, when a savage growl startled him from his dreaming half-consciousness, to realize the terrible fact that the pet *was a lion* after all. With great self-possession, with the other hand he drew carefully from the pillow a revolver, and shot his pet through the head. It was no trivial sacrifice to his feelings, but a moment's delay might have cost him his life.

2. *We must depend upon God's help, and look to him in prayer for his assistance in resisting sin.* Samson slew the lion, not in his own strength, but because "the Spirit of the Lord came mightily upon him." We can only overcome sin by the aid of God's Spirit, &c.

AGAINST TEMPTATION.

BY THE REV. R. T. ROBINSON,
Pastor of the Congregational Church, Winchester, Mass.

. *And lead us not into temptation.* Matt. vi. 13.

What is the text a part of? *The Lord's Prayer.* How many of you, children, are accustomed to say the Lord's Prayer every morning and evening? Hold up your hands. But stop a moment. Let me divide the question. How many of you say the Lord's Prayer at night when you go to bed? Nearly all. How many remember to say it in the morning? Not so many. .... If you study the Lord's Prayer, you will see that, proper as it is at all times, it is better suited to the morning than to the evening. What do we ask of God in this prayer, for ourselves more particularly? "Give us this day our daily bread." That evidently was meant to be said in the morning. We ask for daily bread,—the bread we hope to receive, and which is needful for us through the day. So, too, we pray, "And lead us not into temptation." Now is not that the prayer we should offer in the morning? We go forth to the duties or the pleasures of the day, not knowing what may happen to us, what even an hour may bring forth; how appropriate and beautiful is it that we look up and say, "And lead us not into temptation."

But this prayer should be in our hearts and on our lips, not simply in the morning, but at all times. We should continually say, as we go out, and as we come in, " Lead us not into temptation." ....

In this discourse, I propose to give two or three reasons why all, and children especially, should offer this prayer.

I. And first, because *we are so liable to fall into temptation.* Oh, how easy it is to sin against God! We live in a sinful world. There is sin all around us, and, what is much worse, there is sin in our own hearts. You know how easy it is for the brooks and rivers to run into the sea. They cannot help it, we say. Only let them alone and they are sure to find their way there. So there is in our hearts a constant tendency or proneness to that which is wrong. The current of our thoughts and actions sets in that direction. It is "easy as lying" has passed into a proverb. You have seen a horse-shoe magnet, perhaps. It is a small bar of iron bent into the form of a horse-shoe, and it has this remarkable quality, it attracts other pieces of iron which are brought near to it, and holds them fast. Well, the world is a great magnet, and there is that in our hearts which it attracts, so that we are all the time inclined to do evil. ....

All men and women are pretty much alike in this respect. They are all sinners and prone to sin. So is it with you and me. We are "prone to sin," the Bible says, "as the sparks fly upward." You see some men who are very wicked. They drink and gamble and swear. They break the Sabbath, and do almost everything else that God has commanded men not to do. You shrink from them. You loathe them, and well you may. You have been in the state-prison, perhaps. There are men there who have committed murder and highway robbery; men who have broken into houses in the night time; men who have set buildings on fire; who have forged notes and passed counterfeit money. And there they are—shut out from all the world, for the crimes which they have committed. You would not like to associate with such men. You would think it dreadful if you were obliged to live with them. But did you ever think that these men, steeped to the lips in crime, were once little children like you; that they had each a father and mother, and brothers and sisters, perhaps, who loved them? And then they were comparatively innocent and happy. What makes them to differ from you now? Nothing but the goodness and mercy of God, which have kept you thus far, when tempted, from open sin. If God should leave you to yourselves, you would become just as bad as they. The sweetest child might become the most hardened and blood-thirsty ruffian. How much reason, then, have you to pray continually, "And lead us not into temptation."

II. Another reason why we should offer the prayer of the text is, because *one sin leads to another.* I said it was easy to sin; but how much easier is it to commit a second sin when one has already been committed. Sin is like a chain. Each link is connected with, and draws after it, many others. . . . . Do you know, children, how the suspension bridge below Niagara Falls was built? Let me tell you. It is a light, airy structure to look at, but weighs some seventy-five tons. Over it, heavily loaded cars pass and repass every day. How were these huge, wire cables, each of them as big round as a man's arm, carried across the stream? The span is some seven hundred and fifty feet. The height of the bridge above the water is two hundred and thirty-eight feet,—higher than Bunker Hill monument, higher than the highest of our church steeples. How deep the water is below has never been ascertained. The current is so swift, and the

THE CHILDREN'S PREACHING SERVICE.

pressure of the water between the banks so great, that the lead is thrown to the surface before it reaches the bottom. Now, how were these cables on which the bridge is suspended stretched across this rushing, foaming flood? No boat could cross, of course. I will tell you how it was done. A boy's kite was sent up on one side of the river, and carried by the wind across to the other. There it was suffered to fall. To the string of the kite was attached a cord, and to the cord a rope. Thus a communication was established, and a single cable suspended. On this the daring inventor, in his iron basket, crossed and recrossed, until all the wires were stretched from town to town and the whole structure was complete. So a single sin, even a small sin, may draw after it the most weighty consequences. The only safety is in avoiding, if possible, the *first* sin. It is the first false step, in many cases, that ruins..... Beware, then, children, of the first sin, the first oath, the first cigar, the first glass of strong drink, the first petty dishonesty. If tempted, resist, and call on God to help you resist. Say, "No! I am not going to enter upon that path. I know where it leads. It leads down to death." *Never parley with temptation.* What do I mean by parleying with temptation? I mean stopping to consider whether you will or will not do that which you know to be wrong. You are passing along the road some day, and you see some very tempting fruit just over the fence. You wonder if the owner would miss a few pears or a few peaches, whatever the fruit may be. Don't stop to consider the matter. Run right away. Get out of sight of the fruit as quickly as possible, and don't go round that way again till you know it has all been gathered. Remember, the sight of the eyes leads often to the sin of the heart, and the sin of the heart breaks out into the most flagrant and high-handed iniquities. The various steps in a course of crime have often been detailed. They do not always follow each other in the same order, but they all lead to the same result.

"Crimes lead to crimes and link so straight,
What first was accident, at last is fate."

III. But there is still another reason why we should offer the prayer of the text, "Lead us not into temptation," and that is, *the habit of sin once formed, it is all but impossible to break off from it.* Who can describe the power of habit. "Can the Ethiopian change his skin or the leopard his spots," says the prophet Jeremiah, "then may ye also do good that are accustomed to do evil." I have spoken of sin as a chain. It is a chain that we forge day by day, little thinking to what use it will finally be put. Spurgeon, in one of his sermons, tells of a certain tyrant who ordered one of his subjects, a blacksmith by trade, to make him a chain of a given length. The man made the chain and brought it, but was told to go and make it twice as long, though he received no wages all the while he was at work. Again he brought the chain, and again was told to make it twice as long; and so on, until finally the cruel and wicked monarch said to his attendants, "Take it, and bind him hand and foot with that chain, and cast him into a furnace of fire." Who is the tyrant in this case that orders the chain to be made? *The devil!* Yes, it is the devil. And who makes the chain? *We make it.* And what are the links of the chain? *Our sins.* Very good. Remember, then, every time you commit a sin you add one more link to the chain which will be used when the King shall say to his servants, "Bind him hand and foot, and cast him into outer darkness. There shall be weeping and gnashing of teeth."

We sin, oftentimes, thoughtlessly. We are so accustomed to do that which is wrong, it makes no impression upon our minds, and we straightway forget all about it. In this way the habit of sin is formed. We acquire a facility for wrong-doing. It is like attempting to walk down a steep hill. Did you ever try that, boys? You begin to walk very slowly; but before you are half way down you break into a run, and then there is no such thing as stopping.

An old stage-driver lay dying. His brother "whips" came in to see him, and asked how he was. His reply, as he shook his head, was, "On the down grade, and can't reach the brakes." You know what the brakes are on a railroad car. They stop the train, if put on while the cars are in motion. You are not so familiar with stage-coaches. But some of you may have been up among the mountains, or back in the country, where stage-coaches are still used, and noticed the long handle, with a little step attached, on which the driver puts his foot when going down a steep hill. That is the brake. But what if the driver could not reach it when the stage was under full headway! I once crossed the Alleghany mountains, from Cumberland to Wheeling, in a stage-coach. We started just at night, and rode all night and all the next day. It was in the month of March, and on the mountains it was intensely cold. I was deathly sick inside the coach, and obliged to ride, cold and rough as it was, outside with the driver on the box. He was a drunken, reckless, miserable fellow to have the charge of so many precious lives, for the stage was full of passengers. The grades, ascending and descending, were fearful. It almost made my heart stop beating as I looked down into the black and seemingly bottomless gulfs, now on this side, now on that, into some one of which we must have been plunged, horses, passengers, and all, but for the action of the brake, which the driver, drunk as he was, managed with his foot. Without some such experience as that, I should not have realized the awful sadness of the remark I have quoted —the remark of the old stage-driver as he lay dying, "*On the down grade, and can't reach the brakes.*" Yes, it is indeed fearful, when one feels that he is going swift to destruction, and yet has no power to stop. May God save you, dear children, from any such painful and bitter experience.

I have thus given you three reasons why you should offer the prayer, daily and continually, "And lead us not into temptation." Can you remember and repeat them? What are they?

First, because we are so liable to fall into temptation.

Secondly, because the commission of one sin leads on to another.

And, lastly, because the habit of sin once formed, it is all but impossible to break off from it.

I have only one thing more to say in conclusion. *It is no use to pray,* "*Lead us not into temptation,*" *and then walk straight into it.* Some people do this—they pray to be kept from sin, and then go where they are almost sure to fall into it. Is this consistent? Is it right? It certainly is not. Keep out of the way of temptation, then, children, while you pray to be delivered from it. Give it a wide berth, as the sailors say. Do not go where you will be likely to meet those who would lead you into sin. " Enter not into the path of the wicked, and go not in the way of evil men. Avoid it, pass not by it, turn from it and pass away." Commit that passage of Scripture to memory, and keep it always in mind. Think of it when you are tempted to sin. " How do you manage to get out of scrapes?" one boy said to another. " I never get into them," was the answer. That is the only way of safety. " He that walketh uprightly walketh surely." Lift up your heart to God, and ask Him who guides the stars in their courses, and at the same time watches the sparrow's fall, to keep you; adding always to your prayer for daily bread the petition, " And lead us not into temptation."

TOTAL DEPRAVITY.

BY THE REV. ALFRED TAYLOR,
Secretary of the Pennsylvania S. S. Teachers' Association.

[" *Can the blackboard be used to illustrate doctrinal truth?*" is a question often asked. Let us try to answer the question by a sermon on a subject which some of us are apt to omit, in the instruction of our children.]

There is none that doeth good, no, not one. Psalm xiv. 3.

Perhaps you would like it a great deal better, my dear boys and girls, if I would tell you that you are all very good and very beautiful, and that you are all so sure of going to heaven, that you need give yourselves no concern about it. It would be a delightful thing if we could say that we have never sinned. Is there one of you, here, that can say that? Not one..... Open your Bibles to I. John i. 8; and you find, "if we say that we have no sin, we deceive ourselves, and the truth is not in us."

I am not only going to tell you about your wickedness. I want to tell you about the grace of God..... While I tell you of sin and ruin, I want to tell you, too, of grace and salvation. We are full of sin. But the grace of God is greater than our sin. We are in danger of being lost forever. But the salvation offered us by our Lord Jesus Christ is so rich and full that it takes hold of us, in the depth of our danger, and keeps us for eternal life.

When we talk of our sinful nature, we use the word "*Depravity.*" Let us put that word on the blackboard, so as to remember it. There are some people who stick to it, that there is some little good in them..... Turn to the fifty-first Psalm, and let any boy or girl who first finds it, read the fifth verse. Quick, now, for time is precious! There! you see David had a different view of the matter. He confessed his entire sinfulness, his *total* depravity. Suppose we write that word "*Total*," on the blackboard. Now turn to the account of the Pharisee and the publican in the eighteenth chapter of Luke. Read the thirteenth verse; you, my little man with the bright eyes. Very good, sir, now, why was it that the publican expected God to hear him, and save him? Not because he told how good he was; but because he confessed he was, out and out, a sinner.

Children, we are all sinners, by nature..... Not only sinners on the outside. But through and through. And we need God's grace, through and through, to cleanse us. Let us try to see how.

Here is a dirty black bottle. What do you think it has had in it? Ink. Yes, no mistake about that. Black and dirty enough, is it not? Outside and inside, pretty much alike..... Now let us clean the outside of it. Here is a basin of water and a towel. Rub hard, for the bottle is very dirty, and the dirt does not come off very easily. There it goes, though; now look at the bottle. Clean, isn't it? What? Hold it up to the light, and let us see. Oh! no, it isn't clean at all, when you look through it..... If we want that bottle to be *clean*, we must wash it inside and outside. Now open your Bibles again. Read what Jesus said to the hypocrites, in Matthew xxiii. 27. He told them they were like whited sepulchres, very nice and white, outside; but inside, full of uncleanness. Just so with our hearts. We need to have them washed *entirely*, we are so sinful.

We can wash a dirty bottle with water. For the cleansing of a sinful soul, we need something else. Now let us *all* open our Bibles, and we will *all* read, in concert, a very precious passage. Right alongside of the first passage we looked at, which told us that we are all sinners. (I. John i. 7.) "The blood of Jesus Christ his Son cleanseth us from all sin." Then, if there is something that will clean away *all* our sin, there is no use of trying to keep back any of it from God. We will go to him with the whole guilty load of it, as the publican did, and ask him to be merciful to us, and wash it all away in the blood of his dear Son Jesus Christ. And he will do it, too. . . . .

Let us . . . . note down a few more thoughts about what "total depravity" is.

Turn to what Jeremiah told the Jews, nearly twenty-five hundred years ago. (Jer. xvii. 9.) "The heart of man is deceitful above all things, and desperately wicked." As the human heart is now the same as it was then, we will put down these two ideas on the board. There they are, "*Deceitful*," "*Wicked*." . . . . Read the eighteenth verse of the first chapter of Isaiah. Oh! what a horrible condition the human heart is in, if it is like that! Let us put down one word which will express it. What was the matter with the ink bottle we had, a while ago? *Unclean*, was it not? Well, we will use that word. Now we have it on the board. What then, are we, when we are "totally depraved?" We are "deceitful," "wicked," and "unclean."

But there is one strange thing about this depravity. People think themselves so good. . . . . Now let us see what Paul, who knew all about it, said to the Romans. (Rom. vii. 17, 18.) First he says "sin dwelleth in me." Then he goes on to say, not how good he was, but "I know that in me dwelleth no good thing." We will put that idea on the board. "*Nothing Good*." . . . .

Now turn to Paul's letter to the Ephesians, and we find. . . . .

that when we were (chap. ii. 1) "dead in trespasses and sins," we were (v. 12) "strangers from the covenants of promise, having no hope, and without God in the world." Let us put that idea all in one word, as far as we can. "*Helpless.*" We might say "hopeless;" but when we read (v. 13) about how we are "brought nigh by the blood of Christ," it does not look as if we are without hope, by a great deal. . . . .

Now we have bad things enough to look at, have we not? Isn't there a bright side to it? Yes, thank God! a glorious, beautiful, bright side it is, too!

(Here is the way our blackboard looks, thus far)

```
┌─────────────────────────────────────────────┐
│                                             │
│           Total     Depravity               │
│                                             │
│   Deceitful Wicked     Unclean              │
│                                             │
│                   Nothing Good              │
│                                             │
│   Helpless                                  │
│                                             │
└─────────────────────────────────────────────┘
```

Now for the bright side. . . . . Turn to Isaiah xlv. 22, and read it. "Look unto me, and be ye saved, all the ends of the earth!" Unto whom? "I am God, and there is none else!" "SAVED." We will put that down, for we need to be saved. Saved through Jesus, are we not? Yes, for when we turn to Peter's echo of Isaiah, we read, (Acts iv. 12) "there is none other name under heaven, whereby we may be saved." So we write, "THROUGH JESUS CHRIST."

If we are deceitfully wicked, if our poor hearts are all unclean with sin, we certainly cannot trust to our own righteousness. But there Jesus comes to help us. His righteousness is our plea, as we go before God our Father. His merit is our dependence, "*merit*" is a more convenient word than *righteousness*, so we will write on the board, "JESUS' MERIT."

"Nothing good" in myself? Then some one else must pay the price of my pardon. Open your Bibles again. Paul writes to Timothy, (I. Tim. ii. 5, 6,) that "the man Christ Jesus gave himself a ransom for all." "RANSOMED," then, let us write. And what is the price of our ransom? "Ye are bought with a price," says Paul, (I. Cor. vi. 20,) and Peter follows it up by saying, (I. Peter i. 19,) that the price paid is "the precious blood of Christ." Our "SAVIOUR'S BLOOD" we may write down as the price paid for our rescue from everlasting ruin.

But just another thought, before we stop. We have said we are "*helpless.*" Then we need help..... We need mercy and pardon. What better can we do than as the publican did? Let us come to God and ask his mercy..... We have for a Saviour one who is indeed "mighty to save." With the publican, we will pray,

"O GOD, BE MERCIFUL TO ME!"

Now let us look at our blackboard, and see how beautifully the bright things of God's word lighten up the dark things of our sinful nature.

```
            Total    Depravity
    THROUGH JESUS CHRIST              SAVED
    Deceitful Wicked      Unclean
            JESUS' MERIT
                         Nothing Good
        RANSOMED            SAVIOUR'S BLOOD
    Helpless
    O GOD, BE MERCIFUL TO ME!
```

There we have the leading thoughts of our little sermon. How shall we further impress them on our minds?.... We will *sing* them. What! sing "*total depravity?*" Yes. Or, rather, we will sing the grace of God, that rescues us from it. Sing away, then, children. But first let us fill up the gaps, so that it will sing.

How is it, when we are "totally depraved?" Is it in a state of nature, or a state of grace? "Nature?" Yes. Then we will make the first line read:

"*By nature, totally depraved.*"

But what kind of a salvation is it that Jesus works out for us? It is no half way work. He does not partly save us, and then leave us to ourselves. . . . . No; open your Bibles again; (for if we cannot find it in God's word, there is no use of talking about it). Paul tells us, (Col. ii. 10,) "Ye are complete in him." Then our salvation is a *full* salvation; and we will make our second line read:

"*Through Jesus Christ I'm fully saved.*"

The next line we have all ready to sing, and we will go on, to see just where the righteousness of Christ comes in to help us. It is our sole dependence. We can put our whole trust in it. Then we will sing:

"*On Jesus' merit, let me lean.*"

"Nothing good?" Where? In my own sinful heart. But the goodness of my Saviour, and the worth of his precious blood, are all sufficient. Therefore,

"*Though in myself there's nothing good,
I'm ransomed by my Saviour's blood.*"

And now we see our way right to the cross of Jesus. Helpless, in ourselves, to whom shall we look for the help we need? "I have laid help on one that is mighty to save." Therefore,

"*Helpless, myself, I look to Thee.
O God, be merciful to me!*"

And now, with glad hearts and full voices, let us sing it. . . . . And let us praise God that though we are so full of sin, his grace can reach us, his blood can cleanse us, his spirit can make us holy, till, through the righteousness of Christ, we shall be admitted to reign with him in everlasting glory.

"*There is none that doeth good, no, not one.*" Psalm xiv. 3.

By *nature* **Totally Depraved**,
THROUGH JESUS CHRIST *I'm fully* SAVED.
Deceitful, Wicked, *and* **Unclean,**
On JESUS' MERIT *let me lean.*
Though in myself there's **Nothing Good,**
I'm RANSOMED *with my* SAVIOUR'S BLOOD.
Helpless, *myself, I look to Thee;—*
O GOD, BE MERCIFUL TO ME!

A CHILDREN'S SERVICE.

BY THE REV. J. H. VINCENT,

Editor of the Sunday School Journal, of the M. E. Church.

The following ticket having been issued a week or two in advance, my congregation was large, carefully seated and generally supplied with Bibles, blank-books and pencils.

REV. J. H. VINCENT'S

LECTURE

TO SUNDAY SCHOOL SCHOLARS.

ADMIT THE BEARER.

THE CHILDREN'S PREACHING SERVICE. 301

OPPOSITE SIDE.

> My Dear Friend:
> 1. This ticket is forwarded to you with the expectation that you will attend the lecture, be present in time, and behave with propriety.
> 2. Please bring with you a Bible, a small blank-book, or sheet of paper and a lead pencil. Copy all that is placed on the blackboard.
>
> Yours truly,
> J. H. VINCENT.

After a brief opening service, I placed my text on the blackboard:

M. H. P. S. P. L. L. S.

Attention was fixed, and curiosity excited. I drew a rough outline of Egypt and the Sinaitic peninsula, on the board, indicating the situation of Zoan, Memphis, Suez, Sinai, and the Red and Dead Seas. This occupied less than three minutes.

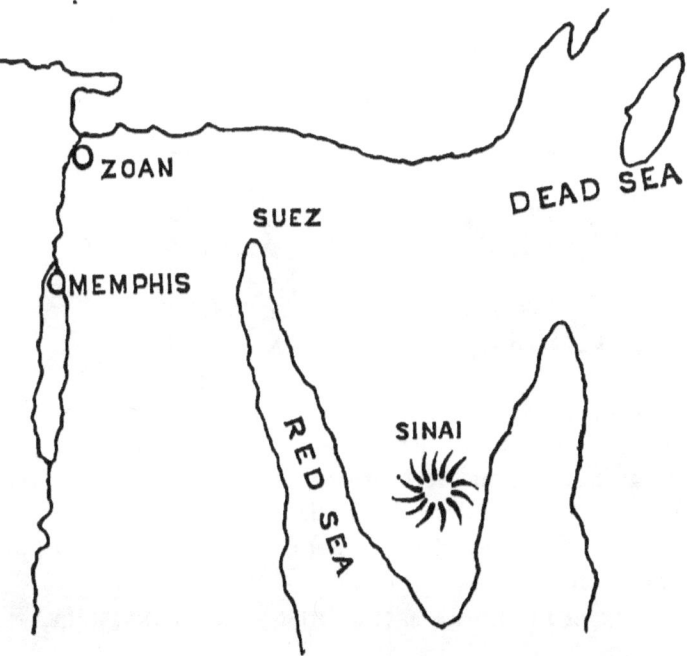

Calling upon all who had Bibles to hold them up as high as possible, the "Swords of the Spirit," in the uplifted hands of the children and youth, furnished an opportunity for alluding to the use of Bibles in the public congregation.

The following scripture was read by the children: Exod. ii. 5-10, and the first three letters of the text found to stand for Moses the Hebrew Prince. We then read in concert Exod. ii. 15-21, about the Shepherd; Exod. v. 1-9 about the Prophet; Exod. xiii. 17-22, about the Leader; Exod. xix. 16-25, xx. 1-21, (we read only parts of this) about the Lawgiver; and Deut. xxxiv. 5-8 and Matt. xvii. 1-5 about the Saint. The initials were arranged differently on the other side of the board; the above-named titles spelled out, and I offered some remarks upon some of the features of Moses' character, adding the descriptive terms as I went on, until the board presented the following arrangement:

Meek **M**oses
Humble **H**ebrew
Pious **P**rince
Self-sacrificing **S**hepherd

Persevering **P**rophet
Laborious **L**eader
Loving **L**awgiver
Sincere **S**aint

This was read over as a sort of historic statement by the congregation. The words were gradually erased, until the lesson was transferred from the board to the minds of the scholars. I closed with an anecdote illustrating faith in God, and called attention to the fact stated by Paul concerning Moses (placing it on the board):

HE ENDURED AS SEEING HIM WHO IS INVISIBLE.

TASTING GOD'S GOODNESS.

BY THE REV. H. D. GANSE,

Pastor of the North-west Reformed Church, New York.

Oh, taste and see that the Lord is good. Psalms xxxiv. 8.

This Psalm was written by King David. If you read it through, you will see that it speaks of great fears and troubles in which David had been. But it also tells how God had "delivered him out of them all." Now, in this verse, David takes it for granted that other persons have their fears and troubles too; and he is trying to persuade them to do just as he had done; that is, to go to God for help. These words were written very long ago—long before Christ was born; long before Daniel or Isaiah was born. It is nearly three thousand years since they were written. And I cannot tell you what multitudes of people from that time to this have been hearing and obeying them. Now it is your turn to obey them, dear children; and David is saying to you, "Oh, taste and see that the Lord is good."

Let us all look carefully at this text, then, and see what it means. It is speaking about something which David had tasted and seen for himself, and which he wished other people to taste and see for themselves.

I. *What was it that David had "tasted and seen?"* Let us see whether it is worth our while to taste it too. He had tasted and seen "*that the Lord is good.*"

But does not everybody know that? Yes, we know it partly; we know it because the Bible says so; and we know it by God's kind acts toward us and toward others. It is God that makes the sun to shine, and the rain to fall. God gives us food and friends. Were you ever sick? and was it not God who made you well? There would be no happiness in the world if God did not give it; no, nor in heaven, either. God's goodness is like the sun; all the light comes from it.

But David meant a great deal more than that. Hear the whole verse. "Oh, taste and see that the Lord is good. Blessed is the man that trusteth in him." No one can know how good God is until he *trusts* in him. Suppose one of your schoolfellows should say to you, "Your mother is good." "Yes," you would say, "she *is* good; she is a great deal better than *you* know. If you were her *child*, and she took care of you and tended you as she tended me when I was sick, then you'd know how good she is." Just so one must be God's child, or he cannot know how good *he* is. The greatest part of God's goodness most men do not understand at all. He gave his dear Son to die to save them. They do not care about that. He has given the Holy Ghost to change their wicked hearts and make them holy. They do not care about that.

But some people *do*. When the Saviour promises to wash away all their sins, and to give them new hearts, they thank him and believe him, and try to serve him; and then God, for Jesus' sake, becomes their Father. They cannot see him, indeed, as we see our parents; but they can see him with their souls,—I mean God makes them sure that he is with them and loves them. They know that they have done many things that are wrong, but God makes them feel that he has forgiven them. They know that they are very weak, and in great danger of doing wrong again. But God promises to help them to do right, and to do good; and he does help them. They may have troubles; but God comforts them, and makes them know that he loves them now, and that by-and-by he will take them where their troubles will all be over. So these Christians live with God every day, almost as you live with your father and mother; and they feel sure that they will live with him and Jesus forever in heaven. Is not that enough to make any one happy? There are thousands of people happy in that way all around you; and that is the happiness or blessedness which this verse speaks of. "Blessed is the man that trusteth in him." That means, "Very, very happy and safe is every man that has God for his father, and feels toward him and obeys him like a loving child. David knew all about such happiness as this; and it was in that way that he tasted that the Lord is good.

Oh, how foolish those people are who do not try to know all about God's goodness. I have seen poor boys in the street pick up pieces of orange peel and eat them. But what would you think of a boy who with a whole orange in his hand, would eat the skin and throw all the rest away. How could you help saying, "Why don't you eat the best?" Now there are thousands of people who never try to get the best part of God's goodness. They try to have a good home, and health, and riches, and good clothes, and good food. But what are such things when you compare them with peace in your heart; with knowing that God loves you; with the pleasure of working with Christ in doing good; and with the sure hope of heaven. Let us get the *best part* of God's love, children. That is the only part that will last. For unless we become God's children, the more kindness he shows us, the more will he punish us for insulting his kindness. All this will help us to understand—

II. The next thing we see in this text; and that is the *anxiety which David felt* that everybody else should know as much about God's goodness as he did. For he said, not to one man, nor to a few men, but to every body that should ever hear his words, "Oh, taste and see that the Lord is good." Do you wonder that he cared so much about other people's happiness? He would not have been a good man if he had cared any less.

There is a story in the book of Genesis about a poor woman who was driven out with her child, into the desert, where they were almost dying with thirst. But God sent an angel to show her a spring. Do you think she went and drank the water herself, and gave none to her child? No: but as soon as she came where the water was, she filled a bottle with it, and carried it back to her boy. No wonder that Hagar did this to Ishmael, for he was her own child. But what if she had never seen him before, and yet knew that he was there and was dying for water, could she help telling him where it could be found?

When the wicked Israelites had been bitten by the fiery serpents, and were suffering and dying all through the camp, you know God commanded Moses to lift up the image of a serpent, and promised to heal all those who would look at it. Suppose one of the wounded men had looked at it, and been healed. Then he would leap up from the ground all strong and glad. Suppose then that he saw lying right before him a poor stranger out of another tribe almost dead, and with his face turned away from the serpent on the pole, what would he do? He would tenderly take that dying man's head in both of his hands; he would turn it toward the brazen serpent; he would point right at it and say "See there! see there! Look at that! It will cure you." That is the way real kindness always does. When we have anything that makes us really happy, if we are kind, we cannot keep it to ourselves. It makes us all the happier when some one else who needs it has a part of it. And that is the reason why David wrote this text. He had found something better than water, better than health; he had found *God's goodness.* Why should he enjoy that goodness all alone? He could not. He *could* not keep it all for himself, even if he tried. The goodness of God is like the ocean. David and Isaiah and Paul and John and all the saints that ever lived could have it for themselves; and yet there would be enough for you and for me and for all the world besides. All Christians know this, and it makes them glad to know it; and so they all join with David in begging us to "taste and see that the Lord is good." Did you ever think of that? There is not a Christian on earth that does not wish *you* to be a Christian. Some of them, like your mother and your Sunday-school teachers, have told you so; and you know that they often speak your name to God, and pray that he would teach you to love him. But there are thousands and thousands of Christians who do not know you; and yet if they *could* know that there was just such a boy or girl as you, there is not one of them that would not wish with all his heart that you might be a Christian. Now listen and it almost seems as if from this church, and from every church, and from every country, yes, and from heaven, too, all the blessed, happy people that love God were saying to you. " *Oh taste and* see that the Lord is good. We have tried it, and we know. Oh taste and see that the Lord is good."

Now, when they say this to you, they show you—

III. The *way* in which any one can get this goodness for himself. It is by *tasting* it.

Let us see, then, what we do when we taste anything. Suppose you wish to taste an orange or a peach, can you do it by hearing about it, or by feeling of it, or by looking at it? You put it in your mouth, and you eat it. You may call the orange yours, while you only have it in your hand. But when you eat it—then, I guess, it's yours in earnest. Now David speaks here as though we could almost take God's goodness into our lips and taste it. Of course we can't do that; but we can take it into our hearts, and taste it there. When a mother has been away all day, and comes home in the evening and takes up her little boy in her lap, and puts her arms around him, and presses him close to her, does not the little child like that? doesn't he *feel* his happiness, as much as if he really could taste it with his lips? Now we see what this text means. It is that we can't know anything about the best part of God's goodness unless we take it right into our hearts as a little child does its mother's love. He does not only think about it, and wish for it, and talk about it, but he just has it. He loves his mother, and she loves him. So when we are Christians, we love God and he loves us, and we take his love into our hearts and taste it.

But, now, is not that something very hard to do! No; for if it was, the Bible would not call it *tasting*. Tasting isn't hard. For, see:

If I ask you to taste anything, it must be *right by you*. While we are here in the church to-day, there are bananas and cocoanuts growing in the West Indies; and there are some bright red apples still hanging on the trees in the country. What if I should ask you to taste *them?* How could you? But if I brought an apple or banana in my hand, and gave it to you and said, "taste it," then I'm sure it would be easy for you to do it. Now you see again what this text means. It means that God and his goodness are not a great way off; so that you will have to go to them, or to wait till they come to you. If it were not for the blessed Saviour, they would be far away—so far that we could never reach them. But Christ has brought salvation to us. And now God is *here;* his love is here; Jesus is here; his Holy Spirit is here—just as near to you as your bread is when you sit down at the table; nearer, too, for you have to take your bread and lift it to your lips. But God comes right home to your heart. His Spirit is now in your bosom, urging you to love God and to give yourself to Christ. And it is because this goodness of God is so near you that we ask you to *taste* it.

But this text means still more than that. For God's goodness might be very near, and yet it might not be for you. I might bring you some delicious fruit, and ask you to pay me for it before you touched it. Then what if you had no money? What good would the fruit do you? Or I might bring you fruit all sealed up in a thick tough husk, that you could not tear open. How could you taste that? But if I bring you a bunch of ripe grapes, and hold them right against your lips, and say, "There, taste them," then you have nothing to pay, and nothing to do, but only to eat them. Would not that be the simplest and easiest thing in the world? It would indeed, because you would be sure to like them. So when this text bids you to taste of God's goodness, it means not only that his goodness is near, but that it is all for *you*, and that you may have it this moment if you only want it.

Now you hardly believe this; but you think you must do something to pay for God's goodness, or to earn it before you can have it. How *can* you pay him for it. Do you pay God for the sun and the light, before you use it to walk by? Do you pay God for water, before you drink it? Do you pay your father and mother for your clothes before you wear them? They *give* them to you. And God *gives* us pardon, and gives us a new heart, and gives us his love. We never can deserve these things. Jesus deserves them for us, and brings them to us.

And so they are all here, and ready; and any one may have them that wants them.

Ah! there is all the difficulty. Can I get you to taste what you don't like? And would you really like to have a new heart, that will love God, and do everything to please him,—a heart willing to take trouble to do right, and unwilling to do wrong even when it is very pleasant? Do you wish to begin right away to be God's child, and never to leave him or to offend him again? What do you say to that question? Some of you say, "I am not sure that I want that now. I don't think I do." Well, that is the whole reason why you do not taste God's goodness. For I tell you again it is all here, and all ready, and ready for you, but you will not have it.

But some of you, I hope, are ready to say, "Oh! yes, that is just what I want. I want to be forgiven, and I want to be a Christian. I wish God to be my Father, and to make me his holy, happy child. I am willing to obey him now, and to believe him, and to love him now, if he only will take me."—He *will* take you. He *does* take you. All the world could not persuade him not to love you, if you really wish to love him. Believe it, and be sure of it. Don't stop and wonder whether that can be so. Believe that God, for Jesus' sake, loves you, and pardons you, and will keep you; and *act* as though you believed it. Go right on and do right, to please him; and be sure that it does please him. When you do wrong, be sorry for it, and ask God, for Jesus' sake, to forgive you; and try to do better. And do all that, not to *make* God love you; but because you know he *does* love you. Are you almost determined to do so? Then, it is the Holy Spirit that is helping you. Now let him lead you right on; and say in your heart, "I take God for my Father and Jesus for my Saviour, *now*."

And that is the way to "taste and to see that the Lord is good."

If you do this you will never be sorry for it. But you will have more and more comfort the longer you live. For notice once more what this text says. If you "taste" you will "*see*"—you will know and be sure—"that the Lord is good." The best way to find out about anything is to try it; and if it is very good you will know about it right away. We often speak about "milk and honey." They are both good and both sweet. Yet if you tasted only a drop of milk, you could hardly tell it from a drop of water. But if you tasted a drop of honey, could you think *that* was water? So there are many things which we expect to make us happy. Yet they do not make us very happy after all. But if we taste of God's goodness, and know that he loves us, there is nothing else like that. When he says to you, "Thy sins are forgiven thee;" isn't that *good?* When he helps you do right, and promises "I will never leave thee nor forsake thee," isn't that good? When he makes you a comfort to your friends, and shows you how to lead others to the Saviour; isn't that good? Never think that if you become a Christian you will have a gloomy life here, and have to wait and make up for it in heaven. A man who loves God cannot be unhappy; and the more he loves him the happier he will be. So as long as you live you will still be "tasting and seeing that the Lord is good."

Yet there is a great difference between *tasting* and *feasting*. God will let you taste of his goodness even here on earth. But he will give you a feast of his goodness forever in heaven.

Now, my dear children, do you know what I have been preaching to you! It is this: That all those who have tasted the love of God and of Christ know that it is better than all the world beside, and that no one can be saved without it; that we all wish you to have it and be happy with it; that we know it is near you, and ready for you, and that if you really wish for it you can have it to-day—this moment—and forever.

But do not think that we say this of ourselves. David spoke in this text only what God taught him to speak. It is God, then, who loves you ten thousand times more than we can—it is Christ who died on the cross to save you, who now offers to you his own precious love and entreats you; "Oh taste and see that the Lord is good."

THE YOUNG FOLLOWER OF CHRIST.

BY THE REV. F. D. HUNTINGTON, D.D.,
Rector of Emmanuel (Episcopal) Church, Boston.

Without forgetting the rest of my congregation, I mean to speak this afternoon especially to the younger part of it—not to the very youngest, perhaps, but to those that are old enough to follow along through a sermon and attend to it.

. . . .

We will have for our text—the first part of the fifth chapter of St. Paul's epistle sent to the Ephesians,—that is, to the Christians of his day who lived at Ephesus, a city in Asia. The Apostle's words are these:

"*Be ye, therefore, followers of God, as dear children, and walk in love, as Christ also hath loved us, and hath given himself for us.*"

What is the first thing to be thought of when you hear these words? It is the word "therefore:" "Be ye, *therefore*, followers of God." When any one says or writes "therefore," it shows that something goes before, and that, to understand it, you ought to go back and look at that. So, looking back to what goes just before this text, we find it is this:

"Let all bitterness, and wrath, and anger, and clamor, and evil-speaking, be put away from you, with all malice: And be ye kind one to another, tender-hearted, forgiving one another, even as God for Christ's sake hath forgiven you."

Everybody can understand that. . . . . Those Ephesians quarreled; and so do men and nations still. Whenever you have asked God in your prayers, here at church, or in your chamber, to forgive your sins, and have felt what you said, God has forgiven you. He has promised that he always will. And he forgives you, he says, for Christ's sake: that is, because Christ has died to bring you out of the punishment of your sins. . . . . Now, then, if God is so willing to forgive us, what ought we to do to each other? Remember that you and I look far worse in his sight than any of our fellow-creatures do in our sight..... If you could see your own heart and life just as God sees it,—he is so much holier and higher than we are,—you would confess that God sees more bad things in you than you can see in the worst people you know. You will feel, then, I am sure, just as the Apostle does, that you ought to forgive everybody, as God, for Christ's sake, hath forgiven you.

But the Apostle says more than that. He says, *therefore*,— that is, for the same reason,—you ought to be "followers of God" in all respects. You ought to be Christians in earnest; .... Christians at home, Christians at school, Christians in company, Christians at church, ... in your heart, and before the world.....

Then you will be ready not only to forgive those that injure you, but to govern and deny yourself, to keep down your temper and appetite, to watch your tongue, ... and to do all other things that a Christian ought to do. The *reason* is, that Christ has loved you, and given himself for you, an offering, or a sacrifice. The *motive* is, that you may please and honor him who has done so much for you..... That is what the "therefore" means. That is what it is to be "followers of God as dear children." .... Now if we act as the Apostle says here, if we "walk in love," ... this grand and glorious motive will lift up our souls and make them bright all the time.....

A great deal of the Bible is written for young people. Sometimes this is said out plainly; so that you cannot help seeing, as you read, that it is meant for you. But I am afraid that in other places you think you are not spoken to when you are. The truth is, about our duties to God, and about the deep feelings in our hearts, young people and older people are more alike than they seem. When our great army sends out recruiting officers to get soldiers for the war, ... they have a rule not to let any young men enlist, unless they are grown stout and old enough to bear the hardships of the camp and the field..... But there is no such rule about enrolling yourselves in this other great army,—

THE CHILDREN'S PREACHING SERVICE. 313

the army of the Cross. . . . . Accordingly, when St. Paul writes to his young friend Timothy, " Thou, therefore, be strong, and endure hardness as a good soldier of Jesus Christ;" . . . . he means *you*. . . . .

The church of Christ to which you belong, then, my young friends, speaks to you as her youthful soldiers. She loves you, and she expects you to show your love for her. She honors you, and she expects honor from you. Now there is only one way to honor her, and in honoring her to honor your Master. You must be her faithful soldiers and servants. What does this mean? Let me tell you what it does *not* mean.

It does not mean that you should take it for granted you have nothing to do for her. . . . . It does not mean that you are too young to be Christians, and so may go on in the wrong way. . . . . When your holy Leader says to you, in his tender and stirring voice, "Come with me; come and take this post of danger or duty; deny yourself; tell the truth; pretend to be only just what you are; do the disagreeable thing if it is only right; do it in faith; do it for my sake!"—it does not mean that you should turn away and pretend you do not hear. What kind of honor is that? . . . .

Half way characters are never honorable. First, you are to be a Christian in your heart, and then you are not to hesitate at all to own yourself one in your manners and your life. Your blood has leaped quicker, I am sure, again and again, ... at reading accounts of young soldiers that have shown this frank fortitude in peril. Some of them are almost equal to the story of the Christian standard-bearer, who had his right arm shot away while he was holding up the slender staff of the banner of his regiment. Determined that his flag should never fall, he then grasped it with his left hand, and pressed on. Presently another shot tore off the left arm. Then he seized it with his teeth, and with both the shortened stumps bleeding, still rushed on with his companions till his blood was gone. This sounds well to you as happening off on some battle-ground. But you have a chance, all of you, to show the same unconquerable spirit in doing right, and doing it fearlessly, for God. Be faithful unto death, and have a crown of life.

You will see that I am anxious to have your decision confessed before men. The best affection for you can ask nothing so good, so blessed, as that. I speak to you in the name of Christ. He wishes it for you. .... He tells you this. He tells you in his Scriptures; he tells you by secret feelings that he puts into your hearts. Let me ask you a question? Sometimes when you have everything bright and comfortable about you, and the world seems to have filled your cup brimful, is there not a feeling of dissatisfaction deep down in your soul? .... What do you think this feeling means? "Blessed are they that hunger and thirst after righteousness." May not that be what it means? .... But will the hunger in your heart be filled, ... and God be found, and your soul rest in him? That depends on yourself. Christ has done his part, in coming to you, and waking up the feeling, knocking at the door of your heart. Will you arise up, and open the door and thankfully let him have your heart, to keep it pure and holy forever? ....

Suppose you are a young man, and that you heard what the greatest and most successful master of brewery in all Europe, once said to a young man who went to him for advice. He said, "I would have you, my young friend, give mind, soul, heart, body to business. That is the way to be happy. Stick to your brewery and you will be the great brewer of London. Be brewer and banker and merchant and manufacturer, and you will soon have your name in the Gazette."

That was the highest thing this successful man of business, with all his millions of money, had to say to an ingenuous youth with a heart in his breast, just starting in life. Would it satisfy you? How does it sound beside that other language of which it is almost a wicked, impious parody, "Thou shalt love the Lord thy God with all thy heart, and with all thy soul, and with all thy mind." A name published with flattery in the Gazette;—a name written in the Lamb's book of everlasting life. Which would you have? That advice was given to Fowell Buxton and, thank

Heaven, it was thrown away upon him, for he had read in his New Testament, "What shall it profit a man if he shall gain the whole world and lose his own soul?" His adviser did become the greatest banker in the world, and had his name every week in the Gazette; and that is all. "Verily they have their reward." Buxton becomes the generous Christian friend of man, walking in love, kind and tender-hearted, a follower of Christ, loved himself and honored everywhere; not only in Europe, but in all Christian countries. . . . .

There used to be, in some old churches, statues of St. Christopher, the martyr. Christopher means *Christ-bearer:* and this holy man was represented as bearing the infant Christ on his shoulders. The story is, that being at first a heathen youth of fine figure, very muscular and active, he was determined to seek out the strongest man in the world, and join him, and follow him. After searching a long time, he found a Christian prince famous for strength, and a great warrior. But one day this prince spoke something about Satan. Then the heathen youth asked him who Satan was. The prince told him Satan was a wicked being, more powerful than any man, and that *he* was afraid of him. "If that is the case," said the young pagan, "I shall leave you, and serve Satan, because he is the strongest." Going through a lonely forest, he met a dark-looking personage, who asked him what he was looking for. "Satan," said the young man, "the strongest being." "I am he," said this person, "follow me." And so he did; but as they went on, and came near to a great city, he noticed that his dark-looking leader struck out of the great highway, and took to by-paths. "Why is this?" he asked. "Because," said Satan, "my greatest enemy who once conquered me, comes that way: I offered him all the kingdoms of the world, and he said 'Get thee behind me.' Three times I tempted him, and three times he overcame me; and I am afraid to meet him." "Oh, then," the youth replied, "I shall leave you, and serve him, because he is stronger than you." So he went on inquiring, till he found that Stronger One, and found he was not like kings or warriors, but was like a little child, the Lamb of God, giving himself an offering and a sacrifice: not strong in the body, but so weak that the young man, the Christ-bearer, could bear him on his shoulders—yet he was Lord of all. Then he believed in his heart, and was baptized by the name of Christopher, bore his cross, and died a glorious martyr. Now, then, if you will serve the strongest, and have the mightiest of all beings in heaven and earth for your Master, whose name is Love, and who is mightiest because he loves most and suffers most, what does the text say? "Be ye therefore followers of God, as dear children, and walk in love, as Christ also hath loved us, and given himself for us, an offering and a sacrifice." Then each of you may be a Christ-bearer, bearing Christ in your heart, and loyal to him as your King; always bearing about in your body the dying of the Lord Jesus: having his life formed in you; and if not one of the noble army of martyrs, yet a confessor of him daily before men.

. . . .

There are only two armies, my dear friends, and you must choose between them. . . . . If you are living all the while as if you did not care which side you are on, you are really on Satan's side, and, coward, thief and traitor as he is, he is glad enough to have you. But are *you* glad? Will you not rather give up anything in the world than be on Satan's side always? Always! No, you mean better than that. But when will you change, if not now in the accepted time? Christ is your only lawful King. . . . . Arise with him, follow after him, fight for him against sin, the world, the devil; walk with him in newness of life, and in love; and let everybody that knows you at all, know that you are his faithful soldier and servant. For how sadly he says, "Whosoever shall be ashamed to confess me before men, of him shall the Son of man be ashamed, when he cometh in the glory of his Father."

. . . .

You know that the Christian poet Keble has made many of the beautiful observances of our Christian year even more beautiful by his chaste imagination. He has put into verse some of the feelings and prayers with which young hearts, mingling in with those of more experience and age, may be supposed to bow their heads in the holy place to receive their Bishop's blessing, and to consecrate themselves to a life-long service of their Saviour.

>Draw, Holy Ghost, Thy seven-fold veil
> Between us and the fires of youth;
>Breathe Holy Ghost, Thy freshening gale,
> Our fever'd brow in age to soothe.
>
>And oft as sin and sorrow tire,
> The hallow'd hour do Thou renew,
>When beckoned up the awful choir
> By pastoral hands, toward Thee we drew;
>
>When trembling at the sacred rail
> We hid our eyes and held our breath,
>Felt Thee how strong, our hearts how frail,
> And longed to own Thee to the death.
>
>Forever on our souls be trac'd
> That blessing dear, that dove-like hand
>A sheltering rock in memory's waste
> O'er-shadowing all the weary land.

But remember there is something greater, holier, deeper than any poetry. It is the question of your soul; life or death. It is the question whether you are *for* Jesus your Lord, or *against* him. It is the question whether you will have the promise and carry it away with you this night to make all the rest of your life strong and happy and to open to you the life eternal. "Whosoever shall confess me before men, him will I confess also before my Father which is in Heaven."

OUTLINE OF A SERMON ON READING.

BY THE REV. JAMES M. FREEMAN,[*]
Of Halsey Street Methodist Episcopal Church, Newark, N. J.

[Put on the blackboard a hand with thumb and fingers

---

[*] Author of The Use of Illustration in Sunday-school Teaching.

extended, and an open book. This may be done in presence of the assembly, or beforehand, as deemed preferable.]

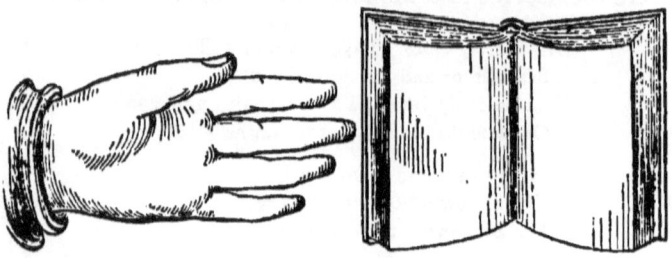

Give attendance to reading. I. Tim. iv. 13.

This the advice of an old minister to a young one.

"Give attendance!" means Give attention! Very hard sometimes for children to do this. Try it all of you, now.

There will be five points to this sermon, just as you have five fingers—including the thumb—on each hand. [Extend the hand, or ask the children to do so; then show the hand on the blackboard.]

I. *Why should we read?* [Show the thumb, and write "Why?" in the thumb on the board.]

1. We can get wiser by reading.

(*a.*) This is only one way of learning, but a very important way.

(*b.*) Story of little Willie Jones, whose mother told him whenever he asked a question, "Read, and you will know." He became a very learned man, and was called "Sir William Jones."

2. We can become better by reading.

a. Reading a good book is like hearing a good man talk to us.

b. Thus, long after good men are dead, we may know what they thought and said while living.

II. *When should we read?* [Show first finger, and write "When?" in it, on the board.]

1. Well to have regular time for reading, if we can; and most children can if they will.

2. Improve the spare moments.

(Story of Ben Johnson, the mason's boy, who carried a book in his pocket while he laid brick, and took it out to read a moment or two at a time while waiting for brick or mortar. Elihu Burritt, the blacksmith's boy, used to have a book before him on his big bellows, and read while he blowed the fire.)

3. Don't read at twilight, for it will hurt your eyes; or late at night, for that is the time to be in bed.

III. *What should we read?* [Second finger.]

This the most important of all.

1. Some children read everything they can get hold of, and boast of it.

(*a.*) As foolish as to eat everything you see.

(*b.*) Should be as careful about reading as about food, for reading is the food of the mind.

2. Some read only new books. But a new book may be a bad book, while an old book may be a good one.

3. Some read only handsome books. But many pretty books are very bad books.

(Like colored candies.)

4. Some want to read only large books. This is very foolish.

5. Read only good books. The Bible is the best of all. It tells us about Jesus. [Write these words in the open book on the board: "The Bible is the book of books."]

IV. *Where should we read?* [Third finger.]

Almost anywhere but in bed, in Sunday-school, or in church—excepting, of course, when we read the Bible lesson in church or Sunday-school.

V. *How should we read?* [Fourth finger.]

1. Not too much at once, any more than you would eat too much at once.

2. Try to understand the meaning of what you read. Do not skip over the hard words.

(*a.*) Look in the dictionary if you have one.

(*b.*) Or, ask some one who knows. (Find it out yourself if you can.)

(*c.*) Better to read only a line and understand it, than to read a whole book through, and not know what it means.

3. When a passage in the Bible is referred to, search it out.

4. Be careful how you use your books.

(Story of Jehudi, who cut the book with a pen-knife. Jer. xxxvi. 23.)

[At the close of the sermon, the blackboard will show thus:

On the other side of the board, have the following synopsis of the sermon; not to be shown until after it is preached. Then, the children to be questioned on it.

I. *Why?*

Two reasons.

Willie Jones.

II. *When?*

The mason's boy.

III. *What?*

Colored candies.

IV. *Where?*

Anywhere but——

V. *How?*

Be careful.

Jehudi.]

BELIEVING IN JESUS.

BY RALPH WELLS,
Superintendent of Grace Mission S. S., New York.

Believe on the Lord Jesus Christ, and thou shalt be saved. Acts xvi. 31.

[The text, displayed on a piece of white muslin, in ornamental letters cut from gilt and colored paper, is suspended before the assembly, thus:]

> **Believe** on the
> Lord **Jesus** Christ,
> and thou shalt be
> **Saved**.

That all may remember the principal words of the text, I have written them out in larger letters than the rest. The first large word is BELIEVE; the second is JESUS; the third is SAVED.

Now, what I say to you, children, I will divide into two parts; and I want you to repeat them after me, and remember them.

I. *What is it to believe?*
II. *Why should I believe?*

First: What is it to believe?

There was a great general, told of in the Bible, who was a famous soldier, and a favorite with his master, the king; but who had a terrible disease, which he longed to be cured of. What was his name? [A pause.] Can't any of you tell it? [Still, no answer.] It began with an N. What was it? "*Naaman!*" Yes. I thought some of you knew it. In the family of this general, there was a little girl, who had been taken prisoner and brought to his home. She saw her master all white with ——. What was the disease? "*Leprosy.*" Yes. Well this little girl said to her mistress, Naaman's wife, "Oh I wish my master could see the great prophet there is in my country. I know he could cure him." The wife told her husband about this. I think Naaman was a kind man, else they wouldn't have cared so much about his being cured. Naaman thought to himself: Well, a great general can be cured if anybody can. So he went to his king, and told him about it, and his king wrote to the king of Israel, and told him he wanted the prophet to cure his general. Then there were two kings at work for his cure. He ought to be cured, now. Riding in his great chariot, with his servants about him, Naaman went to the door of the prophet's house. He sent his servant to tell Elisha to come out, thinking that of course when such a great man as he was there, the prophet would come out very humbly, to see what he could do for him. But Elisha didn't go out of his house—didn't go near the general. He simply sent out word, "Go and wash in the river Jordan, seven times, and you shall be cured." Oh how angry Naaman was, then! "What!" he said, "Go and wash in that little stream, Jordan? What's the use of that? We've a great deal better rivers than that in our country. And then a cold bath is the very worst thing I could take, with this trouble. It's all nonsense. I won't do any such thing." But his servant said, "Look here, master, if you had been asked to try some great thing for a cure, wouldn't you have tried it? Suppose you just try this little thing that the prophet recommends!" "Well, I'll try it," said Naaman, "but I know it's of no use." So down to the Jordan they went. Stepping into the water, he said, "I don't believe it will do any good." He dipped himself in the water, saying the same thing again. He dipped the second time; the third; the fourth. "Oh, it's no use," he said. He dipped the fifth time. "It's all nonsense." The sixth time. "What's the use of trying this over and over, this way. There's nothing in it." Only once more. He trembled a little as he tried it the last time. "What if there should be anything in it?" He dipped the seventh time, just as he was told to. Look at him! Where now is his leprosy? Clean as that little child there! His flesh soft and fair, and he all well again. Oh, how he danced for very joy. Wasn't he glad he had taken the prophet's advice?

Oh, what a simple thing it is to believe! Our souls, children, are sick. No river in all the world will clean them. But "there is a fountain filled with blood," which will cleanse all our souls, if we only believe in it.

[Further illustrations are given of the nature of saving belief. 2. Look and live. Illustration: The brazen serpent uplifted by Moses—presented in a vivid word-picture. 3. Trust him who offers to pay all our soul debts. Illustration: The payment, by an Irish lord, of the entire indebtedness of all of his tenants who would present their cases to him at a given day and hour: only two believing him, they only were relieved. 4. Consider Christ's righteousness *perfect*. Illustration: A young lady dropping a white handkerchief on the fresh fallen snow, and thinking it soiled because of the contrast. Thus with our best conduct by the standard of perfection. All these illustrations are given in full and graphic detail, like that of Naaman.]

And now for the *second* division of the subject. What is it?

"*Why should I believe?*"

Yes, that is it. It is a very simple thing to believe; but *why* should I believe.

1. I should believe because it cost so much for Jesus to bring salvation to me. There was an army once where the soldiers mutinied—rose in rebellion against their commanders, and for this, they were to be punished. All of them deserved death, for all had broken the law. But the general's order was that only every tenth man should die. The other nine should be spared. So the long line of men was drawn up, and the counting commenced.

Anxious times there! One! two! three! four! five! six! seven! eight! nine! *ten!* Let that man step out and be shot. One! two! three! four! five! six! seven!—How the men who were passed breathed free. Eight! nine! Didn't the next man tremble as the call came toward him? *Ten,* and he must step forward and die. In that line stood a father and son, next each other. As the counting came down towards them, the son ran his eye up the line and saw that his father would be the tenth man, and must die, unless he could save him. He resolved to give his life for his father's. Quick! there was no time to be lost. Five! six! seven! came the count on their ten. Eight! nine! and like a flash the son changed places with his father, pushing him one down the line. *Ten!* came the count to the son, and he stepped out to die. His father was saved.

That is the way, children, that Jesus died for us. We were all under sentence of death. Jesus stepped into our places. He died for us. He died in my stead. I ought to believe in a salvation that cost as much as that.

[It is further urged that I should believe, 2. Because of the claims of gratitude. Illustration: The ungrateful guest, branded by Philip of Macedon. 3. Because my soul needs a home. Illustration: A boy in New York without a home or a friend, longing to be sheltered and loved. 4. Because of the end of the believer and unbeliever. Illustration: Cole's three pictures of the two ways of the earthly pilgrim. These illustrations, also, are expanded.

With a word to teachers and another to parents, to urge them to bring their dear children to believe in Jesus, the outline of the subject is again presented to the children, thus:

I. *What is it to believe?*

1. Wash and be clean. Naaman.
2. Look and live. The brazen serpent.
3. Believe in the promised payment of our debts by Jesus. The Irish lord and his tenants.
4. Trust the perfect righteousness of Christ. Handkerchief on the snow.

THE CHILDREN'S PREACHING SERVICE.

II. *Why should I believe?*

1. It cost so much for Jesus to save me. The young soldier dying for his father.
2. Gratitude demands it. The ungrateful guest.
3. My soul needs a home. The homeless and friendless boy.
4. In view of the end of the believer and of the unbeliever. Cole's three pictures, of the two paths.]

THE WILLOW.*

BY E. D. JONES, ST. LOUIS, MO.,
President of the Baptist State S. S. Convention, of Missouri.

And ye shall take you on the first day the boughs of goodly trees, branches of palm-trees, and the boughs of thick trees, and willows of the brook; and ye shall rejoice before the Lord your God seven days. Lev. xxxiii. 40.

---

*One of a series of addresses on The Trees of the Bible, delivered by Mr. Jones before the Benton Street Mission Sunday School, St. Louis, of which he is superintendent.

The shady trees cover him with their shadow; the willows of the brook compass him about. Job xl. 22.

Therefore the abundance they have gotten, and that which they have laid up, shall they carry away to the brook of the willows. Isaiah xv. 7.

And they shall spring up as among the grass, as willows by the water-courses. Isaiah xliv. 4.

He took also of the seed of the land, and planted it in a fruitful field; he placed it by great waters, and set it as a willow-tree. Ezek. xvii. 5.

Let us learn of the willow-tree a few lessons, which its nature may profitably suggest to us.

1. *It thrives best near the water.*

It is called in the Bible, "the willows of the brooks," "willows by the water-courses." David referring to the time when the Jews were in captivity, says, " By the river of Babylon, there we sat down, yea, we wept, when we remembered Zion. We hanged our harps upon the willows." All through the Bible where the willow is mentioned it seems to be associated with living streams of water, as if the tree could not live unless planted where its roots could penetrate the moistened soil, and drink unceasingly of that which should give it a rich and rapid growth. Indeed, the willow cannot flourish upon the mountain top, nor upon the flat prairie lands, no matter how rich the soil may be. It can only thrive in localities that afford an abundance of fresh living water for it to feast upon. Its roots thirst, and will sink themselves, and go long distances, to find water, that seems to be of such importance to its very existence.

So the Christian grows and thrives best, not on the mountain of self-exaltation, not on the barren waste of sin, exposed to the temptations of the evil one, but when planted beside the influences of God's Holy Spirit. David says, "And he shall be like a tree planted by the rivers of water, that bringeth forth his fruit in his season." Rivers and streams of water are used as symbols to represent the happy influences of the Holy Spirit. This blessed Spirit of the living God is what the Christian feeds upon;

he lives by it; he lives upon it; and when he is removed from it he suffers bitterly until he is brought back to its life-giving and life-sustaining power.

When the Christian is on duty, hard at work for Jesus; often in prayer and worship; always present at church, Sunday-school, prayer-meeting, then he may be said to be like the growing, flourishing "willow of the brook." It is when the Christian has sweet and continued intercourse with God that his soul improves, and gains that rich growth in grace, which is so fitting to this life and the life to come. It is reported that when a woman was brought before Bonner, the Bishop of London, to be tried for her religion, he threatened her that he would take away her husband. Said she, "Christ is my husband." Then he threatened to take away her child. Said she, "Christ is better to me than ten sons." Then he threatened to strip her of all earthly comforts. "Yea," said she, "Christ is mine and you cannot strip me of him." So is it with all who live near to Christ; he helps them to grow spiritually, and to become so strong in him that even death can never separate them. Eternity only binds the Christian nearer to Jesus, and the longer they are together, the deeper and more lasting is their love.

2. *It is a thing of joy.*

Willows are mentioned among the trees whose branches were used in the construction of booths, under which the Feast of the Tabernacle was celebrated.

Job says, in speaking of the Behemoth, or Hippopotamus, that the willows afforded him a grateful shade by the side of the rivers.

Isaiah, in speaking of the offspring of the people of Israel, said they should spring up or multiply as rapidly as did "the willows by the water-courses."

It is spoken of as a useful tree. It has been used in roofing the hut of the savage; baskets, chairs, and boats, are made from the wood. The charcoal from the wood is said to be the best to use in making gunpowder.

Poets have sung of the willow in all ages as a beautiful and expressive tree, and as a tree of real virtue, and as a thing of joy.

The Christian may be safely compared to the willow as an object of joy in the world. He affords joy everywhere, especially when he aims to build up the Church of the Lord Jesus Christ; when he is lending comfort to the poor, the sick, the afflicted; when he can render himself useful in any sphere of life, in the church, in the Sunday-school, in the hospital, anywhere that God will be honored and his fellow-men benefited;—happy himself, he helps to make the world around him happy by his usefulness, and especially when he helps poor sinners to Jesus.

One day a hunter, in search of game, had lost his way in an African forest. He was faint and weary. His attention was attracted by the strange twittering and chattering of a little gray bird. It seemed excited about something and anxious to attract his attention. The hunter thought he would follow the little bird. He followed it until it led him to a hollow tree. He examined the tree, and on looking into it found a quantity of honey. He ate of it, and was strengthened. On inquiring, he found the natives called it the honey-bird, and that it seemed to take delight in showing people the trees which had honey in them. So when we see the Christian boy and girl making themselves useful in pointing others to Jesus, we may compare them to the honey-bird, or, the willow of the brooks, things of joy and of great value. The poor anxious honey-bird it is true found something sweet, but he that finds Jesus tastes that which is sweeter than honey. His soul may feast and never tire through an endless eternity.

3. *It is an emblem of mourning.*

The willow is a very graceful tree, with slender swaying branches, long, narrow pointed leaves. Its leaves and branches present a mournful look, as they seem to droop their heads, as if the deepest grief and sorrow and distress were aching its very heart, and it had not the power to hold its head and branches erect, like other trees. The whole expression of the tree gives us an idea of grief and sorrow.

Under these trees, along the banks of the Euphrates, the captive Jews in Babylon, seem to have poured out their sorrow. On these trees they seem to have hung their harps, laying aside these instruments of joy, to give place to sorrow and weeping as they thought of their native land. "By the rivers of Babylon, there we sat down, yea, we wept, when we remembered Zion. We hanged our harp upon the willows in the midst thereof."

The willow tree does not seem to be in mourning for itself. It has a stream of water near to keep its life always fresh, and with all its grief it maintains its beauty and loveliness. It may be said to be sympathizing, weeping in sympathy with others. Let one who is in grief go near the willow, and at once the tree seems to be in sympathy with him, and a relief comes because it appears to share his sorrow with him.

Give me the willow to wave its drooping branches over my simple grave. Give me no cold and cheerless monument of marble, to mark my resting-place. The sympathizing willow shall speak for me—shall act for me when my voice is hushed in the stillness of death. I can then breathe no solace to the mourning hearts of loved ones, but the willow's sweet and tender expressiveness, shall ease the grief and sorrow of those who come to drop the tear of Christian sympathy and love. I would leave behind me no sweeter influence than that which would ease the grief of others.

We might compare the Christian to the willow, as a blessing, because he is a sympathizer and a sharer in the griefs and sorrows of others. It is true that stars and glow-worms shine best in the dark; that spices smell sweeter when crushed; that young trees take root best when shaken; that camomile spreads, the more you trample on it; that afflictions, trials, pains, sorrows, elevate and enrich the Christian; but no sorrowing one is made so strong as when he can find a sympathizing heart to share his griefs and sorrows with him.

So ought we to be like the willow, sharing the afflictions and griefs of those about us. If one is in pain, sickness, disappointment, bereavement, or sorrow of any kind, we should not only lend a word of comfort, a hand to help; but if need be, drop the tear of love and sympathy. Jesus wept with those loving sisters, at the grave of Lazarus, and if the Son of God could sympathize with the poor, the sick, the outcast, and could drop the tear of pity and tender compassion for those in sorrow and affliction, ought we not—when we need it so much ourselves—to imitate him who left us such blessed examples.

SKETCH OF AN ADDRESS ON BESETTING SINS.

BY WILLIAM REYNOLDS, PEORIA, ILL.
President of the Illinois State S. S. Convention.

Wherefore, seeing we also are compassed about with so great a cloud of witnesses, let us lay aside every weight, and the sin which doth so easily beset us, and let us run with patience the race that is set before us, looking unto Jesus the author and finisher of our faith; who for the joy that was set before him endured the cross, despising the shame, and is set down at the right hand of the throne of God. Heb. xii. 1, 2.

Written at the top of the blackboard, on either hand, are the words: *Looking unto Jesus*, and *Besetting sins.*

A description is given, as vividly as possible, of the ancient games, to which allusion is obviously made in the text. For the Olympian races, a severe special training was necessary. "You wish to conquer at the Olympic games?" said Epictetus, "So also do I; for it is honorable; but bethink yourself what the attempt implies, and then begin the undertaking. You must subject yourself to a determinate course; .... must pursue the established exercises at fixed hours in heat and cold; must abstain from all delicacies in meat and drink; yield yourself unreservedly to the control of the presiding physician, and even endure flogging."

At the time of the contest, there was such an assemblage as no other occasion could bring together. Thousands upon thousands were there, to witness the struggle of those who had been so long in preparation for the eventful hour. On a tripod, in the middle of the course, to be seen of all, were the victors' crowns, garlands of wild olive, cut with a golden sickle by a boy, both of whose parents must be living, from a tree in the sacred grove of Altis. Palm branches also were there, to be given into the conqueror's hands when he received the crown of victory. Rich and poor contended for the mastery on equal terms, and the prize was as much desired by the former as by the latter. The names of the different contestants were written on a tablet exposed to public view.

When everything was ready for the start, the judges exhorted all to acquit themselves manfully and nobly, and then gave the signal to commence. The contestants sprang forward in the race. Every nerve was strained; every energy employed. "The cloud of witnesses" used every encouragement in their power, these favoring one competitor, and those another. As they neared the goal, they increased their efforts. Sometimes the whole contest depended on a single final spring; but even life would be gladly risked in such a struggle. "Indeed, one Ladas, a victor at the Olympic games, was so exhausted by his efforts in the long race, that immediately on gaining the honor and being crowned, he fell down dead."

The race once won, and the joys of triumph followed. The victor was crowned on a tripod of bronze, or on a throne of ivory and gold. The palm branch was given him. His name, and that of his father and of his country, were proclaimed by a herald before the assembled representatives of Greece. Loud plaudits came from the delighted throng. Ample reward was his for all the days of privation in training, and for the imminent hour of struggle in the race. "What intense and deep delight must his bosom have been filled with, when the full acclaim of assembled Greece fell upon his ear, coming in loud salutations and applauses from every part of the crowded course! Then came the more private attentions of individual friends. One brought a chaplet of flowers; another bound his head with ribbons. Afterwards came the triumphal sacrifice made to the twelve gods, accompanied by sumptuous feasting. The poet now began his office, gaining in some cases, both for himself and the happy victor, an unexpected immortality. Music also lent her aid, and his name was sung wherever the Greek language was spoken. In order to perpetuate the memory of these great men, their names and achievements were entered in a public register which was under the care of suitable officers. A no less privilege was that of having a statue of themselves placed (either at the expense of the country or their friends,) in the sacred grove of Jupiter."* Victory in such a race, and with such resulting benefits, was deemed worthy of the best efforts and energies of the best men of olden time.

The children are reminded that they also are to strive for a crown, not of fading laurel but of eternal life, which the Lord Jesus Christ, the Judge of the race, will give to them at the door of Heaven. That crown they can gain only by persevering faith. They must make preparation for the race. They must submit themselves obediently to all the requirements of the course. At the word, 'they must spring forward; and in sight of " the cloud of witnesses," they must press on as for their lives. And if they have the victory, they shall be met with rejoicings, when they are crowned before the throne. The very angels of God shall have joy in their triumph, and they shall be as pillars in the house of God forever.· But Satan will try to hinder them in the race.

Suppose, children, says the speaker, a person in running this race should carry a heavy belt of gold around him. Would he be likely to gain the race? "*No, sir!*" Suppose he should hold an armful of books or pictures as he ran. Would he win? "*No, sir!*" Suppose he should often look back to see how far he had come; or should stop a minute to rest himself. Would he probably have victory? "*No, sir!*" No, that is true. Yet Satan is trying to hinder us all, by loading us down or stopping us in some such way. Those things with which he hinders us, we call besetting sins. Let us see what some of these are. Cain lost the race through his besetting sin. What was that? "*Jealousy.*" (This and the following points, as they are brought out,

---

* Encyclopedia Brittanica.

are written on the blackboard.) Gehazi lost his race through another besetting sin. What was it? "*Covetousness.*" What was the besetting sin of the young ruler who came to Jesus? "*Love of riches.*" What was that of Judas? "*Deceitfulness.*" Now, children, what are *your* besetting sins? sins that would hinder you in running the Christian race for the crown of life.

At this question, the children begin to *think.* As there is a pause for the answer, solemnity reigns in the school-room, with its three or four hundred scholars. At length a little boy rises, in the impressive silence of the place, and with tears in his eyes says, "Mr. Reynolds, my trouble is *swearing.* I get mad some times and I swear. I'm afraid Satan tries me in that way." "Swearing" is then written on the board. Perhaps a little girl adds: "Mr. Reynolds, I '*told a story*' to my mother. I am sorry for it, but I think that's my sin." "Story-telling" is written down. And so the children confess their faults one to another, and the confessions are written down, until the board is well-nigh covered. Deep impressions are made. Eyes are filled with tears. The board with its dark record of confessions stands out before the school.

Looking unto Jesus.	*Besetting Sins.*
Cain—Jealousy.	*Swearing.*
Gehazi—Covetousness.	*Story-telling.*
Young Ruler—Love of Riches.	*Sabbath-breaking.*
Judas—Deceitfulness.	*Playing truant.*
	Disobedience.
	Stealing.
	Deceiving.

The children look at it, and their consciences reproach them. The Spirit of God strives with young hearts at such a time. Then the appeal is made: Dear children, God sees this record you have put here,; and he knows a great deal more than is down on the board, for some of you have committed sins which you have not been willing to acknowledge to me,—but God has written them all in his book of remembrance. Now, what will you do? You cannot win the crown with all these besetting sins to hinder you. But see! The Bible tells us of a Friend who can rid you of all these hindrances. Who is that Friend? "*Jesus.*" Yes, Jesus comes, and with his own precious blood blots out the handwriting that is against you—wipes away all these sins; (as he says this, the speaker rubs out the long catalogue of sins, on the board,) wipes them away for all who wish him to do it, and who will believe in and trust him. Are you willing to have him wipe out all your sins? Now?

[This address, given in full detail, and under a sense of responsibility for precious souls, has been blessed of God to the conversion of many. At least twelve, at one time, confessed that that lesson was instrumental to their conversion.]

EXPECT IMMEDIATE RESULTS FROM PREACHING.

The direct appeals to the individual child, in the address of Mr. Reynolds, and the call, in Dr. Huntington's sermon, to his hearers, to choose between the two armies, "now in the accepted time," suggest the importance of looking for speedy results from these public labors with the children. Little good, comparatively speaking, will come of such services, unless those enjoying them are brought into submission to Christ Jesus, as their Lord and Redeemer; and surely the sooner this desired result is attained, the better. Not all seed-sowing should be as bread cast upon the waters, to be found after *many days;* * but some, who go forth weeping, bearing precious seed, should expect to come again with rejoicing, bringing their sheaves with them,†—not necessitated to leave to others the precious harvest gathering. In. young hearts in almost every congregation, the seed has been already long sown, and watered with prayer and tears. Only the removal by loving hands of hindering or obscuring doubts and anxieties, is necessary to show, already developed, the blade, or the ear, or perhaps the full corn in the ear.

There are secret disciples of Jesus among the little ones, needing encouragement to tell of their confiding love for him. There are children who, like Saul of Tarsus, having been called of God, have asked in faith, "Lord, what wilt thou have me to do?"‡ and now wait with closed eyes, in "the street which is called Straight," for Ananias to come and show them more clearly their duty and privileges. And there are others, who lack only the word of the man of God to themselves personally, as Nathan's "Thou art the man!" to the guilty king, to cause them to see their peril and need. Class teaching or pulpit preaching often fails of its proper effect, because it is unappropriated. Sometimes, as quaint John Newton says, it is like "a letter put into a post-office without any direction. It is addressed to nobody, it is owned by no-

---
* Eccl. xi. 1.   † Psalms cxxvi. 6.   ‡ Acts ix. 6.

body, and if a hundred people were to read it, not one would think himself concerned in its contents." And again it needs to be so pressed to the individual conscience of the hearer, as to leave no doubt as to its application. And those who have faith that God will bless the prayerful preaching of his word, and bless it now, are most likely to receive a speedy reward of their labors. For God honors faith, and loves to give best gifts to those who expect him to do so.

Doubtless, no small part of the results for good of the preaching of prominent evangelistic laborers among children, is to be attributed to the faith of these men that God will bless their work, at once. Other men have labored, and these propose to enter into their labors. The field has been long white to the harvest, but there has been no attempt, in faith, to reap, until now. At a meeting of the Superintendents and Secretaries' Association, of London, a year ago, when reports came in from various quarters of the value of the preaching services of the Rev. E. P. Hammond, one brother remarked, that "He believed the success of Mr. Hammond was attributable to the fact that he worked heartily, *expecting* the blessing of God." A letter was then read from Mr. Hammond, "in which he expressed the belief that if the means were used, and earnest believing prayer offered to God, 'tens of thousands of children' might be converted." The chairman of the meeting, F. J. Hartley, added the suggestion, that while the teachers in Sunday-schools had been looking for fruit, one had come among them expecting the blessing, and had secured it.* If ministers and superintendents who object to the introduction of evangelists to their fields, or who question the propriety of some of the modes of such workers, would themselves go to the children in personal inquiry and appeal, after preaching to or teaching them, and this in full and prayerful expectancy of immediate results, it is probable that the highest good would be attained without the intervention of any doubtful expedients.

CHILDREN'S INQUIRY AND PRAYER MEETINGS.

Some of the most successful workers among children, seldom or never preach to them without holding an inquiry meeting at the close of the service—a meeting at which the children may be separately addressed and counseled, by intelligent followers of Christ. The prominence which efforts of this character have obtained, indicates the readiness of the church to avail itself of such an agency. God has seemingly prepared the way by his Spirit and providences for this mode of working to bring little ones into his fold.

There has been a felt want of personal contact of the preacher with the soul preached to.

Says Dr. Duryea, in pressing the advantages enjoyed by the Sunday-school teacher, "While the minister is teaching all about the gospel, here is a soul that wants a direct application of the gospel. The religious teaching from the pulpit is not sufficient. There must

---

* London S. S. Times, Sept. 13, 1867.

be a special teaching, mouth to ear, mind to mind, heart to heart. Just as a student of medicine may want to lecture on medicine, but a sick man knowing his sickness, wants a prescription, so the Christian student may want a lecture on religion, but he wants again and again a prescription for his soul."* And while the minister has thus prized the privileges of the class teacher, that teacher has not been without a longing for yet other advantages in his efforts to win the young to Jesus. "Many a zealous Sunday-school teacher," says an English worker on Mr. Hammond's plan, † "has doubtless often felt the need of something supplementary to the ordinary class teaching and school services—something calculated to give every scholar a medium of sympathy and heart contact with his teacher. He has felt sure that there were some dear scholars in his class who were secret disciples of the Lord Jesus, and others whose minds were evidently impressed with divine truth; and often has he longed for some kind of magnet, so to speak, which would . . . . irresistibly draw forth from the anxious a candid confession of their state of mind. . . . There is about our present Sunday-school system an amount of, perhaps necessary, order and formality, which prevents him from seeing the fruit of his labors, and fails to give him an opportunity of eliciting what impressions have been made on the minds of his scholars." He then argues in favor of the children's meetings instituted by Mr. Hammond, and adduces rea-

---

* Report of New York S. S. Institute, p 137.
† London S. S. Times July 26, 1867.

sons for believing "that in these children's services and inquiry meetings, is to be found the long 'missing link.'"

The meetings thus commended, are more fully described, as follows:*

"The services are held in the school-room of Surrey Chapel [Newman Hall's], on Sunday evening, at half-past six, and on Tuesday evening at seven. On Sunday the attendance averages about three hundred, and would be larger if all applicants were admitted. . . . . On Tuesday there are generally from one hundred to one hundred and twenty, and occasionally as many as one hundred and fifty. . . . . In conducting these meetings the aim has been to make them as varied and interesting as possible, and to bring all the exercises down to the capacity of the children. The prayers and addresses are exceedingly short and simple. There is plenty of singing, and the tunes are lively, many of the hymns having a chorus. . . . .

"But the characteristic feature of the services, and the one which we think has been most productive of good, is that which is called, for want, I think, of a better name, the 'Inquiry Meeting.'† At the close of the preliminary meeting, an invitation is given to the 'children who love Jesus, and those who want to love Jesus' to remain behind, that the teachers may talk to them and pray with them. About half—or sometimes two-thirds—will stop, and the rest leave while a hymn is being sung. The teachers and friends present then

---

* London S. S. Times, May 8, 1868.
† This familiar American title seems to strike the English mind unfavorably.

gather classes round them, and, without taking any formal lesson or subject, speak to the children simply and earnestly about heavenly things, and strive to impress on them individually and personally the duty of giving their hearts to the Saviour. There is not much order or arrangement about these classes—teachers speak to the children nearest them, or to any they may see—but those who come regularly often get the same children from week to week."

The most satisfactory results are reported from similar meetings in other parts of Great Britain, and like services have been richly blessed in various portions of this country. Such an agency, coming thus approved, should not be lightly passed by by those desiring greatest good to the children.

House and Pardee and other prominent American writers on Sunday-school themes, commend, warmly, regular prayer-meetings for the children, and many pastors and superintendents make much of them. "Some of our Sabbath-schools," says Pardee, "hold such a meeting at the close of each afternoon session." The boys and girls being in separate rooms, under leaders of their own sex, respectively, "the meeting opens with singing a familiar hymn, and then a few appropriate verses and remarks just adapted to kindle devotion in the little hearts, and then the little prayers follow freely and almost spontaneously. They soon learn to love to pray, and pray in real faith too, for the whole life of a little child is a life of faith."*

---

* S. S. Index, p. 20.

In some churches at the West, an organization known as "The Faithful Band," gathers young believers for culture in the Christian life. This resembles the Methodist class-meeting in its main features, and serves as a training school for youthful disciples, directing them in active effort for other souls, while aiding them in the cultivation of grace in their own renewed hearts.*

Thus, in various ways, the children are finding their proper place in the temple, and their part in all its services. Through Bible study and recitation, in prayer and praise, as listeners to the preached word and to its application to their individual consciences, as helpers of each other in the divine life, and as workers together with each other and with Jesus, they are being won to the Redeemer, and upreared in his service. So are being answered the prayer of the Psalmist, and of so many who have come after him: "That our sons may be as plants grown up in their youth; that our daughters may be as corner-stones, polished after the similitude of a palace." †

---
* See House's S. S. Hand Book, p. 123-127.   † Psalms cxliv. 12.

APPENDIX.

ADDITIONAL historical notes as to church care for children, and religious services for their benefit, which could not well be inserted in the body of the work, are here appended, as is also a list of books for the benefit of those attempting to lead children's religious meetings.

WORSHIP BY THE YOUNG IN THE SCHOOLS OF THE PROPHETS. A school thus formed is referred to undoubtedly in the First Book of Samuel, situated near the holy tabernacle. Samuel when quite young was placed and educated at this school, received while there a call from heaven, and became a prophet of the Lord. Previously to this time according to Jahn, "there had been many other schools of this kind, which had fallen into discredit, but which were restored again by the prophet Samuel, after whose time the members of the seminaries in question, who were denominated by way of distinction, the *Sons of the Prophets*, acquired no little notoriety." One of these seminaries was at Naioth, a suburb of Ramah, where Samuel lived; another was at Bethel; another at Gilgal, and others perhaps at Jericho and Jerusalem. . . . . "It is pretty evident," says Dr. J. P. Smith, "from various intimations, that some eminent persons, such as Samuel or Elijah presided over them, and undertook the charge of communicating instruction to these young persons." . . . . Among the ancient Israelites, it was a common practice in seasons of worship to chant their prayers and praises, accompanied by instruments. This music was a source of high national enjoyment, and the taste for it probably was perfected, if not formed, at these schools. . . . . This singing or chanting by the whole school is called in the Scriptures *prophesying;* as when Saul sent messengers to arrest David, who had taken refuge in the school at Ramah. . . . . "And when they saw the company of prophets prophesying, and Samuel standing as appointed over them, the Spirit of God was upon the messengers of Saul, and they also prophesied;"—that is, united with Samuel and the whole school in the recitation or chanting of some sacred composition in praise of the wisdom and wonderful works of Jehovah. . . . . In this kind of prophesying or chanting, the whole school were initiated and constantly practiced. By this means much sacred thought and wisdom was committed to memory, made popular by recitation and widely diffused. [*The History of Sunday Schools, By Lewis G. Pray, Chap. iv.*

CARE OF CHILDREN BY MINISTERS IN THE EARLY CHURCH. No sooner had their Master ascended . . . . than they [the Apostles] entered upon the great work of evangelization. They commenced it by public teaching—by preaching the Gospel everywhere; . . . . and so different was the notice which they took of the young from the course of all previous prophets or teachers, that we can ascribe it, without hesitation, to the example of their ascended Master . . . . Paul . . . . teaches in more than one of his epistles [preaching directly to the young] "Children, obey your parents in the Lord for this is right." . . . . Peter also . . . . addressing himself particularly to children, adds, "Ye younger, submit yourselves unto the elder." . . . . And so . . . . John, ... how beautifully he writes on the subject! "I write unto you little children, because your sins are forgiven you for his name's sake." [*Ibid.* p. 41.

CHILDREN'S WORSHIP COMMENDED IN THE SECOND CENTURY.

  Shepherd of tender youth!
  Guiding in love and truth,
   Through devious ways.
  Christ, our triumphant king!
  We come thy name to sing,
  And here our children bring,
   To shout thy praise.

[*Translated from a Greek Hymn of Clement of Alexandria about A. D. 200.*

CHILDREN'S CLAIMS NEVER WHOLLY IGNORED BY THE CHURCH. In the first few centuries of the Christian era, the church provided for the young of its charge by the Catechumenical Schools. Even during the Dark Ages, from the fourth to the twelfth centuries, Cathedral and Conventual Schools, and, later, the schools of the Universities, secured at least nominal religious instruction, directly from the church, to the young.

Indeed, all study of church history shows clearly, that the Christian church has never fallen so low as to formally deny the children's claim to a place in the temple, and a share in its pulpit ministrations, and that where spiritual life has been fullest, there those claims have been most clearly recognized. Children's worship, and Sunday teaching of the children by the church, have had no *beginning* since the days of Jesus.

BIBLE TEACHING AND RECITATIONS AMONG THE WALDENSES, IN THE THIRTEENTH CENTURY. From a very early period of their history, the Vaudois have been distinguished for the attention which they have given to education. . . . . According to the statements made by Reinerius [in the thirteenth century,] in his work against them,* they had anciently something like a system of mutual education, and devoted much of their time to the work. " He who has been a disciple for seven days looks out some one whom he may teach in his turn, so that there is a continual increase. If any one would excuse himself they say to him: Only learn one word every day, and at the end of the year you will have three hundred, and so make progress. . . . . I have heard one of those poor peasants repeat the whole book of Job by heart without missing a single word; and there are others who have the whole of the New Testament at their fingers' ends. . . . . The Vaudois know the whole of the New Testament by heart, and much of the Old; nor . . . . will they listen to anything else, saying that all sermons which are not proved by Scripture, are unworthy of belief." [*The Vaudois, Henderson, p.* 102. *London,* 1858.

IGNATIUS LOYOLA'S JESUIT SCHOOLS, IN THE SIXTEENTH CENTURY. Only seven years had elapsed [1546] since the foundation of the Society. . . . . One thing was hitherto wanting, great in itself, but greater still in its endless consequences to the Company and to men. I allude to the *public instruction of youth.* On this foundation the Jesuits will build their fortress of influence. Youth will be trained to love, to admire their teachers, and the Company to which these teachers belong; for the Jesuit method will be one of fascination— a heart-penetrating, bewitching inculcation—full of sweets and flowers, natural and artificial—all that the young love dearly and parents love to see. . . . . The rising generation will thus be in her interest; and, therefore, in process of time the risen generation will not be against her, but will rather fill her schools with another, and so on for ever. . . . .

The morals of youth were formed and promoted as follows: . . . . the pupils were to hear mass daily, and go to confession every month. . . . . At the commencement of class-hours, all should recite a devout prayer, to beg the grace of profiting by their studies. Once a week they should be catechised in the doctrines of faith, and the principles of morality. In addition to this, the masters were to take every opportunity, in and out of class, to converse familiarly with their pupils on religious matters. [*Steinmetz's History of the Jesuits, Vol. I. pp.* 346-50.

CARLO BORROMEO'S IDEA OF PRIESTLY RESPONSIBILITY FOR CHILDREN, 1560-84. The number of schools and seminaries which he founded is almost incredible; 740 schools with 3,040 teachers and 40,098 scholars are recorded. It was his theory that every child belonged to the church, and the priest had special care of the souls of children. And while he in no degree abated the splendor of the metropolitan ritual, and left the choir of the cathedral that marvel of magnificence which it still remains, he would have its institutions of religious training only the centre of a system which should penetrate the remotest parts of his diocese, so that the poorest boy in the entire district might

---

* Rein. De Hæret, p. 300.

I *

reach the highest doctor's place in the metropolitan chapter. Neglect of teaching was to him a graver offense than neglect of prayer, when he took account of his priesthood. [*New American Cyclopedia.*

ROMISH ZEAL FOR YOUTH IN BOHEMIA STIMULATED BY LUTHERAN FAITHFULNESS. On the 16th of August, 1584, the curate Erhard, by advice of Cardoneus, drew up Latin regulations for the future conduct of the curate of Nicolsburg. In which . . . . "the clergy are . . . . reminded that it is their solemn duty . . . . diligently to teach Canisius' catechism to the young, and insist upon their regular attendance at church; for since the *Lutherans are so diligent to instil into their children* their abominable doctrines, the Catholic clergy ought not to be behind them in zeal." [*The Reformation and Anti-Reformation in Bohemia, p.* 121. *London,* 1845.

REVIVAL AMONG MORAVIAN CHILDREN, 1727. The same grace which the congregation had experienced on the 13th of August, their children experienced likewise. There appeared, already on the 26th of May, 1727, the first emotions in their hearts, by occasion of a discourse which the Count [Zinzendorf] delivered in the œconomy of girls in the house of Baron De Watteville at Bertholdsdorf. . . . . This emotion was the more joyous to him, as he had hitherto been deeply concerned on account of the evident want of spiritual life in their hearts.

But the real and abiding awakening of these children did not take place till the 17th of August, which arose from the testimony of a simple brother, *Grumpe,* whom the Count had sent to Bertholdsdorf in June the same year, to instruct them in the principles of the Christian religion. In the meantime, the memorable work of grace in the soul of a girl of eleven years, proved on the 6th of August, the occasion of the beginning of an extraordinary awakening among some girls who lived with their parents at Herrnhut, which had also a great influence upon those at Bertholdsdorf, and upon their parents and the rest of the inhabitants. On the 29th of August these children were heard praying on the Hutberg with such fervor, tears, and singing of hymns, that, as it is related in the diary of Herrnhut, "it is impossible to describe it in words."

They entered at the same time into a covenant together, that they would be the entire property of our Saviour. It is worthy of being taken notice of, as something particular, that though the most powerful emotions in children are apt to die away as they advance in years, yet none of these children ever broke their covenant; and most of them became blessed handmaids of Jesus in the congregation of the Brethren.

There was also, during this period, a great emotion and awakening among the little boys at Herrnhut: yet this had not such blessed consequences, or such an abiding fruit as attended the awakening among the girls. [*History of the Brethren, by David Cranz, p.* 119. *London,* 1780.

CHILDREN'S MEETING IN PENN., 1829. A worthy clergyman in Pennsylvania writes: "The monthly concert of prayer for the heathen, and for Sabbath-schools, are interesting seasons among us. When we came here they were nearly run down. I commenced giving information and relating anecdotes appropriate to each of these occasions. I require the children at the next concert for Sabbath-schools to relate what was said at the last. In this way not only have the children become interested, but also the parents and the teachers. The last meeting was held in the church, the session house would not hold them. Many were in tears. Only let ministers of the Gospel do their duty, and Sabbath schools will flourish wherever ministers are found, and the concerts of prayer will be well attended." [*New Jersey S. S. Journal, Dec*., 1829.

SERVICES FOR CHILDREN IN BOSTON, 1834-5. Religious services appropriate to children are still continued, morning and afternoon, at the Friend St. Chapel. There are generally from one hundred and twenty to one hundred and fifty children present. Many of the parents attend with the children, and seem much pleased; in the visits to them, they often speak of their children's interest in these services. Though we may not have accomplished all that we could wish, and cannot present to view all we could desire, yet we have had much to encourage us; and have become each Sabbath more and more impressed with the importance of these services and the good that may result from them. . . . The field for usefulness in this respect is great, and it is to be hoped that the plain and simple manner adopted of illustrating religious truth may in some cases produce that happy result, which is so earnestly to be desired. . . .

Rev. Mr. Wright is employed by the Society for the Moral and Religious Education of the Poor. He is effecting a great deal of good at West Boston. His congregation of children in the morning and afternoon of the Sabbath is very large. [*Report of the Ministers-at-Large.* 1835.

WORSHIP FOR CHILDREN, NISMES, FRANCE, 1846. Although the instruction given to the catechumens is extensive, regular, and varied, according to their different degrees of intelligence, the Consistory has nevertheless thought that it was insufficient; and the means which they have adopted to secure a more solid development of their religious character has been the establishment of a religious service adapted to the young, celebrated on every Wednesday, at the small temple, at eleven o'clock A. M. [*Translation from French Report, by Pray.*

ENGLISH PLAN FOR CHILDREN'S SERVICES, 1847. In lieu of the adult public service, it would be well to hold at the same time, every Sabbath morning, a *separate* religious service for children, *adapted to their tender capacities.* The children should have a sermon preached to them by a regularly appointed party; a text should be taken and a discourse delivered, matter, manner, and style suited to their infantile minds: but even at this juvenile service the smallest children should not be present; the *infants* should be taught in a separate room by an infant teacher, as *preaching* of any sort is an unsuitable mode of instruction for very little children. There is no objection, on the contrary a great advantage, in two or three schools taught in the same vicinity, meeting, if convenient, at the appointed hour, in one central spot, that all may share in the same service. As preaching is God's appointed means for spreading the knowledge of the truth, and as more souls have been brought to Jesus through its instrumentality than by all other agencies,—for "it hath pleased God, through the foolishness of preaching, to save those who believe"—we assert that preaching to children in a style which they can understand must be productive of good to them. and results must follow its general adoption that shall cause the hearts of parents and teachers to sing for joy. [*The Sunday School*, *by Louisa Davids, p. 225.*

ANOTHER PLEA FOR SEPARATE SERVICES. Services adapted to children can alone be expected to beget among the young the habit of attending public worship. . . . Separate services can alone speak with children to God, or speak for God to children. . . . There is no abstract or absolute God's house. . . . God's house is that spot or structure which to our hearts is a meeting-place with God. The building which is "amiable" to the Christian through associations of God's presence therewith, is not lovely to the mind that has not connected with it corresponding thoughts. ["*Separate Services*," *by the Rev. Samuel Martin, Westminster, Eng.*

CALL FOR A CHILDREN'S CHAPEL. Since the institution of the Sunday-school system, what wonderful changes has this progressive principle wrought! . . . . All these changes we owe to this same principle, which now, in this age of earnest thought, advances with steady step, and asks, as a matter of consistency, a separate service for young children; and as a matter of convenience and economy, in some places, a Children's Chapel. . . . The object we have in view is to make the Sabbath a delight, and that the *whole* of it may be so, this substitute for the ordinary public worship is proposed. So popular is this separate service, that elder children beg hard to stay. On every hand the prejudice against it is giving way, and many ministers are not only consenting to its adoption, but taking their turn in its performance, becoming, like the venerable Charles of Bala, as "children for the children's sake;" or, as the tender-hearted Doddridge, who said, "I am not ashamed of these little services, for I had rather feed the lambs of Christ than rule a kingdom." ["*The Infant Class.*" *By Charles Reed, Hackney, Eng., p. 84-96.*

"CHILDREN'S CHURCH" IN GLASGOW, SCOTLAND, 1861-3. During the two years we occupied the City Hall we carried on a special service, which was soon attended by about five hundred. This was conducted not as a Sabbath-school, but as a children's. church, and was wondrously helpful in training the children into church-going habits, and bridging the chasm between the school and the church. This service became very popular. Conductors of Sabbath-schools frequently visited it, and in a short time nearly sixty similar though smaller meetings were organized throughout the city. Some of the children, above twelve years of age, were trained as a visitation agency, after the model of our adult method, and thus about thirty of these young visitors would issue after morning service and bring in children from the houses and the streets. This service continues now..... Various office-bearers and Sabbath-school teachers take part. They meet still at two o'clock, but in the hall under the church, and we hear the young voices rising in their happy hymns and mingling faintly with our service above. Parents often leave their children there, and get them as they leave. [*Maccoll's "Among the Masses," p.* 355.

SEPARATE SERVICES FOR CHILDREN IN LONDON, 1868. At the meeting of the London S. S. Superintendents and Secretaries' Association, Aug. 28, 1868, the subject for discussion was, "What means might be used to induce the youthful class more generally to devote the evening of the Sabbath to religious objects."

Mr. C. A. Comyn opened the question. The best antidote to the evil appeared to him to be the establishment of juvenile Sunday-evening services for worship..... The hymn-book decided upon should not be too childish, and a number of Bibles should be provided for the use of those who might come unprovided with a copy of the Scriptures. The prayers should be short and clothed in the simplest language, but above all things they should be prayers *with* and not *for* the congregation; not, "Bless these dear children, bless their parents and friends," but, "Bless us, our parents and friends." All peculiar figurative expressions as "giving their hearts to God, and themselves to His people," should be reduced to their meaning of conversion, change of disposition, and active service. Scriptural truths should be explained in the ordinary phraseology of the day. The reading should be natural and without affectation. A few of the older boys and girls should be selected to form a choir. The hymns, portions of Scripture, and addresses, should be arranged so as to bear upon one idea or lesson..... The order of service adopted by the East London Auxiliary and which was found eminently successful ... was divided into two parts. The first was taken by the superintendent, who had his separate and distinct table on a level with the congregation, and the second part by the teacher who officiated as minister, and who had his desk on a slightly raised platform behind. The doors were opened at about a quarter or half-past six, and at a quarter to seven, Bibles, &c., having been previously distributed, a call-bell was touched as a signal for silence. The time devoted to the service was thus apportioned: The superintendent after kneeling for a minute or two in silent prayer, announced the opening hymn. Singing hymn, about five minutes. Reading a psalm, the superintendent and congregation reading alternate verses (congregation sitting), seven minutes. *Gloria Patri*, &c., chanted, standing, one minute. Prayer and thanksgiving by the superintendent kneeling, the congregation sitting, five minutes. Hymn sung, all standing, five minutes. First lesson from Old Testament, by superintendent, five minutes. Hymn chanted, all standing, three minutes. Second lesson from New Testament by minister or superintendent, five minutes.

Hymn sung, all standing, five minutes. Very short prayer for wisdom, attention, etc., by minister, one minute. Address by minister, twenty to twenty-five minutes. Hymn sung, five minutes. Prayer and benediction by minister, three minutes. The books were then collected and the congregation dispersed. A service, thoroughly diversified, thus occupied about an hour and a quarter. [*London S. S. Times, Sept.* 4, 1868.

WESTERN ADVOCACY OF CHILDREN'S CHURCH. The *time* of holding these services cannot be determined by any fixed rule. .... I would only stipulate for this as an essential, viz: that it be in lieu of an ordinary service of the church; and that children and congregation all understand that this is a common and regular church service. Any other course is very likely to defeat one of the good purposes of such meetings, [that of] identifying the children with the ordinances of God's house. The right *place* for the children's church, is the place for the adults' assembling; not in the chapel, but in the main auditorium. This may seem a little matter, and so it is relatively; but it has its importance in the formation of right religious habits, in training the footsteps of the young to tread the path that leads "up Zion's hill.".... Let the children's church be held regularly. Let its claims to observance be borne in mind and respected by all. If it is forgotten, omitted, or unceremoniously jostled aside a few times to make way for some other special or regular service, it will be treated by the children in the same spirit. And why not? ....

Let it be a pleasant and judicious blending of the methods of church and Sunday-school, both in worship and instruction. Thus the children will be led imperceptibly from the school-house to the house of God, and these services will be the stepping-stones. The church will have a place in their thoughts and loves. The sanctuary and its order of worship will become a part of their habits. The minister will take his lawful place in their minds as their pastor and God's ambassador to them. And in after years, fewer of them will be alienated from the counsel of the minister and the ordinances of God's house. [*Rev. H. C. McCook, of St. Louis, in S. S. Times, Dec.* 5, 1868.

BOOKS FOR THE LEADER OF CHILDREN'S MEETINGS.—The books here named are only such as will be of service in preparing for or conducting general meetings of children, as advocated in this work. Usual helps to Bible study are not included, nor are many periodicals and volumes on Sunday-school and class management, which are essential to the superintendent and teacher in their ordinary Sunday-school labor. The list makes no pretence of completeness. It merely gives a few works familiar to the author of this volume, as suitable for the specific purpose indicated.

FOR HINTS ON CHILDREN'S SERVICES, OPENING AND CLOSING EXERCISES, &c. House's Sunday-School Hand-book, Hitchcock & Walden; Pardee's

APPENDIX. 351

Sunday-school Index, Garrigues; Sunday-school Hand-book, London S. S. Union; Serjeant's Sunday-school Teaching, London; The Sunday-school, by Louisa Davids, London S. S. Union; Our Sunday-school, Waldo Abbot, Hoyt; Steel's Christian Teacher in Sunday-schools, T. Nelson & Sons; Todd's Sabbath-school Teacher, Bridgman & Childs; The Teacher Taught, Am. S. S. Union; Alfred Taylor's Sunday-school Photographs, Hoyt; Tyng's Forty Years' Experience in Sunday-schools, Sheldon & Co.; Report of the General Sunday-school Convention, London, 1862; Pray's History of Sunday-schools, Crosby & Nichols; Spooner's Parson and People, F. J. Huntington; Country Sunday-school, Carlton & Porter; Sunday-school Work in the Benton Street Mission, St. Louis, by E. D. Jones; Johnson's Manual of the Lee Avenue Sabbath-school, Randolph; Beal's Manual of the Cong. Sabbath School, Cohasset, Mass.; Vincent's Sunday-school Reader, Carlton & Porter; Walden's Sunday-school Prayer-Book, E. P. Dutton & Co.; Newton's Offices of Devotion for Sunday-schools; and Short Responsive Liturgy for Sunday-schools, Prot. Epis. Book Society; New Sunday-school Manual, Carlton & Porter; Worship in the School-room, W. J. Holland & Co.; The Singing Pilgrim, by Philip Phillips; The Infant Class, Charles Reed, London S. S. Union; Martin's Separate Services for Children, London; Hart's Thoughts on Sabbath Schools, Presb. Board.

MATERIAL AND SUGGESTIONS FOR ILLUSTRATION IN ADDRESSING CHILDREN. Hartley's Pictorial Teaching, London S. S. Union; Dowling's Power of Illustration, Sheldon & Co.; Groser's Illustrative Teaching, London S. S. Union; Freeman's Use of Illustration in S. S. Teaching, Carlton & Porter; Newcomb's Teachers' Aid, Mass. S S. Soc.; Bible Illustrations, introduction by Rev. Dr. Newton; and Bate's Cyclopædia of Illustrations, Smith, English & Co.; Biblical Treasury, (annual volumes.) London S. S. Union; The Land and the Book, by Thomson, Harpers'; Illustrative Gatherings, (two series,) Perkinpine & Higgins; Cranfield's Branches Running over the Wall, London S. S. Union; Parables of Krummacher, Lindsay & Blakiston; Gotthold's Emblems, Gould & Lincoln; Good News, and Things New and Old, (annual volumes,) London; Todd's Stories on the Shorter Catechism, Bridgman & Childs; Sunday-school Anecdotes, London S. S. Union; Book of Anecdotes, London; Peep of Day Series; Stories on the Parables, by A. L. O. E., Carter; Arvine's Cyclopædia of Moral and Religious Anecdotes; Buck's Religious Anecdotes; Anecdotes for the Family; and Sketches from Life, Am. Tract Soc., N. Y.; Parley's Book of Fables.

SPECIMEN SERMONS AND ADDRESSES. Dr. Newton's series of Sermons, Carters'; The Child's Preacher, Carlton & Porter; The Children's Church at Home, by Rev. J. Edmond, T. Nelson & Sons; Boyd's Food for the Lambs, Church & Goodman; McLean's Food for the Lambs, N. Tibbals & Co.; Grapes from the Great Vine, and Under the Oak, by Rev. Dr. Breed, Presb Board; Plumer's Sermons for Children, Am. S. S. Union; Greenwood's Sermons for Children, and Peabody's Sermons for Children, Am. Unit. Assoc.; S. G. Green's Addresses to Children, Pearls for the Little Ones, and other volumes, London; The Children and the Lion, Rev. Samuel Wilberforce, Carlton & Porter; Brace's Sermons to Newsboys, Scribner; Peirce's Stories from Life, Hoyt; Todd's Lectures to Children, and Truth Made Simple, Bridgman & Childs; Collier's Little Crowns, Carters'; Disosway's Children's Book of Sermons, Carlton & Porter.

HELPS IN PREPARING CONCERT EXERCISES. Eadie's Analytical Concordance, Gould & Lincoln; Simmons' Scripture Manual, Dodd; Index to the Persons, Places and Subjects mentioned in the Holy Scriptures, Eyre & Spottiswoode, London, (re-published as The Bible Text Book, Am. Tract Soc., N. Y.); Curious and Useful Questions on the Bible, (three series,) Carlton & Porter; 1000 Questions and Propositions, Am. S. S. Union; Sunday-school Concert Exercises, (monthly series,) H. Hoyt; Sunday-school Exhibition Exercises, (three numbers,) Carlton & Porter; Brooks' Concert Exercises for the Use of Sunday-schools, N. Tibbals & Co.

BIBLE LESSONS

FOR THE

Sunday-School Concert

OR

THE CHILDREN'S SERVICE.

A Cheap Edition in Paper Covers.

On the author's recommendation, the publishers of "CHILDREN IN THE TEMPLE" have issued Part III. of that book, comprising the Bible Lessons, by itself, in paper covers. This will put the Lessons within reach of every Teacher, that they may be used at Sunday-School Concerts, or other Meetings of the Children, in accordance with the suggestion on page 85.

Copies of these Lessons—Part III. complete—can be obtained of the publishers direct or of any bookseller, at Fifty Cents per copy, or twelve copies for Five Dollars, postage paid.

AGENTS WANTED.

"The Book for the Times."

"IMMANUEL,"
OR
The Life of Jesus Christ,

Our Lord.

BY

ZACHARY EDDY, D. D.

WITH AN INTRODUCTION BY

RICHARD S. STORRS, JR., D. D.

Christians of all orthodox denominations will read this excellent work with delight and profit. I wish God speed to this and every similar effort to lift up Christ before men.—*Rev. Richard Newton, D. D., Rector of the Church of the Epiphany, Philadelphia, Pa.*

It cannot fail to interest the most cultivated minds, and its general circulation must accomplish great good.—*Rev. Daniel March, D. D., Philadelphia, Pa.*

The engravings of Jerusalem in the frontispiece are almost the best we have ever seen.—*Standard, Chicago, Ill.*

We welcome this volume. It is a valuable contribution to the literature of the world.—*Pittsburgh Advocate, Pittsburgh, Pa.*

It meets a want which none others in the language supplies so well.—*Rev. George Barton Ide, D. D., Springfield, Mass.*

Sold Only by Subscription.

Liberal Premiums will be paid Pastors and Sunday-School Superintendents to recommend Agents for the work.

W. J. HOLLAND & CO., PUBLISHERS,
SPRINGFIELD, MASS.

www.ingramcontent.com/pod-product-compliance
Lightning Source LLC
Chambersburg PA
CBHW030256240426
43673CB00040B/986